AN ANTHOLOGY OF TWENTIETH CENTURY NEW ZEALAND POETRY

THIRD EDITION

AN ANTHOLOGY OF
TWENTIETH CENTURY
NEW ZEALAND POETRY

THIRD EDITION

SELECTED BY

VINCENT O'SULLIVAN

AUCKLAND
OXFORD UNIVERSITY PRESS
OXFORD MELBOURNE NEW YORK

Oxford University Press

OXFORD   NEW YORK   TORONTO
DELHI   BOMBAY   CALCUTTA   MADRAS   KARACHI
PETALING   JAYA   SINGAPORE   HONG KONG   TOKYO
NAIROBI   DAR ES SALAAM   CAPE TOWN
MELBOURNE   AUCKLAND
and associated companies in
BEIRUT   BERLIN   IBADAN   NICOSIA

Oxford is a trade mark of Oxford University Press

First published by Oxford University Press 1970
Second edition published 1976,
reprinted 1979, 1983, 1986
Third edition first published 1987
Introduction and selection ©Oxford University Press
1970, 1976, 1987

ISBN 0 19 558163 6

Cover designed by Neysa Moss
Printed in Hong Kong
Published by Oxford University Press
5 Ramsgate Street, Auckland, New Zealand

CONTENTS

INTRODUCTION

A new anthology of New Zealand poetry demands a clear-cut choice. Should its editor select a body of verse on lines that follow the contours of the country's development, the kind of collection that also provides material for the sociologist and historian, or one where each poem is included simply because it seems good poetry?

This selection is very much the second.

I have tried to represent each poet by a selection large enough to suggest his range in theme, and the variety of his form. There are some poets who have written their finest work in a short space of time, and I have made no attempt to spread their representation wider. With poets such as Curnow and Brasch a wide selection is still limiting. Other poets have put into a few poems all that is valuable in their work. A few may have just begun.

I do not believe that any anthology selected while three-quarters of its poets are still living, and while many of those are comparatively young, can claim any kind of finality. I prefer to regard this volume as a considered report on how New Zealand poetry stands now, and how it appears, looking back, from the end of the 1960s.

I

There were scores of colonists who published verse in the nineteenth century. They wrote poems which made New Zealand exotic, and poems which said how different from home. Yet as long as these things could be said, there was little more than physical conflict between man and environment. It was easy to acknowledge certain obvious contrasts between home and colony. One could enjoy nostalgia for one hemisphere, fascination with another. There was little tension, little uneasiness, that filtered through to poetry. Only seldom did a poem such as Edward Tregear's 'Te Whetu Plains' break through to a response that owed more to the awareness of an individual mind than to what currently was thought poetry's due. The apprehension of 'such ghastly peace', in a land for the most part too strange even to be misunderstood in a meaningful way, must have been a not uncommon feeling in colonial life. It is almost unique as it appears in verse.

Something inherent in the average British mind, once removed from home, and the tedium of a diction that was thought appropriate only to verse, continue to make the reading of nineteenth-century New Zealand verse an imposition. The landscape itself could be appreciated as the work of God, and a happy consequence of colonial policy. But chauvinism and evangelism stood between European and Maori before land disputes, the clamour for quick returns, and incomprehension hardened into war. Nothing in education or contemporary literature could prepare men to see their new country on any terms but their own, or with sensibilities uncluttered by what may have been relevant no longer.

Alfred Domett was the most ambitious of the colony's poets, and the man whose gifts were large enough to suffer the most. His *Ranolf and Amohia*, outrunning *Paradise Lost* in the number of its lines, drew from the Poet Laureate in 1872 the appraisal that he 'but wants limitation to be a very considerable poet'. That long idyllic epic, heavy with philosophy and erudition, is of some historical interest; but the poem had no machinery for experience, and remains a museum piece. The language had little in common with language used for anything else. Maoris remain the children of Rousseau, having nothing to do with the severity of Domett's racial views in parliament and press.

One feels that Tennyson's 'Enoch Arden' must acknowledge paternity for a great deal of bad verse where homesickness and a superficial exoticism were the areas attended. Such rhymes were the work of those who had crossed the world. The feeling of alienation, when it comes, is a more indigenous thing. It begins when what went before is not remembered at all, or is recalled through a sentimentality that sees things as they never were. When only hearsay, or reading, or a brief voyage of homage, is set against what is continually before one's eyes, reality is no longer exotic. It is all we have.

At this point there begins what one may call the colonial neurosis—regret for what one has not had, and yet an obsession with it; self-consciousness about what is one's own, and cannot be given. This leads to that most typical paradox: gaucherie and local assertiveness, on the one hand, and on the other, the rabid support of imperialism caught in Allen Curnow's line 'Seddon howling empire from an empty coast'.

The problem—one which a certain kind of New Zealander has never solved—was where to draw the line between those Englishmen who settled overseas, and those born overseas who claimed they were Englishmen. Many of the poems in this country's first anthology, Alexander and Currie's *New Zealand Verse* in 1906, insist on a vision that now seems as false to one country as it is to another. The England celebrated in 'an English lane, Where the primrose patches blow', is not the England many settlers, or their parents, had left behind them. Nor is the New Zealand where 'honey-loving wild birds kiss The kowhai's cups of gold' the land they came to, or were reared in. With the exception of Blanche Baughan, no poet before the First World War looked squarely at what was done, thought, and felt, in the full context of colonial or early Dominion life.

II

The first poets who almost consistently wrote well were R. A. K. Mason, who was born and educated in Auckland, and the older Englishwoman, Ursula Bethell. Neither paid service to predetermined diction or theme. They made it clear that a more rigorous use of language precludes, as a matter of course, what is second-hand in response.

Ursula Bethell is at her weakest when her voice is raised for public or traditional statement. When her poems begin at her fingertips, among her plants and shrubs, they ring most true. That garden in the Cashmere Hills in Christchurch is not simply an extension of an English personality. It declares the uneasy truce between beauty watched over and cultivated, and the raw push of the seasons that offered Ursula Bethell involvement at the centre of growth, change, decline.

Tutored by the classics, and without Bethell's trust in natural beneficence, Mason often did not enjoy what he saw, but recorded the sight with extraordinary honesty and skill. It is no literary cliché to compare Mason's response to life with Thomas Hardy's. The same harshness informs them both, and a sympathy too profound to settle for any but the details of truth. A human Christ, and his extension in the lost, the betrayed, the intellectually honest, stands at the centre of Mason's refusal to concede comfort on the strength of hoping for it. Myth may have tailed off in the new world, yet the repetition of circumstances again initiates its relevance. What is biblical, what antipodean, in Christ on the swag, or in Judas that 'most sporting bird', are not questions we need to ask.

Eileen Duggan's was an equally honest mind, but one whose poems were muted by convention. Yet from a Georgian and Celtic inheritance she evolved, in a number of poems, and over many years, a hard-edged lyricism. At her best she brought a tougher grain to the tradition she had served.

The early 1930s saw a fresh excitement among students and younger writers. New Zealand, like everywhere else, was touched by the literary events of the decade before. A number of young men were to look at writing more critically, at their country less complacently.

As New Zealand approached its official centenary, Allen Curnow's was the voice to take up the complexities of a people for whom history continued to hold more reserved decisions than it did certainties. Curnow was fortunate in having Mason as an elder, and was gifted with linguistic and rhythmic resources of a high order. He turned to his country's past with a feeling of entailed involvement; to its present with the conviction—at times begrudged—that his reality as a man was here, or not at all.

The guilt that comes with a coastline appropriated through bloodshed, and the discovery that what these islands held out was 'something different, something Nobody counted on', are central to a myth, and to a corpus of verse, more compelling than anything else we have. Curnow's persistence in tracking New Zealand reality to its particulars, contracted in his later work to what lay within a man's own grasp, what passed before his eyes. It is as though reality, once assured in a broader context, must submit, step by step, until nervous responses, memory, and habit have been tested, and found not wanting.

The 1930s hold the beginnings of much else that we cannot now imagine ourselves without. A. R. D. Fairburn's output in poetry, satire, and occasional prose bear witness to a many-sided mind. He wrote more extensive political verse than did any other New Zealander. He castigated the society he lived in, yet his commitment was such that criticism at times brought him close to the elegiac. He saw in a decent regard for nature the basis of a finer national life. And when he confined himself to where his truest gift lay, he wrote from his preoccupation with love and death lyrics like 'Tapu' and 'The Cave'.

Denis Glover shared Fairburn's penchant for satire, and an eye acutely focused on what surrounded him. In the early 1950s he was to find, in sequences grouped about the legendary figures of gold-digger and solitary, a form superbly fitted to his spare, lyrical voice. Nowhere else do the land's lock upon mind and body, and the liberation possible within its bond, work so memorably into poetry.

In Charles Brasch natural beauty frequently becomes a touchstone for what man has not lived up to in his uneasy tenure. Brasch's verse is thoughtfully wrought and for the most part meagre in metaphor. In five volumes, over thirty years, he has asked, and suggested, where in the intricacies of history and time, human values reside. More recently, his poetry has sought to build, from what the emotions have verified, a bulwark that at least ensures breathing space in a world where questions, if put at all, seldom can be put with expectation of reply.

III

A man who lives in this country today does not generally have to come to terms with the land. For better or worse, that land, for the time being, offers those who live with her too comfortable a life to talk of hostility. There is still hard physical work, but there is little feeling of a battle to be won, unless self-imposed by mountaineering, the vagaries of the sea, or the choice of back-country jobs. Not man and the land, but man in a welfare state society, man in love, man in the flow of a larger world around him, are the concerns of most of our poets since 1950. The look of New Zealand, the feel of it, must continue to furnish the staple of much impulse, to serve as the mould where much feeling settles most effectively. To go that one step farther, and claim that only in what is recognizably New Zealand can valid poetry begin, has come to be more than a little narcissistic.

It is self-definition that occupies the greater part of our poetry. To harden this into defining national consciousness, along particular lines, now seems too crude. Often critical insistence presses on the supposed common experience of being a New Zealander, and on the demand for evidence in a poem that is consistent with it. This is trying to wring community statement from a number of individual necks. There is not much that could be called a cultural inheritance in the New Zealand pakeha way of life. There is no folk-tradition, and there are aspects of life in these islands that no writer, in verse or prose, has yet touched on. What we have to look to are a number of fine individuals, in writing, painting, and music. The sum to which such individuals tend, a distinct quality of life, cannot be presumed.

I take at random four of the poets represented in this collection. The grandparents of the first were Jewish, and settled in the South Island. The second, whose father was Scottish and mother Polynesian, has lived the greater part of his life in Wellington. The third's grandparents came from Sweden on one side, his great-grandparents from Ireland on the other, and the family was settled in the Waikato. The fourth, who now lives in England, had English forebears, and grew up on the east coast of the North Island. To try to find points of similarity between these men is difficult. To elicit from their poems, from their imagery or language or themes, something of which we can say 'yes, this is New Zealand, and what we value', seems not so much impossible as to direct attention falsely. It is possible that some racial inheritance, some detail from mythology or folk-lore unknown to the majority of his countrymen, just as some half-remembered incident from childhood, or by-way of education, may be central to each poet. These materials may be of far greater importance to poetry than what he has looked at often, what he has read in other poems, or what touches his life from day to day.

Glover, Baxter, Campbell, to select names at random, are three fine poets. Try to link them through some thread of imagery, some common areas of interest, in the cause of national consciousness, and each poet is diminished. To go further, and say that in certain elements of each, one detects the flow of a 'tradition', is not to concern ourselves with what is valued most in each man's work.

IV

Charles Spear's one small volume, *Twopence Coloured*, was published in 1951. Spear, who grants little to metrical innovations, and uses language with *fin-de-siècle* preciousness, is modern for more than his wry distortions, or the panoply of erudition ironically trifled with. He persuades us to accept seriously a contemporary tone that penetrates his unaccommodating form and diction. The reality of detail, the relevance of mood, survive among the slanted mirrors of fairy-tale, historical snippet, and pose. In the minute clarity of a glass-paperweight world, feeling evokes a strange wasteland, a fantasy that one accepts as life. Only he and M. K. Joseph can so lightly employ learning, touch deeply with it, and lay claim to overtly scholarly verse.

Kendrick Smithyman emerged as a writer at much the same time. He is capable of more genuinely complex verse than any of his contemporaries. Almost as often, he continues to publish poems that seem unrewardingly obscure, where even syntax is not assured safe conduct. Yet there is a considerable *oeuvre* of dexterity and wit, which examines man in terms of the places and activities he is most at ease with, or works the kind of myth sustained in 'Parable of Two Talents'.

A good deal of our prose has insisted that New Zealand life has little emotional resonance. Because of society's disparateness, its divided ambitions, its inability in recent years to define with much enthusiasm or precision what those ambitions are, social verse has vast tracts to exercise it. In the wake of the failed socialist dream, the years from 1950 have less optimism to show on many levels than the preceding twenty.

Louis Johnson is the most consistent in the attention he directs to the hollowness of our social life, and regret for what it stifles. A large part of James K. Baxter's work shares the same concern. But Johnson's values, when they can be detected, are humanist. Baxter draws on another view of man which a histrionic Catholicism cannot altogether obscure. His morality is a Hebraic wolf in New Testament fleeces. The fall of man, emotionally, takes precedence over the efficacy of grace. Baxter's increasing tendency—particularly in his several plays—is to locate value only in the social outcast, the habitual sinner. God's justice has further to relent, his mercy more to redeem. The poet does, of course, go beyond the limits of his theology. He is capable of uncovering areas of response, and embodying them in poems of such formal rhetorical skill, that no other New Zealand poet can keep him company. Baxter's ballads, far from his least achievements, bring poetry closer to the language and conceptions of the people he writes of than has been common with our verse. They are among that very small body of New Zealand poetry of which it makes sense to say that it speaks for a community, and is literary work.

It is ironical that at a time when so many writers have misgivings at their country's increasing dependence on the United States, American poetry is the strongest influence on our recent verse. There is no reason to expect that this will change while Americans continue to write so much that is among the best. Although Gloria Rawlinson has written a fine sequence about childhood in Tonga, no European New Zealand poet has drawn successfully on Polynesian poetry or lore. (This, of course, does not apply to much of Campbell's work, nor to all of Tuwhare's. In different ways, they *are* that tradition. There is no question of their merely deriving from it.) And those poems of Robin Hyde's that found so much of value in China are now thirty years old, and remain all that has come from contact with Asia.

Poetry here, as elsewhere, recently has tended away from public statement, or from too loud a declaration of beliefs. Anything that passes as large political comment has attracted little literary talent. Apart from well-established names such as Baxter, Smithyman, and Campbell, one now looks to strong, personal work like Fleur Adcock's; Gordon Challis's quasi-scientific gutting of neuroses; to Hubert Witheford's singular precision in his continual whittling of language; or to poems like K. O. Arvidson's declension of a symbol, in 'Fish and Chips on the Merry-go-round', to register an amused distaste at the way ideals turn out. In Michael Jackson's African poems, for example, one sees clearly the open-ended range of current verse.

Europe is the closest that a New Zealander has to an extensive birthright. How each poet goes about constructing for himself a coherent body of verse, aware that geography and history have deprived him of much that is valuable, even as they give what cannot be done without, is of permanent interest in New Zealand verse. And what at first appears to be a cultural penalty may in fact be construed as rigorous liberty.

A poet anywhere is free to adapt from what has been central, or peripheral, to his tradition. In a milieu with not only fewer of the usual pressures, but the actual absence of such pressures at work upon him, even a very minor poet may find that simply to adapt is to construct. It is to do, in the poetry that springs from the men with whom he shares time and place, something that may not have been done before, or not done in such a way as to mean the same thing. This constant relation to poetry written in English, anywhere, as well as to the poetry of his own countrymen, does not, except for a particular mind that would be patriotic even in this, involve double standards. It is only by accepting each as naturally one's own that richness and uniqueness evolve. It offers a double interest which is far from the least excitement of New Zealand poetry.   *1970*

Note to the Third Edition

If we accept that poetry in English by consistently serious poets began in New Zealand with Ursula Bethell and R. A. K. Mason, then the first edition of this anthology drew on the work of slightly more than forty years. Each of those poets understood thoroughly what it meant to practise a claim on tradition, on poetry at large, just as each felt poetically at ease in her or his own country. They knew that what poets write anywhere relates primarily to other poems, however much it may also take them to those gaps where the previously unspoken, the local and the quotidian, draw them on to something new.

Discussion of New Zealand poetry begins at that point, and demands that from time to time we bear it in mind. When one notices that of the 57 poets in this volume, 41 are still alive, it seems a fairly obvious requirement that we go cannily with whatever we want to say about New Zealand poetry as a free-standing tradition. Rather than some drift towards collective evidence, I would prefer to think of strong individual poets working on their own terms. From first to last, New Zealand poetry of consistent interest covers a good deal less than the lifespan of its oldest living writer.

In a note to the second edition in 1976 it seemed appropriate to record the major occurrences between then and the original collection put together six years before. One was the prolific final work of James K. Baxter, a production of such range and impressiveness, as well as such implication for ordinary New Zealand life, that his work continues to dominate so much of this volume. The other was the later work and death of Charles Brasch. As editor of *Landfall* for twenty years, he was the one effective patron New Zealand writing has had. Part of that patronage had been to direct scrutiny to whatever *context* might mean in what was written here. For most of those years up to 1970, our criticism tended to fret over how, how much, and in what form, self-definition emerged in our poetry.

There were obvious historical reasons why a comparatively new country and its writers were drawn to and repelled by their European ties, attracted to and ill at ease with indigenous presence. The intention of most criticism, like the efforts of so much fiction, was to polish up a mirror that would show who was at home. Even recently it has been tempting enough to substitute an echo chamber for that mirror, to strain after some notion of 'the demotic' so that the same sigh can go up—'Ah, that's *us.*' The family album syndrome dies hard. But there are many poets who are not particularly concerned with mimetic postures. Again, history proposes reasons why this might be so, from a country's increasing self-confidence on a world political stage, to the wider horizons pointed to by the small literary magazines of the seventies. At least we can now more easily see that the quest for the definingly recognizable is one among several alternatives.

I believe more strongly than I did in my earlier introduction that the differences between most New Zealand poets are deeper and are more interesting than whatever it is they demonstrate when they are assumed to move as a kind of poetical posse, trailing the 'authentic' New Zealand experience, ready to throw 'reality' for appropriate branding. Those writers without the true markings—traces of the vernacular, images of local density, evidence of Polynesian awareness, or whatever—may be less likely to be favoured when nationally-minded critics make their round-up.

All poets, of course, write from what they know and see around them. That is the one thing we *can* take for granted. Their own country, or that part of it which matters to them, inevitably will emerge in some form. So will the network of values and possibilities that they work either with or against, the way things are said, the pressures they find important.

It is proper that we take such things seriously, and find their presence or absence at certain times a matter of some interest. They are not however the factors which make a poem necessarily good, although some of our feebler verse will demonstrate them generously. Nor does their being shared by certain good poets tell us much that is crucial. Smithyman and Baxter, more than any others, take on history and geographic exactness as constant and attractive elements in their poetry. Yet there are probably no two poets in this volume who share less in other respects, who diverge so widely in their technique and in their expectations of language. Again, it may be of some interest to know that Curnow and Stead share certain critical preferences, a coincidence of 'views' which lie prior to the poems of each of them and which appear in works by both. Yet there is no more than a cursory closeness between a major writer for whom poetry is also a primary philosophical act, and one whose interest may be his deft instruction in how pastiche was among the minor veins of Modernism. New Zealand poetry, then, I take in its broadest sense to mean either poetry written in this country, or by New Zealanders who choose to live somewhere else. A privileging of certain adjectives, of certain supposedly inherent characteristics, strikes me more and more as exclusive rather than useful.

Some years ago, after reading the first edition of this anthology, Northrop Frye remarked that 'the poetry was rather discursive, wasn't it?' To some extent one takes that to mean there was an ample survival of nineteenth-century and Georgian traits, a concern with sequential statement and demonstration rather than with the autonomous Image, juxtaposition, the structures of irony, and the formal experiments which at that time (the early seventies) were much talked of in defining modern twentieth-century poetry. Certainly the 'story' element, that part of the poem which is paraphrasable, was of more importance to earlier New Zealand poets than it is at present. There is now more consciousness of the deliberately fabricated, a confident defiance of formal anticipations, a greater sense of poetry as play. And that does not in the least prevent poets like Wedde and Turner, as much as Baxter a generation before them, or Fairburn again before that, from writing with sustained ethical energy, with their issuing moral directives as an assumed literary right.

It has become more obvious that poetry by women has offered an impressive alternative to more declarative verse. From Bethell and Hyde to Smither and McQueen, the intricately personal has proved quite as compelling as an overtly public stance. There is, I think, very little fuss about theory, and a scepticism among writers themselves that any one style should call the tune. It is the persuasively individual that we look for in any writer. For, as Wallace Stevens wrote, a poet's cast of mind 'is born with him and persists, and penetrates the ameliorations of education and the experience of life. His species is as fixed as his genes. . . . What is the poet's subject? It is his sense of the world. For him it is inevitable and inexhaustible, and his work is autobiographical in spite of every subterfuge.'

What brings us to any anthology is the likelihood of those differences, the fact that even writers of the same nationality and age and sex and predilections are read, finally, for what they do *not* have in common. It is a plurality of views and styles, an unconfined possibility of voices, which now seems to me so much more commanding than the recognizable logo in the locally patterned. What I value most about New Zealand poetry in 1986 is that its diversity quite undercuts any ground for the prescriptive; the fact that Curnow and O'Brien are writing at the same time in one city, Manhire and Lauris Edmond in another. There is no 'approach' which will ever position those four in the same square, or hold them beneath the same critical net. What prevents the attempt is the enduring certainty of reading, that a text will outmanoeuvre whatever we try to do to it.

This anthology lays no claim, then, to an 'interpretation' of New

Zealand writing, although inevitably it must be tempered by what contemporary philosophers might call its editor's 'enabling prejudices', those biases and turns which any one reader brings to selecting from what he reads. As the editorial role has never seemed to me to incorporate either the auctioneer or the officer on point duty, I like to think the business of selecting poems one admires, or one believes an audience should be given the chance to assess (they are not always the same thing), can be done with an eye both to fairness and to range. But as the origin of anthology implies, it would be rash to think the field may not have a good deal more to it than what, for the moment, is collected for display.

In order to represent several younger poets, and because space as ever inflicts ruthless demands, two poets from the earlier editions who now seem of less importance than was then the case regrettably have been withdrawn. For similar reasons neither poems by Len Lye nor Douglas Stewart's long poem "Rutherford" could be included, although that too was decided with regret.

Vincent O'Sullivan
October 1986

EDWARD TREGEAR

Te Whetu Plains

A lonely rock above a midnight plain,
  A sky across whose moonlit darkness flies
No shadow from the 'Children of the Rain',
  A stream whose double crescent far-off lies,
  And seems to glitter back the silver of the skies.

The table-lands stretch step by step below
  In giant terraces, their deeper ledges
Banded by blackened swamps (that, near, I know
  Convolvulus-entwined) whose whitened edges
  Are ghostly silken flags of seeding water-sedges.

All still, all silent, 'tis a songless land,
  That hears no music of the nightingale,
No sound of waters falling lone and grand
  Through sighing forests to the lower vale,
  No whisper in the grass, so wan, and grey, and pale.

When Earth was tottering in its infancy,
  This rock, a drop of molten stone, was hurled
And tost on waves of flames like those we see
  (Distinctly though afar) evolved and whirled
  A photosphere of fire around the Solar World.

Swift from the central deeps the lightning flew
  Piercing the heart of Darkness like a spear,
Hot blasts of steam and vapour thunder'd through
  The lurid blackness of the atmosphere.
  A million years have passed, and left strange quiet here.

Peace, the deep peace of universal death
  Enshrouds the kindly mother-earth of old,
The air is dead, and stirs no living breath
  To break these awful Silences that hold
  The heart within their clutch, and numb the veins with
    cold.

My soul hath wept for Rest with longing tears,
  Called it 'the perfect crown of human life'—
But now I shudder lest the coming years
  Should be with these most gloomy terrors rife;
  When palsied arms drop down outwearied with the strife.

May Age conduct me by a gentle hand
   Beneath the shadows ever brooding o'er
The solemn twilight of the Evening Land,
   Where man's discordant voices pierce no more,
   But sleeping waters dream along a sleeping shore.

Where I, when Youth has spent its fiery strength
   And flickers low, may rest in quietness
Till on my waiting brow there falls at length
   The deeper calm of the Death-Angel's kiss—
   But not, oh God, such peace, such ghastly peace as this.

B. E. BAUGHAN

The Old Place

New Zealand

So the last day's come at last, the close of my fifteen year—
The end of the hope, an' the struggles, an' messes I've put in
here.
All of the shearings over, the final mustering done,—
Eleven hundred an' fifty for the incoming man, near on.
Over five thousand I drove 'em, mob by mob, down the coast;
Eleven-fifty in fifteen year . . . it isn't much of a boast.

Oh, it's a bad old place! Blown out o' your bed half the nights,
And in summer the grass burnt shiny an' bare as your hand, on
the heights:
The creek dried up by November, and in May a thundering roar
That carries down toll o' your stock to salt 'em whole on the
shore.
Clear'd I have, and I've clear'd an' clear'd, yet everywhere, slap
in your face,
Briar, tauhinu, an' ruin!—God! it's a brute of a place.
. . . An' the house got burnt which I built, myself, with all that
worry and pride;
Where the Missus was always homesick, and where she took
fever, and died.

Yes, well! I'm leaving the place. Apples look red on that
bough.
I set the slips with my own hand. Well—they're the other man's
now.
The breezy bluff: an' the clover that smells so over the land,
Drowning the reek o' the rubbish, that plucks the profit out o'
your hand:
That bit o' Bush paddock I fall'd myself, an' watch'd, each year,
come clean
(Don't it look fresh in the tawny? A scrap of Old-Country
green):
This air, all healthy with sun an' salt, an' bright with purity:
An' the glossy karakas there, twinkling to the big blue twinkling
sea:
Ay, the broad blue sea beyond, an' the gem-clear cove below,
Where the boat I'll never handle again, sits rocking to and fro:
There's the last look to it all! an' now for the last upon
This room, where Hetty was born, an' my Mary died, an'
John . . .

Well! I'm leaving the poor old place, and it cuts as keen as a
　　knife;
The place that's broken my heart—the place where I've lived
　　my life.

from *A Bush Section*

Logs, at the door, by the fence; logs, broadcast over the paddock;
Sprawling in motionless thousands away down the green of the
　　gully,
Logs, grey-black. And the opposite rampart of ridges
Bristles against the sky, all the tawny, tumultuous landscape
Is stuck, and prickled, and spiked with the standing black and
　　grey splinters,
Strewn, all over its hollows and hills, with the long, prone, grey-
　　black logs.

　　　　For along the paddock, and down the gully,
　　　　Over the multitudinous ridges,
　　　　Through valley and spur,
　　　　Fire has been!
　　Ay, the Fire went through and the Bush has departed,
　　The green Bush departed, green Clearing is not yet come.
　　　　'Tis a silent, skeleton world;
　　　　Dead, and not yet re-born,
　　　　Made, unmade, and scarcely as yet in the making;
　　　　Ruin'd, forlorn, and blank.

　　　　　　　*　　　*　　　*

Day after day,
The hills stand out on the sky,
The splinters stand on the hills,
In the paddock the logs lie prone.
The prone logs never arise,
The erect ones never grow green,
Leaves never rustle, the birds went away with the Bush,—
There is no change, nothing stirs!
And tonight there is no change;
All is mute, monotonous, stark;
In the whole wide sweep round the low little hut of the settler
No life to be seen; nothing stirs.

　　　　　　　*　　　*　　　*

. . . It is stiller than ever; the wind has fallen.
The moist air brings,
To mix with the spicy breath of the young break-wind macro-
　　carpa,

Wafts of the acrid, familiar aroma of slowly-smouldering logs.
And, hark, through the empty silence and dimness
Solemnly clear,
Comes the wistful, haunting cry of some lonely, far-away
     morepork,
'*Kia toa!* Be brave!'
—Night is come.
Now the gully is hidden, the logs and the paddock all hidden.
Brightly the Stars shine out! . . .
The sky is a wide black paddock, without any fences,
The Stars are its shining logs;
Here, sparse and single, but yonder, as logg'd-up for burning,
Close in a cluster of light.
And the thin clouds, they are the hills,
They are the spurs of the heavens,
On whose steepnesses scatter'd, the Star-logs silently lie:
Dimm'd as it were by the distance, or maybe in mists of the
     mountain
Tangled—yet still they brighten, not darken, the thick-strewn
     slopes!
But see! these hills of the sky
They waver and move! their gullies are drifting, and driving;
Their ridges, uprooted,
Break, wander and flee, they escape! casting careless behind them
Their burdens of brightness, the Stars, that rooted remain.
—No! they do not remain. No! even they cannot be steadfast.
For the curv'd Three (that yonder
So glitter and sparkle
There, over the bails),
This morning, at dawn,
At the start of the milking,
Stood pale on the brink of yon rocky-ledged hill;
And the Cross, o'er the viaduct
Now, then was slanting,
Almost to vanishing, over the snow.
So, the Stars travel, also?
The poor earthly logs, in the wan earthly paddocks,
Never can move, they must stay;
But over the heavenly pastures, the bright, live logs of the
     heavens
Wander at will, looking down on our paddocks and logs, and
     pass on.
'O friendly and beautiful Live-Ones!
Coming to us for a little,
Then travelling and passing, while here with our logs we remain,
          What are you? Where do you come from?
          Who are you? Where do you go?'

          *   *   *

O pioneer Soul! against Ruin here hardily pitted,
What life wilt thou make of existence?
Life! what more Life wilt thou make?

*   *   *

Here in the night, face to face
With the Burnt Bush within and without thee,
Standing, small and alone:
Bright Promise on Poverty's threshold!
What art thou? Where hast thou come from?
How far, how far! wilt thou go?

ARTHUR H. ADAMS

The Dwellings of our Dead

They lie unwatched, in waste and vacant places,
In sombre bush or wind-swept tussock spaces,
  Where seldom human tread
And never human trace is—
  The dwellings of our dead!

No insolence of stone is o'er them builded;
By mockery of monuments unshielded,
  Far on the unfenced plain
Forgotten graves have yielded
  Earth to free earth again.

Above their crypts no air with incense reeling,
No chant of choir or sob of organ pealing;
  But ever over them
The evening breezes kneeling
  Whisper a requiem.

For some the margeless plain where no one passes,
Save when at morning far in misty masses
  The drifting flock appears.
Lo, here the greener grasses
  Glint like a stain of tears!

For some the quiet bush, shade-strewn and saddened,
Whereo'er the herald tui, morning-gladdened,
  Lone on his chosen tree,
With his new rapture maddened,
  Shouts incoherently.

For some the gully, where in whispers tender,
The flax-blades mourn and murmur, and the slender
  White ranks of toi go,
With drooping plumes of splendour,
  In pageantry of woe.

For some the common trench where, not all fameless,
They fighting fell who thought to tame the tameless,
  And won their barren crown;
Where one grave holds them nameless—
  Brave white and braver brown.

But in their sleep, like troubled children turning,
A dream of mother-country in them burning,
   They whisper their despair,
And one vague, voiceless yearning
   Burdens the pausing air . . .

'Unchanging here the drab year onward presses;
No Spring comes trysting here with new-loosed tresses,
   And never may the years
Win Autumn's sweet caresses—
   Her leaves that fall like tears.

And we would lie 'neath old-remembered beeches,
Where we could hear the voice of him who preaches
   And the deep organ's call,
While close about us reaches
   The cool, grey, lichened wall.'

But they are ours, and jealously we hold them;
Within our children's ranks we have enrolled them,
   And till all Time shall cease
Our brooding bush shall fold them
   In her broad-bosomed peace.

They came as lovers come, all else forsaking,
The bonds of home and kindred proudly breaking;
   They lie in splendour lone—
The nation of their making
   Their everlasting throne!

MARY URSULA BETHELL

Response

When you wrote your letter it was April,
And you were glad that it was spring weather,
And that the sun shone out in turn with showers of rain.

I write in waning May and it is autumn,
And I am glad that my chrysanthemums
Are tied up fast to strong posts,
So that the south winds cannot beat them down.
I am glad that they are tawny coloured,
And fiery in the low west evening light.
And I am glad that one bush warbler
Still sings in the honey-scented wattle . . .

But oh, we have remembering hearts,
And we say 'How green it was in such and such an April',
And 'Such and such an autumn was very golden',
And 'Everything is for a very short time'.

Pause

When I am very earnestly digging
I lift my head sometimes, and look at the mountains,
And muse upon them, muscles relaxing.

I think how freely the wild grasses flower there,
How grandly the storm-shaped trees are massed in their gorges
And the rain-worn rocks strewn in magnificent heaps.

Pioneer plants on those uplands find their own footing;
No vigorous growth, there, is an evil weed:
All weathers are salutary.

It is only a little while since this hillside
Lay untrammelled likewise,
Unceasingly swept by transmarine winds.

In a very little while, it may be,
When our impulsive limbs and our superior skulls
Have to the soil restored several ounces of fertilizer,

The Mother of all will take charge again,
And soon wipe away with her elements
Our small fond human enclosures.

Detail

My garage is a structure of excessive plainness,
It springs from a dry bank in the back garden,
It is made of corrugated iron,
And painted all over with brick-red.

But beside it I have planted a green Bay-tree,
—A sweet Bay, an Olive, and a Turkey Fig,
—A Fig, an Olive, and a Bay.

Soothsayer

I walked about the garden in the evening,
And thought: How Autumn lingers—
Still a few gold chrysanthemums—
Still one late rose—
The old blackbird still has voice.

I walked back down the pathway,
The evening light lay gently on the orchard;
Then I saw a redness on the peach boughs,
And bulb-spears pushing upwards,
And heard the old blackbird whistle—
'Get ready. Get ready. Get ready.
Quick. Quick. Spring.'

So I cut down the last chrysanthemums,
Pulled up their stakes and piled them in the shed,
At hand to serve me soon for young delphiniums.

Erica

Sit down with me awhile beside the heath-corner.

Here have I laboured hour on hour in winter,
Digging thick clay, breaking up clods, and draining,
Carrying away cold mud, bringing up sandy loam,
Bringing these rocks and setting them all in their places,
To be shelter from winds, shade from too burning sun.

See, now, how sweetly all these plants are springing
Green, ever green, and flowering turn by turn,
Delicate heaths, and their fragrant Australian kinsmen,
Shedding, as once unknown in New Holland, strange scents
    on the air,

And purple and white daboecia—the Irish heather—
Said in the nurseryman's list to be so well suited
For small gardens, for rock gardens, and for graveyards.

Fall

Autumn, I think, now.

Rose hues assume a deeper intensity.
Little birds flying in from far in the wild bush
Pursue insects boldly even into our parlours.

The play of the winds is less turbulent:
They scatter gently forspent petallage,
And a scent of ripe seeds is borne on their soft gusts.

Today I do not perceive the outcry of young folk;
Perhaps they are helping to get in some harvest,
Or far afield for important ball-games.

Only old men pause by the sunny roadside
Noticing the same sights that I have noticed,
And listening to the same quietness.

We do not regret that we are of ripe years;
We do not complain of grey hairs and infirmities;
We are drowsy and very ready to fall into deep sleep.

Trance

While others slept I rose, and looked upon the garden,
Lying so still there in the rare light of the soon-to-be-setting moon.

The soft, sharp shadows marked a familiar pattern,
But not a leaf stirred, not a blade of grass quivered,
The trees seemed petrified, and the hedges cut out of black glass.

So still it lay, it suffered an enchantment.
It was the dimly mirrored image of a grove laid up in heaven,
Or the calm mirage of a long-since-lost oasis,
Or the unflickering dream of a serene midnight
Dreamt by one falling into profound sleep.

It was the spectral vision of a work accomplished, done with.
Veiled in the silvery mists of very long past years;
Myself the wraith, from all vicissitude abstracted,
Of one who had, perhaps, once known expectance,

Had sown in tears and learnt the grave joys of harvest,
Had long ago, perhaps, an enclosed garden tended,
Had for a short while, perhaps, been happy there.

The Long Harbour

There are three valleys where the warm sun lingers,
gathered to a green hill girt-about anchorage,
and gently, gently, at the cobbled margin
of fire-formed, time-smoothed, ocean-moulded curvature,
a spent tide fingers the graven boulders,
the black, sea-bevelled stones.

The fugitive hours, in those sun-loved valleys,
implacable hours, their golden-wheeled chariots'
inaudible passage check, and slacken
their restless teams' perpetual galloping;
and browsing, peaceable sheep and cattle
gaze as they pause by the way.

Grass springs sweet where once thick forest
gripped vales by fire and axe freed to pasturage;
but flame and blade have spared the folding gullies,
and there, still, the shade-flitting, honey-sipping lutanists
copy the dropping of tree-cool waters
dripping from stone to stone.

White hawthorn hedge from old, remembered England,
and orchard white, and whiter bridal clematis
the bush-bequeathed, conspire to strew the valleys
in tender spring, and blackbird, happy colonist,
and blacker, sweeter-fluted tui echo
either the other's song.

From far, palm-feathery, ocean-spattered islands
there rowed hither dark and daring voyagers;
and Norseman, Gaul, the Briton and the German
sailed hither singing; all these hardy venturers
they desired a home, and have taken their rest there,
and their songs are lost on the wind.

I have walked here with my love in the early spring-time,
and under the summer-dark walnut-avenues,
and played with the children, and waited with the aged
by the quayside, and listened alone where manukas
sighing, windswept, and sea-answering pine-groves
garrison the burial-ground.

It should be very easy to lie down and sleep there
in that sequestered hillside ossuary,
underneath a billowy, sun-caressed grass-knoll,
beside those dauntless, tempest-braving ancestresses
who pillowed there so gladly, gnarled hands folded,
their tired, afore-translated bones.

It would not be a hard thing to wake up one morning
to the sound of bird-song in scarce-stirring willow-trees,
waves lapping, oars plashing, chains running slowly,
and faint voices calling across the harbour;
to embark at dawn, following the old forefathers,
to put forth at daybreak for some lovelier,
still undiscovered shore.

Warning of Winter

Give over, now, red roses;
Summer-long you told us,
Urgently unfolding, death-sweet, life-red,
Tidings of love. All's said. Give over.

Summer-long you placarded
Leafy shades with heart-red
Symbols. Who knew not love at first knows now,
Who had forgot has now remembered.

Let be, let be, lance-lilies,
Alert, pard-spotted, tilting
Poised anthers, flaming; have done flaming fierce;
Hard hearts were pierced long since, and stricken.

Give to the blast your thorn-crowns
Roses; and now be torn down
All you ardent lilies, your high-holden crests,
Havocked and cast to rest on the clammy ground.

Alas, alas, to darkness
Descends the flowered pathway,
To solitary places, deserts, utter night;
To issue in what hidden dawn of light hereafter?

But one, in dead of winter,
Divine *Agape*, kindles
Morning suns, new moons, lights starry trophies;
Says to the waste: Rejoice, and bring forth roses;
To the ice-fields: Let here spring thick bright lilies.

Decoration

This jar of roses and carnations on the window-sill,
Crimson upon sky-grey and snow-wrapt mountain-pallor,
(Sharp storm's asseveration of cold winter's on-coming,)
How strange their look, how lovely, rich and foreign,
The living symbol of a season put away.

A letter-sheaf, bound up by time-frayed filament,
I found; laid by; youth's flowering.
The exotic words blazed up blood-red against death's shadow,
Red upon grey. Red upon grey.

Midnight

All day long, prismatic dazzle,
Clashing of musics, challenge, encounter, succession;
Gear-change on the up-and-down hill of hypothesis;
Choice, choice, decision, events rivetting shackles;
Hazardous tests, new wine of escape . . .
              oh, strange noviciate!
Bright stimulus, venture, tension, poised preparedness.

But at midnight, infinite darkness,
Opulent silence, liberty, liberty, solitude;
The acrid, mountainy wind's austere caresses;
Rest, rest, compensation, very suspension of death;
Deep stillness of death, dark negation . . .
              ah, thy heart-beat,
Origin, Signification, dread Daysman, Consummator.

Lever de Rideau

Today
the clocks strike
seven, seven, seven, and church-bells
chime busily, and the plain-town heavily wakes;
a salt-sharp east wind flicks and swells
and tosses my emerald silk curtains;
translucent green on blue the empyrean, and lo!
north and west, endlessly limned and painted,
my mountains, my mountains, all snow.

Now a change begins in the heavenly tone-chord;
to the east, eyes! where the sea is incised
like azure ice on sky of vermeil;

oh, dream on prolonged, beautiful prelude!
hushed still, delay, summoning bird-song!
hold, magic touch, be arrested, lovely crisis of sunrise!
when yonder death-white summits are rose-flushed
and glittering, I must
away.

October Morning

'All clear, all clear, all clear!' after the storm in the morning
The birds sing; all clear the rain-scourged firmament,
All clear the still blue horizontal sea;
And what, all white again? all white the long line of the
      mountains
And clear on sky's sheer blue intensity.

Gale raved night-long, but all clear, now, in the sunlight
And sharp, earth-scented air, a fair new day.
The jade and emerald squares of far-spread cultivated
All clear, and powdered foot-hills, snow-fed waterway,
And every black pattern of plantation made near;
All clear, the city set—but oh for taught interpreter,
To translate the quality, the excellence, for initiate seer
To tell the essence of this hallowed clarity,
Reveal the secret meaning of the symbol: 'clear'.

Evening Walk in Winter

Tussock burned to fine gold, and the sheep bore golden fleeces
by the sudden alchemy of wintry waning sun,
and stepping eastwards
My arrowy shadow sapphire led me on.

So airy light I seemed to climb, the earthy path so gilded,
the illumined hill appeared in that transmuted hour
olympian,
the self a quenchless effluence of fire.

But overhead marmoreal white now hung the cold moon ominous
in ashen blue of empty dome, our doom
exhibit thus
even so to frozen death we must all come.

Now lost the living orb, and all his spacious ardours
concealed behind black rocky alps in wintry grave.

Falling darkness
possessed the plain, pale streams, sad fields and groves.

Now stars rushed out to fill the void with sparkling affirmations,
their cold acumen spoke no comfort, as before,
the heavens vacant;
mirror-moon shone false from fire afar.

Darkly alone, the errant hour outspent, led downwards
by homing track, the lowly glittering chain
lit round
hearth-fastness beckoned there was warmth within.

Oh not by late-launched planets flung in heavens equivocal
may we, or making moonlight wan and wild
oracular,
be certified of life or death, of heat or cold.

The bright particular hearts mysteriously enkindled
for us—the daily love, like fire that glows and runs
half hidden
among the embers—this the warmth we live by, our unsetting sun.

What if the light go out? What if some black disaster
of total nightfall quench the vivid spark?
Oh might we hearken,
then, with night-initiate Spaniard to the Answerer
who said: I am the dark.

from *By the River Ashley*

VI

The hour is dark. The river comes to its end,
Comes to the embrace of the all enveloping sea.
My story comes to its end.

> Divine Picnicker by the lakeside,
> Familiar friend of the fishermen,
> Known and yet not known, lost and yet found,
> The hour is dark, come down to the riverside,
> The strange river, come find me.
> Bring if it might be companions
> In the tissue of the Kingdom, but come thou,
> Key to all mystery, opening and none shall shut again,
> Innermost love of all loves, making all one.
> Come.

KATHERINE MANSFIELD

The Man with the Wooden Leg

There was a man lived quite near us;
He had a wooden leg and a goldfinch in a green cage.
His name was Farkey Anderson,
And he'd been in a war to get his leg.
We were very sad about him,
Because he had such a beautiful smile
And was such a big man to live in a very small house.
When he walked on the road his leg did not matter so much;
But when he walked in his little house
It made an ugly noise.
Little Brother said his goldfinch sang the loudest of all birds,
So that he should not hear his poor leg
And feel too sorry about it.

Sanary

Her little hot room looked over the bay
Through a stiff palisade of glinting palms,
And there she would lie in the heat of the day,
Her dark head resting upon her arms,
So quiet, so still, she did not seem
To think, to feel, or even to dream.

The shimmering, blinding web of sea
Hung from the sky, and the spider sun
With busy frightening cruelty
Crawled over the sky and spun and spun.
She could see it still when she shut her eyes,
And the little boats caught in the web like flies.

Down below at this idle hour
Nobody walked in the dusty street
A scent of dying mimosa flower
Lay on the air, but sweet—too sweet.

To L. H. B.

Last night for the first time since you were dead
I walked with you, my brother, in a dream.
We were at home again beside the stream
Fringed with tall berry bushes, white and red.

'Don't touch them: they are poisonous,' I said.
But your hand hovered, and I saw a beam
Of strange, bright laughter flying round your head,
And as you stooped I saw the berries gleam.
'Don't you remember? We called them Dead Man's Bread!'
I woke and heard the wind moan and the roar
Of the dark water tumbling on the shore.
Where—where is the path of my dream for my eager feet?
By the remembered stream my brother stands
Waiting for me with berries in his hands . . .
'These are my body. Sister, take and eat.'

To Stanislaw Wyspianski[1]

From the other side of the world,
From a little island cradled in the giant sea bosom,
From a little land with no history,
(Making its own history, slowly and clumsily
Piecing together this and that, finding the pattern, solving the
    problem,
Like a child with a box of bricks),
I, a woman, with the taint of the pioneer in my blood,
Full of a youthful strength that wars with itself and is lawless,
I sing your praises, magnificent warrior; I proclaim your
    triumphant battle.
My people have had nought to contend with;
They have worked in the broad light of day and handled the clay
    with rude fingers;
Life—a thing of blood and muscle; Death—a shovelling under-
    ground of waste material.
What would they know of ghosts and unseen presences,
Of shadows that blot out reality, of darkness that stultifies morn?
Fine and sweet the water that runs from their mountains;
How could they know of poisonous weed, of rotted and clogging
    tendrils?
And the tapestry woven from dreams of your tragic childhood
They would tear in their stupid hands,
The sad, pale light of your soul blow out with their childish
    laughter.
But the dead—the old—Oh Master, we belong to you there;
Oh Master, there we are children and awed by the strength of a
    giant;

[1] Stanislaw Wyspianski was born in the 1860s and died prematurely in 1907.
He was a dramatic poet and has been described as the greatest literary genius
produced by modern Poland. The keynote of his work is an unconquerable faith
in the future of his country.

How alive you leapt into the grave and wrestled with Death
And found in the veins of Death the red blood flowing
And raised Death up in your arms and showed him to all the
    people.
Yours a more personal labour than the Nazarene's miracles,
Yours a more forceful encounter than the Nazarene's gentle
    commands.
Stanislaw Wyspianski—Oh man with the name of a fighter,
Across these thousands of sea-shattered miles we cry and proclaim
    you;
We say 'He is lying in Poland, and Poland thinks he is dead;
But he gave the denial to Death—he is lying there, wakeful;
The blood in his giant heart pulls red through his veins'.

J. R. HERVEY

Somnambulist

He could not fall so far,
Nor ever be so lost in a murmuration
Of dreams as not to lie
Still on the startled path of evocation.

Whose voice was it that scattered
The deep defence of sleep, that flattered
The dubious brain into escapade?

It was the frigid hour of resurrection
When he arose, and night drew back
From the body that slid from all correction,
Whose implacable face
Knew the blotted road and the empty appointed place.

Two Old Men Look at the Sea

They do not speak but into their empty mood
    Receive the leaden utterance of waves,
    And intimations blowing from old graves,
    Men who have already crossed to the torpid sandspit
    Between life and death, whose cold rejected hands
    Have flung farewell to passion, the brassy lands
    Of love and pursuit, who even taste not life
    In the pomp of passing synopsis, but only savour
    The salty wind and sand swirling up to claim
    The total mystery masking in a name.

How shall we live and hold, how love and handle
    To the last beach the dark and difficult gleanings?
    For so must we come, hugging our recompense,
    To the unfeeling shore, to the bleak admonitory tide,
    Our fear being as a hand that cups a candle
    Against the winds that whiff away pretence,
    And the sea whose sentence strikes like a leaden wave.

Man on a Raft

Not out of the war, not out of the agitated
House of life and wearing the brand of love,
He is yet no more than the diving bird between
    Wave and wave.

Only one is near, only one regards, death,
In the stare of the sky, in the cold watch of water:
And who but death trundles the eccentric toy,
    The dancing timber.

But always he skirted the vortex of disaster,
For the crazy earth carried him and lost him
Among the witless stars and hostile calms,
    Smothering knowledge.

His days have sickened in the heavy perfume
Of death hanging a flower on every season:
His hope has stumbled over crooked stones,
    Pretending sleep.

Where shall be his landfall who resigns
The rudder, whose hands, twin-gods of design,
Are but fists that threaten doom and beat like flowers
    On the iron doors?

Yet the rag at the mast was valid, it persuaded
The clean prow of love, and the man on the raft
Climbed to the assured deck, the rational voyage,
    Drowning fear.

The Empty Valley

Yeats could not walk in the disarming field without
Feeling at elbow spirit or devil,
Nor hear an idle shout
But he proclaimed a shred of ghostly revel.

If but the countryman, he said,
Had the keen ear and eagle sight
Of Swedenborg he would hear the noise
Of swords in the empty valley—shall we go at the side
Of the poet and mingle
With marches of spirit or stand
With the countryman who sees as single
The abundant land?

This beauty shall be my love, I shall not ask
If nature be an ineffectual mask
Through which death-chastened eyes
Persuade the wise,

I shall not look to left or right
For a cold companion nor suspect the night,
Nor regard the rally
Of irrelevant swords—
What so replete as the empty valley?

Children Among the Tombstones

The O so gay
Among the text-strewn graves at play—
Says nothing the heaven-telling story
To inmates of the earlier glory.

Mourning the wrangle
Between life and death a carven angel—
Too near the beginning to see the end
They danced with time the trumped up friend.

And sprinkled over
With loves and flowers and songs to cover
From ghosts and stones so down to death,
And mounded hints that hold their breath.

To party laughs
They could invite the epitaphs,
Wiseacre text and monument—
No death, no death, the word was sent.

From the wide eyed
Of world without end was nothing to hide,
Necropolis nurse of endless play,
No death, no death whistled the day.

EILEEN DUGGAN

Booty

Ah not as plains that spread into us slowly
But as that mountain flinging at the skies
And not as merchantmen which trundle in the offing
But as a privateer that boards a prize,
Let song come always at me and not to me
And, coming, let it plunder, burn, and flay,
For beauty like heaven by violence is taken
And the violent shall bear it away.

Pilgrimage

Now are the bells unlimbered from their spires
In every steeple-loft from pole to pole:
The four winds wheel and blow into this gate,
And every wind is wet with carillons.
And two Americas at eagle-height,
The pure, abstracted Himalayan chimes,
Great ghosts of clappers from the Russian fries,
And sweet, wind-sextoned tremblers from Cathay;
The bells of Ireland, jesting all the way,
The English bells, slowbosomed as a swan,
The queenly, weary din of Notre Dame,
And the Low Countries ringing back the sea.
Then Spain, the Moor still moaning through the saint,
The frosty, fiery bells of Germany,
And on before them, baying, sweeping down,
The heavy, joyful pack of thunder-jowls
That tongue hosannas from the leash of Rome—
All float untethered over Jaffa Gate
To fling one peal when angels cheat the stone.
But if one little gaping country bell,
Blown from its weather-boarding in the south,
Should be too lost to keep its covenant,
Or lift its heart and reins up to the hour,
Know that its dumbness riots more than sound.

The Tides Run up the Wairau

The tides run up the Wairau
That fights against their flow.

My heart and it together
Are running salt and snow.

For though I cannot love you,
Yet, heavy, deep, and far,
Your tide of love comes swinging,
Too swift for me to bar.

Some thought of you must linger,
A salt of pain in me,
For oh what running river
Can stand against the sea?

The Bushfeller

Lord, mind your trees today!
My man is out there clearing.
God send the chips fly safe.
My heart is always fearing.

And let the axehead hold!
My dreams are all of felling.
He earns our bread far back.
And then there is no telling.

If he came home at nights,
We'd know, but it is only—
We might not even hear—
A man could lie there lonely.

God, let the trunks fall clear,
He did not choose his calling;
He's young and full of life—
A tree is heavy, falling.

Have No Fear!

In any element, you are scot-free.
Whatever faction triumphs you are safe.
Matching its medium,
What is abeyant
Assumes responsibility.
The switch from gill to lung
To you is nothing.
Behold the complete axolotl!
And should, as some say,

The world end by fire,
You, a salamandrine,
Would usurp the powers of fable
By wits alone;
If wits could flick up fire
As smooth as breath to nostril,
Your ribs would glow,
Your chest become a brazier—
Of all mankind
The final opportunist!

Truth

Some can leave the truth unspoken.
Oh truth is light on such!
They may choose their time and season,
Nor feel it matters much.

I am not their judge, God help me!
Though I am of the crew
For whom is only truth or treason—
No choice between the two.

But pity wrestles with my fury
Till, spent and dumb and dry,
I envy bees which, barbed with reason,
Give the whole sting and die.

Victory

It comes to this, in plain words,
You will be defeated
By those who have no arms
And have not even retreated.

Back to original night
You will drive each defenceless city,
But in the eyes underground
There will be only pity.

Though, in contempt of life,
You slew the last defying,
Into your very ranks
His spirit would come flying.

When the learned have all despaired
For liberty departed,
This planet will be saved
By the simple-hearted.

More even, the universe,
Since space and time are shrinking!
What our star takes to heart
Its kind may yet be thinking.

The gentle are used to destroy
But the ultimate peace shall hinge
By an awful equity
On their unsought revenge.

It may even be
That under their frozen woe,
Bearing and bearing down,
You will snap like boughs in snow.

The humble shall sentence in kind
Those who winter the world by law,
Some may not be slain but live,
Forgotten in the thaw.

A. R. D. FAIRBURN

Rhyme of the Dead Self

Tonight I have taken all that I was
and strangled him that pale lily-white lad
I have choked him with these my hands these claws
catching him as he lay a-dreaming in his bed.

Then chuckling I dragged out his foolish brains
that were full of pretty love-tales heigho the holly
and emptied them holus bolus to the drains
those dreams of love oh what ruinous folly.

He is dead pale youth and he shall not rise
on the third day or any other day
sloughed like a snakeskin there he lies
and he shall not trouble me again for aye.

Winter Night

The candles gutter and burn out,
   and warm and snug we take our ease,
and faintly comes the wind's great shout
   as he assails the frozen trees.

The vague walls of this little room
   contract and close upon the soul;
deep silence hangs amid the gloom;
   no sound but the small voice of the coal.

Here in this sheltered firelit place
   we know not wind nor shivering tree;
we two alone inhabit space,
   locked in our small infinity.

This is our world, where love enfolds
   all images of joy, all strife
resolves in peace: this moment holds
   within its span the sum of life.

For Time's a ghost: these reddening coals
   were forest once ere he'd begun,
and now from dark and timeless boles
   we take the harvest of the sun;

and still the flower-lit solitudes
    are radiant with the springs he stole
where violets in those buried woods
    wake little blue flames in the coal.

Great stars may shine above this thatch;
    beyond these walls perchance are men
with laws and dreams: but our thin latch
    holds all such things beyond our ken.

The fire now lights our cloudy walls,
    now fails beneath the singing pot,
and as the last flame leaps and falls
    the far wall is and then is not.

Now lovelier than firelight is the gleam
    of dying embers, and your face
shines through the pathways of my dream
    like young leaves in a forest place.

from *Dominion*

Utopia

III

In the suburbs the spirit of man
walks on the garden path,
walks on the well-groomed lawn, dwells
among the manicured shrubs.
The variegated hedge encircles life.
In the countryside, in shire and county,
the abode of wind and sun, where clouds trample the sky
and hills are stretched like arms heaped up with bounty,
in the countryside the land is
the space between the barbed-wire fences,
mortgaged in bitterness, measured in sweated butterfat.

VI

The press: slow dripping of water on mud;
thought's daily bagwash, ironing out opinion,
scarifying the edges of ideas.
And the hirelings; caught young;
the bough bent and twisted
to the shape of evil; tending the oaf
who by accident of birth has property
in the public conscience, a 'moulder of opinion';
turning misshapen vessels, and jars for subtle poisons;

blinde mouthes;
insulated against discontent
born dumb and tractable, swift to disremember
the waif, and the hurt eyes of the passing stranger,
and the statistics of those who killed themselves
or were confined in asylums for the insane.
And the proletarian animal,
product of perversion and source of profit,
with a net paid circulation of a million,
and many unsold, or lying about the streets
bearing the marks of boot-protectors;
a crucified ape, preached by Darwinian bishops,
guarded by traitorous pens, handed the vinegar
of a 'belief in the essential goodness of human nature'.

IX

This is our paper city, built
on the rock of debt, held fast
against all winds by the paperweight of debt.
The crowds file slowly past, or stop and stare,
and here and there, dull-eyed, the idle stand
in clusters in the mouths of gramophone shops
in a blare of music that fills the crumpled air
with paper flowers and artificial scents
and painless passion in a heaven
of fancied love.
                    The women come
from the bargain shops and basements
at dusk, as gazelles from drinking;
the men buy evening papers, scan them
for news of doomsday, light their pipes:
and the night sky, closing over, covers like a hand
the barbaric yawn of a young and wrinkled land.

from Album Leaves

Imperial

In the first days, in the forgotten calendars,
came the seeds of the race, the forerunners:
offshoots, outcasts, entrepreneurs,
architects of Empire, romantic adventurers;
and the famished, the multitude of the poor;
crossed parallels of boredom, tropics
of hope and fear, losing the pole-star, suffering
world of water, chaos of wind and sunlight,
and the formless image in the mind;
sailed under Capricorn to see for ever
the arc of the sun to northward.

They shouted at the floating leaf,
laughed with joy at the promise of life,
hope becoming belief, springing
alive, alight, gulls at the masthead crying,
the crag splitting the sky, slowly
towering out of the sea, taking
colour and shape, and the land
swelling beyond; noises
of water among rocks, voices singing.

Haven of hunger; landfall of hope;
goal of ambition, greed, and despair.

In tangled forests under the gloom
of leaves in the green twilight,
among the habitations of the older gods
they walked, with Christ beside them,
and an old enemy at hand, one whose creed
flourished in virgin earth. They divided the land;
some for their need, and some
for aimless, customary greed
that hardened with the years, grew taut
and knotted like a fist. Flower and weed
scattered upon the breeze
their indiscriminate seed; on every hillside fought
God's love against the old antagonist.
They change the sky but not their hearts who cross the seas.

These islands;
the remnant peaks of a lost continent,
roof of an old world, molten droppings
from earth's bowels, gone cold;
ribbed with rock, resisting the sea's corrosion
for an age, and an age to come. Of three races
the home: two passing in conquest
or sitting under the leaves, or on shady doorsteps
with quiet hands, in old age, childless.
And we, the latest: their blood on our hands: scions
of men who scaled ambition's
tottering slopes, whose desires
encompassed earth and heaven: we have prospered greatly,
we, the destined race, rulers of conquered isles,
sprouting like bulbs in warm darkness, putting out
white shoots under the wet sack of Empire.

Back Street

A girl comes out of a doorway in the morning
with hair uncombed, treading with care
on the damp bricks, picks up the milk,
stares skyward with sleepy eyes;
returns to the dewy step; leaves
with the closing of the door
silence under narrow eaves
the tragic scent of violets on the morning air
and jonquils thrust through bare earth here and there.

At ten o'clock a woman comes out
and leans against the wall
beside the fig-tree hung with washing; listens
for the postman's whistle. Soon he passes,
leaves no letter.
She turns a shirt upon the barren tree
and pads back to the house as ghost to tomb.
No children since the first. The room
papered in 'Stars', with Jubilee pictures
pasted over the mantel, spattered with fat.

Up the street
the taxi-drivers lounging in a knot
beside the rank of shining cars
discuss the speed of horses
as mariners the stars in their courses.

Conversation in the Bush

'Observe the young and tender frond
of this punga: shaped and curved
like the scroll of a fiddle: fit instrument
to play archaic tunes.'
                    'I see
the shape of a coiled spring.'

Elements

I

In the summer we rode in the clay country,
the road before us trembling in the heat
and on the warm wind the scent of tea-tree,
grey and wind-bitten in winter, odorous under summer noon,
with spurts of dust under the hoofs
and a crackle of gorse on the wayside farms.
At dusk the sun fell down in violet hills
and evening came and we turned our horses
homeward through dewy air.

In autumn, kindness of earth, covering life,
mirrored stillness,
peace of mind, and time to think;
good fishing, and burdened orchards. Winter come,
headlands loomed in mist,
hills were hailswept, flowers were few;
and when we rode on the mountains in frosty weather
the distant ranges ran like blue veins through the land.
In spring we thrust our way through the bush,
through the ferns in the deep shadow angled with sunbeams,
roamed by streams in the bush, by the scarred stones
and the smooth stones water-worn, our shoulders wet
with rain from the shaken leaves.

O lovely time! when bliss was taken
as the bird takes nectar from the flower.
Happy the sunlit hour, the frost and the heat.
Hearts poised at a star's height
moved in a cloudless world
like gulls afloat above islands.

Smoke out of Europe, death blown
on the wind, and a cloak of darkness for the spirit.

II

Land of mountains and running water
rocks and flowers
and the leafy evergreen, O natal earth,
the atoms of your children
are bonded to you for ever:
though the images of your beauty lie in shadow,
time nor treachery, nor the regnant evil,
shall efface from the hearts of your children
from their eyes and from their fingertips
the remembrance of good.

Treading your hills, drinking your waters,
touching your greenness, they are content, finding
peace at the heart of strife
and a core of stillness in the whirlwind.
Absent, estranged from you, they are unhappy,
crying for you continually
in the night of their exile.

III

To prosper in a strange land
taking cocktails at twilight behind the hotel curtains,

buying cheap and selling dear, acquiring customs,
is to bob up and down like a fisherman's gaudy float
in a swift river.

He who comes back returns
to no ruin of gold nor riot of buds,
moan of doves in falling woods
nor wind of spring shaking the hedgerows,
heartsache, strangling sweetness: pictures
of change, extremes of time and growth,
making razor-sharp the tenses,
waking remembrance, torturing sense;

home-coming, returns only
to the dull green, hider of bones,
changeless, save in the slight spring
when the bush is peopled with flowers,
sparse clusters of white and yellow
on the dull green, like laughter in court;
and in summer when the coasts
bear crimson bloom, sprinkled like blood
on the lintel of the land.

IV

Fairest earth,
fount of life, giver of bodies,
deep well of our delight, breath of desire,
let us come to you
barefoot, as befits love,
as the boy to the trembling girl,
as the child to the mother:
seeking before all things the honesty of substance,
touch of soil and wind and rock,
frost and flower and water,
the honey of the senses, the food
of love's imagining; and the most intimate
touch of love, that turns to being;
deriving wisdom, and the knowledge of necessity;
building thereon, stone by stone,
the rational architecture of truth, to house
the holy flame, that is neither reason nor unreason
but the thing given,
the flame that burns blue in the stillness, hovering
between the green wood of the flesh and the smoke of death.

Fair earth, we have broken our idols:
and after the days of fire we shall come to you
for the stones of a new temple.

Full Fathom Five

He was such a curious lover of shells
and the hallucinations of water
that he could never return out of the sea
without first having to settle a mermaid's bill.

Groping along the sea-bottom of the age
he discovered many particulars he did not care to speak about
even in the company of water-diviners
things sad and unspeakable
moss-covered skulls with bodies fluttering inside
with the unreality of specks moving before the eyes of a
    photograph
trumpets tossed from the decks of ocean-going liners
eccentric starfish fallen from impossible heavens
fretting on uncharted rocks
still continents with trees and houses like a child's drawing
and in every cupboard of the ocean
weary dolphins trapped in honey-coloured cobwebs
murmuring to the revolution Will you be long.

He was happy down there under the frothing ship-lanes
because nobody ever bothered him with statistics
or talk of yet another dimension of the mind.

And eventually and tragically finding he could not drown
he submitted himself to the judgement of the desert
and was devoured by man-eating ants
with a rainbow of silence branching from his lips.

Tapu

To stave off disaster, or bring the devil to heel,
    or to fight against fear, some carry a ring or a locket,
but I, who have nothing to lose by the turn of the wheel,
    and nothing to gain, I carry the world in my pocket.

For all I have gained, and have lost, is locked up in this
        thing,
    this cup of cracked bone from the skull of a fellow long
        dead,
with a hank of thin yellowish hair fastened in with a ring.
    For a symbol of death and desire these tokens are wed.

The one I picked out of a cave in a windy cliff-face
   where the old Maoris slept, with a curse on the stranger
        who moved,
in despite of tapu, but a splinter of bone from that place.
   The other I cut from the head of the woman I loved.

Epithalamium

We have found our peace, and move with a turning globe;
the night is all about us, the lovers' robe.

Mortal my love, my strength: your beauty their wound.
Strip quickly darling, your fingers be the wind

undressing a snowy peak to the sun's love,
scatter your clouds, be Everest, O my Eve.

Leap on the bed, lie still, your body truth become dream
torturing my arms before their kingdom come.

Give the wise their negations, the moralists their maps;
our empire the moment, the geometer's point where all shapes

of delight are hidden as joy sleeps in the vine.
I tell you again, what the poor have always known,

that this is all the heaven we shall ever find
in all our footsore and fatal journey and beyond,

and we shall never have enough to keep out foul weather,
or to eke out age, will perish forgetful of each other,

yet breeding saints or subduing Asia set against this
were violating our lives with littleness.

Now at the brink of being, in our pride of blood
let us remember lost lovers, think of the dead

who have no power, who aching in earth lie,
the million bones, white longings in the night of eternity.

O love, how many of our faith have fallen!
Endless the torrent of time, endless and swollen

with tributaries from the broken veins of lovers.
I kiss you in remembrance of all true believers.

Midnight thoughts. Dark garlands to adorn your flesh
so it shine like snow, like fire. Flakes of ash

blowing from doom's far hill. Such wisps of terror
gazed at too long even in your body's mirror

would disrupt our continent, drain our seas,
bring all to nothing. Love, let us laugh and kiss,

only your lips but not with speech can tell
moving in the darkness what is unspeakable,

and though your eyes reflect spring's green and yellow like a pool
I cannot see them, can only guess at what is more beautiful

than home at last, than a child's sleep, more full of pity
and gentleness than snow falling on a burning city.

The Cave

From the cliff-top it appeared a place of defeat,
the nest of an extinct bird, or the hole where the sea hoards
    its bones,
a pocket of night in the sun-faced rock,
sole emblem of mystery and death in that enormous noon.

We climbed down, and crossed over the sand,
and there were islands floating in the wind-whipped blue,
and clouds and islands trembling in your eyes,
and every footstep and every glance
was a fatality felt and unspoken, our way
rigid and glorious as the sun's path,
unbroken as the genealogy of man.

And when we had passed beyond
into the secret place and were clasped
by the titanic shadows of the earth,
all was transfigured, all was redeemed,
so that we escaped from the days
that had hunted us like wolves, and from ourselves,
in the brief eternity of the flesh.

There should be the shapes of leaves and flowers
printed on the rock, and a blackening of the walls
from the flame on your mouth,
to be found by the lovers straying
from the picnic two worlds hence, to be found and known,

because the form of the dream is always the same,
and whatever dies or changes this will persist and recur,
will compel the means and the end, find consummation,
whether it be
silent in swansdown and darkness, or in grass moonshadow-
    mottled,
or in a murmuring cave of the sea.

We left, and returned to our lives:

the act entombed, its essence caught
for ever in the wind, and in the noise of waves,
for ever mixed
with lovers' breaths who by salt-water coasts
in the sea's beauty dwell.

A Farewell

What is there left to be said?
There is nothing we can say,
nothing at all to be done
to undo the time of day;
no words to make the sun
roll east, or raise the dead.

I loved you as I love life:
the hand I stretched out to you
returning like Noah's dove
brought a new earth to view,
till I was quick with love;
but Time sharpens his knife,

Time smiles and whets his knife,
and something has got to come out
quickly, and be buried deep,
not spoken or thought about
or remembered even in sleep.
You must live, get on with your life.

For an Amulet

What truly is will have no end,
although denied by friend or foe,
and this I tell to foe and friend
as onward to the grave we go.

The candle in my little room
gives light but will not bake the host.
I share my certainty with Hume,
my candle with the Holy Ghost.

The Estuary

The wind has died, no motion now
in the summer's sleepy breath. Silver the sea-grass,
the shells and the driftwood, fixed in the moon's vast
    crystal.
Think: long after, when the walls of the small house
have collapsed upon us, each alone,
far gone the earth's invasion
the slow earth bedding and filling the bone,
this water will still be crawling up the estuary,
fingering its way among the channels, licking the stones;
and the floating shells, minute argosies
under the giant moon, still shoreward glide
among the mangroves on the creeping tide.

The noise of gulls comes through the shining darkness
over the dunes and the sea. Now the clouded moon
is warm in her nest of light. The world's a shell
where distant waves are murmuring of a time
beyond this time. *Give me the ghost of your hand:*
unreal, unreal the dunes,
the sea, the mangroves, and the moon's white light,
unreal, beneath our naked feet, the sand.

Solitude

The curtains in the solemn room
    are drawn against the winter dusk;
the lady sitting in the gloom
    has hair that faintly smells of musk.

As in some dim romantic night
    the mist will not divulge the moon,
around her unbetrothèd plight
    her thoughts have woven a cocoon.

Now recollection brings again
    the distant hour, the tide that flowed,
the word that might have flowered then
    as epic or as episode.

Half proud because the thing she sought,
   still lacking, is inviolate,
half puzzled by that eerie thought
   she rocks her chair and scans the grate.

Then suddenly she sees it clear,
   the monstrous image, cold, precise—
the body of the mountaineer
   preserved within the glacial ice,
      for ever safe, where none shall seek,
      beneath the unattempted peak.

I'm Older than You, Please Listen

To the young man I would say:
Get out! Look sharp, my boy,
before the roots are down,
before the equations are struck,
before a face or a landscape
has power to shape or destroy.
This land is a lump without leaven,
a body that has no nerves.
Don't be content to live in
a sort of second-grade heaven
with first-grade butter, fresh air,
and paper in every toilet;
becoming a butt for the malice
of those who have stayed and soured,
staying in turn to sour,
to smile, and savage the young.
If you're enterprising and able,
smuggle your talents away,
hawk them in livelier markets
where people are willing to pay.
If you have no stomach for roughage,
if patience isn't your religion,
if you must have sherry with your bitters,
if money and fame are your pigeon,
if you feel that you need success
and long for a good address,
don't anchor here in the desert—
the fishing isn't so good:
take a ticket for Megalopolis,
don't stay in this neighbourhood!

Down on My Luck

Wandering above a sea of glass
   in the soft April weather,
wandering through the yellow grass
   where the sheep stand and blether;
roaming the cliffs in the morning light,
   hearing the gulls that cry there,
not knowing where I'll sleep tonight,
   not much caring either.

     I haven't got a stiver
       the tractor's pinched my job,
     I owe the bar a fiver
       and the barman fifteen bob;
     the good times are over,
       the monkey-man has foreclosed,
     the woman has gone with the drover,
       not being what I supposed.

     I used to set things spinning,
       I used to dress like a lord,
     mostly I came out winning,
       but all that's gone by the board;
     my pants have lost their creases,
       I've fallen down on my luck,
     the world has dropped to pieces,
       everything's come unstuck.

Roaming the cliffs in the morning light,
   hearing the gulls that cry there,
not knowing where I'll sleep tonight,
   not much caring either,
wandering above a sea of glass
   in the soft April weather,
wandering through the yellow grass
   close to the end of my tether.

R. A. K. MASON

Old Memories of Earth

I think I have no other home than this
    I have forgotten much remember much
    but I have never any memories such
    as these make out they have of lands of bliss.

Perhaps they have done, will again do what
    they say they have, drunk as gods on godly drink,
    but I have not communed with gods I think
    and even though I live past death shall not.

I rather am for ever bondaged fast
    to earth and have been: so much untaught I know.
    Slow like great ships often I have seen go
    ten priests ten each time round a grave long past

And I recall I think I can recall
    back even past the time I started school
    or went a-crusoeing in the corner pool
    that I was present at a city's fall

And I am positive that yesterday
    walking past One Tree Hill and quite alone
    to me there came a fellow I have known
    in some old times, but when I cannot say:

Though we must have been great friends, I and he,
    otherwise I should not remember him
    for everything of the old life seems dim
    as last year's deeds recalled by friends to me.

Body of John

Oh I have grown so shrivelled and sere
    But the body of John enlarges
    and I can scarcely summon a tear
    but the body of John discharges

It's true my old roof is near ready to drop
    But John's boards have burst asunder
    and I am perishing cold here atop
    but his bones lie stark hereunder.

Sonnet of Brotherhood

Garrisons pent up in a little fort
    with foes who do but wait on every side
    knowing the time soon comes when they shall ride
    triumphant over those trapped and make sport
    of them: when those within know very short
    is now their hour and no aid can betide:
    such men as these not quarrel and divide
    but friend and foe are friends in their hard sort

And if these things be so oh men then what
    of these beleaguered victims this our race
    betrayed alike by Fate's gigantic plot
    here in this far-pitched perilous hostile place
    this solitary hard-assaulted spot
    fixed at the friendless outer edge of space.

The Spark's Farewell to Its Clay

I

Well clay it's strange at last we've come to it:
    after much merriment we must give up
    our ancient friendship: no more shall we sup
    in pleasant quiet places wanly-lit
    nor wander through the falling rain, sharp-smit
    and buffeted you, while I within snug-shut:
    no longer taste the mingled bitter-sweet cup
    of life the one inscrutable has thought fit

To give to us: no longer know the strife
    that we from old have each with each maintained:
    now our companionship has certain end
    end without end: at last of this our life
    you surely have gained blank earth walls
        my friend
    and I? God only knows what I have gained.

II

There is no thought that any hope can give
    for this fine hair and these long pliant hands
    and this proud body that so firmly stands
    these eyes deep delicate and sensitive:
    vain vain for such in mind towards hope to strive.
    What if my body has at its commands
    strength beauty knowledge rule of many lands
    still is not any hope that it can live.

Perhaps I seek myself and am not whole:
    times think I in some pure place there can wait
    a far surpassing fellow for my soul
    and joy to think when I shall find that mate—
    still you good easy earth must pay earth-toll
    I recollect and so am desolate.

Latter-day Geography Lesson

This, quoth the Eskimo master
    was London in English times:
    step out a little bit faster
    you two young men at the last there
    the Bridge would be on our right hand
    and the Tower near where those crows stand—
    we struck it you'll recall in Gray's rhymes:
    this, quoth the Eskimo master
    was London in English times.

This, quoth the Eskimo master
    was London in English days:
    beyond that hill they called Clapham
    boys that swear Master Redtooth I slap 'em
    I dis-tinct-ly heard—you—say—Bastard
    don't argue: here boys, ere disaster
    overtook her, in splendour there lay
    a city held empires in sway
    and filled all the earth with her praise:
    this, quoth the Eskimo master
    was London in English days.

She held, quoth the Eskimo master
    ten million when her prime was full
    from here once Britannia cast her
    gaze over an Empire vaster
    even than ours: look there Woking
    stood, I make out, and the Abbey
    lies here under our feet *you great babby*
    Swift-and-short do—please—kindly—stop—poking
    vour thumbs through the eyes of that skull.

Song of Allegiance

Shakespeare Milton Keats are dead
    Donne lies in a lowly bed

Shelley at last calm doth lie
    knowing 'whence we are and why'

Byron Wordsworth both are gone
    Coleridge Beddoes Tennyson

Housman neither knows nor cares
    how 'this heavy world' now fares

Little clinging grains enfold
    all the mighty minds of old . . .

They are gone and I am here
    stoutly bringing up the rear

Where they went with limber ease
    toil I on with bloody knees

Though my voice is cracked and harsh
    stoutly in the rear I march

Though my song have none to hear
    boldly bring I up the rear.

Oils and Ointments

Let me fall down about your feet oh Christ
    that have bruised and bled along the lonely way,
    wait here my bringing forth those highly priced
    treasures I have saved up this many a day.

The ointments I bring up to you my lord
    gleam jewels like a steel-flashing beetle shard
    lo! I shower down cascading the rich hoard
    frankincense aloes myrrh cassia spikenard,

Sluggish oil that glints oh look rainbows and gold
    gently assailing unguents the orient has spiced
    slow pouring balm smooth smearing calm behold
    and stretch out your soothful longing foot oh Christ.

Nails and a Cross

Nails and a cross and crown of thorn,
    here I die the mystery-born:
    here's an end to adventurings
    here all great and valiant things
    find as far as I'm concerned a grave.

God, I may say that I've been brave
    and it's led me——? Damned and deified
    here I spurt the blood from a riven side:
    blood, never revisit my heart again
    but suck the wisdom out of my brain
    I got in so many lonely days
    bruising my feet with flinty ways.

For I left my boyhood dog and fire
    my old bed and him I called my sire
    my mother my village my books and all
    to follow the wild and lonely call
    luring me into the solitary
    road that has brought me here to die.

And I see, if I squint, my blood of death
    drip on the little harsh grass beneath
    and friend and foe and men long dead
    faint and reel in my whirling head:
    and while the troops divide up my cloak
    the mob fling dung and see the joke.

If the Drink

If the drink that satisfied
    the son of Mary when he died
    has not the right smack for you
    leave it for a kindlier brew.

For my bitter verses are
    sponges steeped in vinegar
    useless to the happy-eyed
    but handy for the crucified.

On the Swag

His body doubled
    under the pack
    that sprawls untidily
    on his old back
    the cold wet dead-beat
    plods up the track.

The cook peers out:
    'oh curse that old lag—
    here again
    with his clumsy swag
    made of a dirty old
    turnip bag.'

'Bring him in cook
    from the grey level sleet
    put silk on his body
    slippers on his feet,
    give him fire
    and bread and meat.

Let the fruit be plucked
    and the cake be iced,
    the bed be snug
    and the wine be spiced
    in the old cove's night-cap:
    for this is Christ.'

Judas Iscariot

Judas Iscariot
    sat in the upper
    room with the others
    at the last supper

And sitting there smiled
    up at his master
    whom he knew the morrow
    would roll in disaster.

At Christ's look he guffawed—
    for then as thereafter
    Judas was greatly
    given to laughter,

Indeed they always said
    that he was the veriest
    prince of good fellows
    and the whitest and merriest.

All the days of his life
    he lived gay as a cricket
    and would sing like the thrush
    that sings in the thicket

He would sing like the thrush
    that sings on the thorn
    oh he was the most sporting bird
    that ever was born.

Footnote to John ii. 4

Don't throw your arms around me in that way:
    I know that what you tell me is the truth—
    yes I suppose I loved you in my youth
    as boys do love their mothers, so they say,
    but all that's gone from me this many a day:
    I am a merciless cactus an uncouth
    wild goat a jagged old spear the grim tooth
    of a lone crag . . . Woman I cannot stay.

Each one of us must do his work of doom
    and I shall do it even in despite
    of her who brought me in pain from her womb,
    whose blood made me, who used to bring the light
    and sit on the bed up in my little room
    and tell me stories and tuck me up at night.

Ecce Homunculus

Betrayed by friend dragged from the garden hailed
    as prophet and as lord in mockery
    hauled down where Roman Pilate sat on high
    perplexed and querulous, lustily assailed
    by every righteous Hebrew cried down railed
    against by all true zealots—still no sigh
    escaped him but he boldly went to die
    made scarcely a moan when his soft flesh was nailed.

And so he brazened it out right to the last
    still wore the gallant mask still cried 'Divine
    am I, lo for me is heaven overcast'
    though that inscrutable darkness gave no sign
    indifferent or malignant: while he was passed
    by even the worst of men at least sour wine.

The Young Man Thinks of Sons

Did my father curse his father for his lust I wonder
    as I do mine
and my grand-dad curse his sire for his wickedness his weakness
  his blunder
    and so on down the whole line

Well I'll stop the game break the thread end my race: I will not
  continue
    in the old bad trade:
I'll take care that for my nerveless mind weakened brain neglected
  sinew
    I alone shall have paid.

Let the evil book waste in its swathings the ill pen write not one
  iota
    the ship of doom not sail,
let the sword rot unused in its scabbard let the womb lack its
  quota:
    here let my line fail:

Let the plough rust untouched of the furrow, yea let the blind
  semen
    stretch vain arms for the virgin:
I'll hammer no stringed harps for gods to clash discords, or
  women:
    my orchard won't burgeon.

I'll take care that the lust of my loins never bring to fruition
    the seed of a son
who in his nettle-grown kingdom should curse both my sins of
  commission
    and what I left undone.

Lugete O Veneres

With his penis swollen for the girl on the next farm and rigid
        here he lies on his bed
motionless dumb and his naked corpse goose-fleshed and as frigid
        as if he were dead:

Only at times a great sob rises up in his drawn aching throttle
        and dies like his hope
or the tear of his anguish drips down on his arm cold and mottled
        like a bar of blue soap.

For the people next door have packed up their pots and their
    table
        and their mats and their ploughs
they have brought up their pigs from the sty their steeds from
    the stable
        and driven off the cows.

Tomorrow strange people will reign there tomorrow the stranger
        will inherit their places
other cows know the shed where they milk, new horses the
    manger
        and dogs with unknown faces.

Mark how dejected tormented he lies poor lad while shivers
        run and shake his fat arse:
for a space let us mourn here this tortured boy's slobbering
    quivers
        as we laugh at the farce.

Our Love was a Grim Citadel

Our love was a grim citadel:
    no tawdry plaything for the minute
    of strong dark stone we built it well
    and based in the ever-living granite:

The urgent columns of the years
    press on, like tall rain up the valley:
    and Chaos bids ten thousand spears
    run to erase our straw-built folly.

Flow at Full Moon

Your spirit flows out over all the land between
    your spirit flows out as gentle and limpid as milk
    flows on down ridge and through valley as soft and serene
    as the light of the moon that sifts down through its light
            sieve of silk

The long fingers of the flow press forward, the whole hand follows
    easily the fingers creep they're your hair's strands that curl
    along the land's brow, your hair dark-bright gleaming on
            heights and hollows
    and the moon illumines the flow with mother of pearl

Beloved your love is poured to enchant all the land
    the great bull falls still the opossum turns from his chatter
    and the thin nervous cats pause and the strong oak-trees
            stand
    entranced and the gum's restless bark-strip is stilled from its
            clatter

Your spirit flows out from your deep and radiant nipples
    and the whole earth turns tributary all her exhalations
    wave up in white breath and are absorbed in the ripples
    that pulse like a bell along the blood from your body's
            pulsations

And as the flow settles down to the sea it nets me about
    with a noose of one soft arm stretched out from its course:
    oh loved one my dreams turn from sleep: I shall rise and
            go out
    and float my body into the flow and press back till I find
            its source.

ROBIN HYDE

The Bronze Rider, Wellington

Riding wooden horses from the hot Christmas Caves,
The children came laughing out into the Quay,
With a prance at their hills, and a dash at their waves,
And the broad street between shining peaceful and free.
Cheeks nipped in the wind, and their curls sailing gold,
Rode the sons and the daughters . . . (Come home, dears,
       come home.)
But a wind from the sea blows, a thin mist blows cold . . .
Faint down the Quay sounds the tuck of a drum.

Children, come home, and be kissed as you're told.
(Ah, but who said it? A child could grow old.)
Home when you're bid, or the length of my tongue.
(Ah, but who said it? A child could die young.)
Now the bronze Rider comes to stay awhile,
In our hilly heart, so haunted by running feet;
Turns to the dusk his young, mysterious smile,
Implacably, unanswerably sweet.
He props the sky up with his stiff young arm,
Lest down it drop on cradled cottages,
Do our poor groping ways of living harm,
Vex with a light our city, that was his.
O forfeit of this world. . . . The great bronze hooves,
Soundless, yet trampling air as they aspire,
Fling shame on us, who tread the ancient grooves;
Dawn is his stirrup, and his reins are fire.

Riding painted horses from town to Island Bay,
Mouths pink as moss-roses, hair sailing free,
Past the penny-shops, awning-shops, red shops and grey,
Past the vast jars of peppermint down to the sea;
Past the Blue Platter Inn, that's been burnt seven year,
Ride the sons and the daughters. (Come home, loves,
       come home.)
But the sound of a bugle folds crisp on the air,
The swish of a keel cutting out in the foam.

Children, come home, will you hear your Dad shout?
(Ah, but who said it? A ship could glide out . . .)
Home to your broth and your books, as you're bid . . .
(Ah, but who cried it? Our lamps could be hid.)

Faint on the Quay sounds the throb of the drum.

The Last Ones

But the last black horse of all
Stood munching the green-bud wind,
And the last of the raupo huts
Let down its light behind.
Sullen and shadow-clipped
He tugged at the evening star,
New-mown slivers swished like straw
Across the manuka.

As for the hut, it said
No word but its meagre light,
Its people slept as the dead,
Bedded in Maori night.
'And there is the world's last door,
And the last world's horse,' sang the wind,
'With little enough before,
And what you have seen behind.'

from *The Beaches*

VI

Close under here, I watched two lovers once,
Which should have been a sin, from what you say:
I'd come to look for prawns, small pale-green ghosts,
Sea-coloured bodies tickling round the pool.
But tide was out then; so I strolled away
And climbed the dunes, to lie here warm, face down,
Watching the swimmers by the jetty-posts
And wrinkling like the bright blue wrinkling bay.
It wasn't long before they came; a fool
Could see they had to kiss; but your pet dunce
Didn't quite know men count on more than that;
And so just lay, patterning the sand.
                        And they
Were pale thin people, not often clear of town;
Elastic snapped, when he jerked off her hat;
I heard her arguing, 'Dick, my frock!' But he
Thought she was bread.
I wished her legs were brown,
And mostly, then, stared at the dawdling sea,
Hoping Perry would row me some day in his boat.

Not all the time; and when they'd gone, I went
Down to the hollow place where they had been,
Trickling bed through fingers. But I never meant

To tell the rest, or you, what I had seen;
Though that night, when I came in late for tea,
I hoped you'd see the sandgrains on my coat.

from *The Houses*

I

Old nursery chair; its legs, cut down, are broken:
Old timepiece, out-of-date, forlorn and slow:
Slow creaking shadow; somebody unawoken.
Trumpet: don't touch it, soldier, it won't blow.

III

Adolicus; that's a creeper rug, its small
Pink-and-white piecemeal flowers swarm down a fence:
So little, no scent to be by; show, pretence—
Nothing to do, but hide the rotting wall.
Three slats were broken: but the street-boys' eyes
Can't climb in here like ants and frighten us.
Stare if they like: we've the adolicus.

V

None of it true; for Christ's sake, spill the ink,
Tear out this charnel's darnel-root, that lingers
Sprouting words, words, words! Give me cool bluegum
       leaves
To rub brittle between my fingers.

I had the touch of hillside once: the ever-
So-slender cold of buttercup stems in brink:
Pebbles: great prints in mud: Oh, Lazarus, bring me
Some mountain honesty to drink!

Pihsien Road

Old men in blue: and heavily encumbered
Old shoulders held by shadowy whips in sway,
Like ox and ass, that down this road have lumbered
All day: all the bright murderous day.
More than their stumbling footprints press this clay.

And light in air, pure white, in wonder riding,
Some crazy Phaeton these have never known
Holds by a lever their last awe, deciding
How flesh shall spurt from sinews, brain from bone—
Crushing desolate grain with a harder stone.

What Is It Makes the Stranger?

What is it makes the stranger? Say, oh eyes!
Because I was journeying far, sailing alone,
Changing one belt of stars for the northern belt,
Men in my country told me, 'You will be strange—
Their ways are not our ways; not like ourselves
They think, suffer, and dream.'
So sat I silent, and watched the stranger, why he was strange.
But now, having come so far, shed the eight cloaks of wind,
Ridden ponies of foam, and the great stone lions of six strange
          cities.
What is it makes the stranger? Say, oh eyes!
Eyes cannot tell. They view the self-same world—
Outer eyes vacant till thoughts and pictures fill them,
Inner eyes watching secret paths of the brain.
Hands? But the hands of my country knit reeds, bend wood,
Shape the pliable parts of boats and roofs.
Mend pots, paint pictures, write books
Though different books; glean harvests, if different harvests,
Not so green as young rice first shaking its spears from water.
Hands cannot say. Feet then? They say
In shoe, not sandal, or bare if a man be poor,
They thread long ways between daylight and dark,
Longer, from birth to death.
Know flint from grasses, wear soles through, hate sharp pebbles,
Oftentimes long for the lightness of birds.
Yet in my country, children, even the poor
Wear soft warm shoes, and a little foot in the dance
Warms the looks of young men, no less than here.
In my country, on summer evenings, clean as milk poured out
From old blue basins, children under the hawthorne trees
Fly kites, lacing thin strings against the sky.
Not at New Year, but at other festivals
We light up fire-crackers
In memory of old buried danger, now a ghost danger.

On a roof garden, among the red-twigged bowing of winter
          trees,
The small grave bowls of dwarf pines (our pines grow tall
Yet the needle-sharp hair is the same) one first star swam,
Silver in lily-root dusk. Two lovers looked up.
Hands, body, heart in my breast,
Whispered, 'These are the same. Here we are not so strange—
Here there are friends and peace.
We have known such ways, we in our country!'
Black-tiled roofs, curled like wide horns, and hiding safe
From the eyes of the stranger, all that puts faith in you.

Remember this, of an unknown woman who passed,
But who stood first high on the darkening roof garden looking
      down.
My way behind me tattered away in wind,
Before me, was spelt with strange letters.
My mind was a gourd heavy with sweet and bitter waters.
Since I could not be that young girl, who heedless of stars
Now watched the face of her lover,
I wished to be, for one day, a man selling mandarins,
A blackened tile in some hearth place; a brazier, a well, a good
      word,
A blackened corpse along the road to Chapei,
Of a brave man, dead for his country.
Shaking the sweet-bitter waters within my mind,
It seemed to me, all seas fuse and intermarry.
Under the seas, all lands knit fibre, interlock:
On a highway so ancient as China's
What are a few miles more to the ends of the earth?
Is another lantern too heavy to light up, showing the face
Of farers and wayfarers, stumbling the while they go,
Since the world has called them stranger?

Only two rebels cried out 'We do not understand.'
Ear said, 'China and we
Struck two far sides of a rock; music came forth,
Our music and theirs, not the one music.
Listening in street and stall I hear two words,
Their word and mine. Mine is not understood,
Therefore am I an exile here, a stranger,
Eaten up with hunger for what I understand,
And for that which understands.'
Tongue said, 'I know
The sweet flavours of mandarin or fish. But mouth and I,
Speaking here, are mocked. Looks fall on us like blows.
Mistress, we served you well, and not for cash,
But free men. Therefore, beseech you, let us go on.'

Heart, lowlier, said, 'There is a way of patience—
Let ear study the door to understanding.
Mouth, there is silence first, but fellowship
Where children laugh or weep, the grown smile or frown,
Study, perceive, and learn. Let not two parts
Unwisely make an exile of the whole.'
But still the rebels bawled, and so I saw
How in a world divorced from silences
These are the thieves.
Ear, who no longer listening well, sniffs up
The first vain trash, the first argument into his sack.

Mouth, who will spew it forth, but to be heard—
Both ill-taught scholars, credulous liars,
Seizing on, flinging up fuel.
There flamed the restlessness of such sick worlds,
As cannot know their country or earth's country;
Their moment or an age's moment.
Having such brawling servants in my train
I can be neither tile nor lamp.
Only a footprint. Some boy sees it at dawn
Before his high-wheeled cart creaks over it;
Only a sped and broken arrow,
Pointing a way where men will come in peace.

The Deserted Village

In the deserted village, sunken down
With a shrug of last weak old age, pulled back to earth,
All people are fled or killed. The cotton crop rots,
Not one mild house leans sideways, a man on crutches,
Not a sparrow earns from the naked floors,
Walls look, but cannot live without the folk they loved—
It would be a bad thing to awaken them.
Having broken the rice-bowl, seek not to fill it again.

The village temple, well built, with five smashed gods, ten whole ones,
Does not want prayers. It's last vain prayer bled up
When the women ran outside to be slain.
A temple must house its sparrows or fall asleep,
Therefore a long time, under his crown of snails,
The gilded Buddha demands to meditate.
No little flowering fires on the incense-strings
Startle Kwan-Yin, whom they dressed in satin—
Old women sewing beads like pearls in her hair.
This was a temple for the very poor ones:
Their gods were mud and lathe: but artfully
Some village painter coloured them all.
Wooden dragons were carefully carved.
Finding in mangled wood one smiling childish tree,
Roses and bells not one foot high,
I set it back, at the feet of Kwan-Yin.
A woman's prayer-bag,
Having within her paper prayers, paid for in copper,
Seeing it torn, I gathered it up.
I shall often think, 'The woman I did not see
Voiced here her dying wish.
But the gods dreamed on. So low her voice, so loud
The guns, all that death-night, who would stoop to hear?'

CHARLES BRASCH

The Islands (ii)

Always, in these islands, meeting and parting
Shake us, making tremulous the salt-rimmed air;
Divided, many-tongued, the sea is waiting,
Bird and fish visit us and come no more.
Remindingly beside the quays the white
Ships lie smoking; and from their haunted bay
The godwits vanish towards another summer.
Everywhere in light and calm the murmuring
Shadow of departure; distance looks our way;
And none knows where he will lie down at night.

Great Sea

Kona Coast, Hawaii

Speak for us, great sea.

Speak in the night, compelling
The frozen heart to hear,
The memoried to forget.
O speak, until your voice
Possess the night, and bless
The separate and fearful;
Under folded darkness
All the lost unite—
Each to each discovered,
Vowed and wrought by your voice
And in your life, that holds
And penetrates our life:
You from whom we rose,
In whom our power lives on.
All night, all night till dawn
Speak for us, great sea.

from *Nineteen Thirty-nine*

I

The City

The walls divide us from water and from light,
Fruits are sold but do not ripen here;
We cannot tell the time of year,
And lamps and traffic estrange us from the night.

What of our fellow-citizens, the doves
And sparrows that seem now to belong here? Could
They live as freely in hedgerow and in wood
After generations of town lives?

For we have shut ourselves off from the larger world
And grown hearts narrow like alleys; we are afraid
Of quiet, emptiness, the far away.

No one knows what his neighbour is called,
But fears him; defences go up; weapons are made
To keep the unknown constantly at bay.

III

Far on the mountains of pain there may yet be a place
For breath, where the insensate wind is still,
A hollow of stones where you can bow your face
And relax the quivering distended will.

There earth's life will speak to you again,
An insect in the grasses, a meagre bird,
That in that outpost faithfully maintain
The pulse of being so slowly, weakly heard.

And they remain. But you go on, and bear
The frail life farther yet, blindly and slow,
Into the pitiless mountains and the glare
Of deathly light, ceasing to know or care
If you are still man; but the frozen rocks know,
And the white wind massing against you as you go.

Photograph of a Baby

Round-head round-eyed Sebastian,
Wrinkling his eyes against the sun,
Looks into the distance and will not see anyone.

What does he find there
At the end of his absorbing stare,
Where Mt. Herbert floats weightless in the glass-clear air?

It is something he does not meet
Among us, that he will not be asked to greet,
To laugh at or yield to, because it knows how to treat

Him as an equal, as fact,
The present and plain, which neither bluffness nor tact
Can make more real or charm away or even distract.

Such he can understand,
It is primal like himself, like the sun on his hand,
Disdaining to raise a smoke-screen of reasons for what must
        be, and

Ignores all conditions. For though objects are multiplied
Hourly in his world, he cannot put them aside,
But always must try to see them as clearly as though they
        had died,

As still and as final; and he
Has the air of one looking back, by death set free,
Who sees the strangeness of life, and what things are trying
        to be.

Word by Night

Ask in one life no more
Than that first revelation of earth and sky,
Renewed as now in the place of birth
Where the sea turns and the first roots go down.

By the same light also you may know yourselves:
You are of those risen from the sea
And for ever bound to the sea,
Which is but the land's other and older face.

It is time to replant the seed of life
At this rich boundary where it first sprang,
For you are water and earth,
Creatures of the shore, disputed ground.

For too long now too many have been deceived,
Renouncing the bare nursery of the race,
Trying to shed the limiting names
That link them to their kind;

Have sought sufficiency
In the contingent and derivative,
Wishing to rise from doubtful earth
And move secure among the abstract stars;

But faltering, losing the prime sense of direction,
Fell at last in mindless lassitude
Among the traffic,
Chattering, withered, unrecognizable.

Come again to the shore, the gathering place,
Where cries of sea-birds wring the air,
And by the poverty of rocks remember
Human degrees.

Water rises through the sand, but near
Are the first pastures,
Dyed by the shadow of a leaf,
Promise of the mind's kingdoms.

Seasons that bore you bring renewal,
But do not alter
The nature of your never-finished nature,
Nor the condition of time.

Oreti Beach

Thunder of waves out of the dying west,
Thunder of time that overtakes our day;
Evening islands founder, gold sand turns grey
In ocean darkness where we walk possessed.

What does it mean, this clamorous fall of night
Upon the heart's stillness? What pledge can they give,
These passionate powers of the world, that we might live
More surely than by the soul's solitary light?

Letter from Thurlby Domain

I walk among my great-grandfather's trees.
Through poplar and pine pour the steady seas
Of mild mountain wind, norwester, in long-
Breathed tide and calm of voice shaking their strong
Rock-bedded roots; yet, below, the air is still
In this orchard-harbour deep embayed in the hill-
Terrace, where cattle graze in thick grass
By pear-tree, apricot, walnut, and through the ground-bass
Swell of the wind quivers and rings a thread
Of song from leaf-lost birds. But dumb and dead
In this quick summer stir the old house decays,
Hollow, unroofed, with staring window-bays

And boards torn up; from fallen foundations the stone
Walls lean outward; garrulous starlings own
It as home now, but after ninety years
No man any more.

                When a long-lived house disappears,
Ruined, into this raw-man's-land, and grows
New harvests of elder and thistle and briar rose,
An air of contentment breathes from it, almost
Of reconciliation, the laying of a ghost—
That figure of brute man breaking in on nature,
Defiling its sanctities, altering rhythm and feature,
That represents us all, that haunts all
Our works till they too are proved natural
By their decay, and so are lost to us
And given back to nature; like this house.

A debt is paid here then, a silent wrong
Atoned in silence, and one man's works belong
At last to earth. But man's earth: is it not now
Man's, marked with the sign of axe and plough,
Watered, shaded, settled? For men have brought
Ripe gifts to soften the rigours that contort
This towering snow-dazzled sun-shot world
Of rock on rock, mountain on mountain hurled,
Cupping cold lakes, bare valleys curved for sleep.

Look, he who built here planted: road, hedge, and sweep
Of fields, garden, and stable; this avenue
All summer sounding, cool in the blazing blue,
Its poplar-fountains soaring from some green well
Under the waste where there was nothing to tell
Of water's sweetness; and hill of twilight pine,
And the wind-censing gum's tattered ensign
Over the running grasses; ash, acacia,
Lime, and tall towers of wellingtonia—
All his; and he in Lebanon plucked the cone
From which that masterful cedar sprang alone;
He, my great-grandfather whom I did not know,
Who built and sowed and left his seed to grow
Cradling the land. So these rich groves (and those
That crown now the bare peninsula he chose
For Queenstown Park) make him a monument,
And marry us to this earth; but for the spent,
The sober house, that held so mildly together
Brunswick and Lincolnshire in colonial tether—
All trace of person gone, all family pride,
Call it man's first-fruits offered and not denied.

Cast on this Eden we must violate still,
Where shall we find that good for which we do ill
By necessity, but so long? Where, if not in
The heart's peace from which all worlds begin,
Our wrong and loss and pain with a due kiss
Sealed in acknowledgement of our genesis;
Not by inflaming nor by stilling desire,
But learning in the fire the nature of fire,
Upon the wheel replenishing the wheel,
Caught in the dance that sifts unreal from real.
Dead house and living trees and we that live
To make our peace on earth and become native
In place and time, in life and death: how should
We entertain any other goal or good
Than this, than here?
                        From Crown to Coronet
The sun has swung overhead, and burning yet
Thirsts for western waters; the wind will soon die
In the trees; at my foot a lizard slides among dry
Stalks and is gone with a flickering good-bye.

Autumn, Thurlby Domain

What news for man in a broken house, old trees
And ruined garden dying among the hills?
Nothing is here to distract or to surprise,
Nothing except the plainness of stone walls
And trunks unleafing, what has been planted and grows,
What has been built to stand; that now fails,
Having served its time,
And goes back ripe to the earth from which it came.

What news? Are old age and decay so new
They put us out of countenance, offend
Lives that have long forgotten how to grow
And die, and do not care to understand
The elemental language of sickle and plough,
Of nursery and orchard, sun and wind,
That speak to us everywhere
With the same untroubled intimacy as here?

What we have found before we shall find again,
No new thing; age and youth seem strange to us
Who can no longer relight the morning sun,
Bring each day to birth in that bitter stress
And eddying joy that mark the life of a man
As years ring a tree; only in loss,

All knowledge stripped away,
We stumble towards our naked identity.

All civilizations, all societies,
Die with a dying house. These walls beheld
Rites of birth, marriage and death, customary days
Of equable happiness, dear hope unfulfilled,
Heart practised in patience and hand grown wise;
All riddling glory men have dreamed or hailed
Lived here in embryo or
Epitome, and dies in character.

What ceremony does autumn hold this afternoon
With green-gold bough and golden spire—what rite
Of pirouetting poplar-dancers, to crown
The dying year, the death of man's estate,
With brilliance so raptly and so lightly worn?
In celebration of death we consummate
Our vows to place and time,
In sickness and in health to live and die with them.

Self to Self

'Out of this thoughtless, formless, swarming life
What can I find of form and thought to live by,
What can I take that will make my song news?'

'Where nothing is, a seed may yet be sown.
Does not chaos cry for the forming hand?
Thought and form be the new song you choose.'

'But if this outward chaos only mirrors
Chaos within, confusion at the heart,
How can I start, where settle to begin?'

'The formless and the thoughtless then your theme;
Knowing disorder like the palm of your hand,
Set up house there, amid the stench and din,

And be at home in your own darkness, naming
Hand and mouth first, wall and ceiling, then all
That hurts you or offends, without as within,

All that you hate, that maddens, that merely is—
The ants, the dumb oxen, the golden calves
(For there is nothing you have the right to refuse);

And when you have bent before them, made them one
With the waste heart, they will obey your word,
Out of disorder bring you song for news.'

'To work in what I fear, subject my weakness
To power, surrender speech for an idiot dumbness?—
O worse than death, the very self to abuse.'

'What have you left to lose, disorder's own?
Only from incarnation of disorder
Can order spring, and you must end to begin,
If you would sing you must become news.'

from *The Estate*

xxii

Once more as I gather about me the cloak of the evening,
Fastening windows, drawing curtains, and moving
Arm-chair, paper, and books to the lamp and the fireside
That now till morning shall be a world sufficient,
I turn to you calmly, after the day's distractions,
And picture you as I would, alert and thoughtful,
Almost unchanged since dawn, or only changed by
Putting on more completely the rounded nature
So seldom visible to me undistorted
Because I see it in many climates and under
Changing aspects, each with its partial purpose
(For though we divine the nature of those who are near to
    us
We do not see it entire, never exhaust it,
Not in a lifetime: to see another completely
Would mean to reveal oneself to him completely
—Or to see with a god's eye, stilled and unjudging—
And that is not in our power, not in the lover's
Nor in the mother's power, neither by willing
Nor yet by surrender); find you although familiar
Fresh, dewed with surprises, as if you bore the
Archaic smile of the morning-marvelling kouroi;
You take possession again of my city of silence;
You are the limitless dark defining the circle
Of fireside, lamplight; you the inconceivable
Guest out of nowhere suddenly fiery and singing
Before me, midnight word of transfiguration.

What have you seen on the summits, the peaks that plunge
    their
Icy heads into space? What draws you trembling
To blind altars of rock where man cannot linger
Even in death, where body grows light, and vision
Ranging those uninhabitable stations
Dazzled and emulous among the rage of summoning
Shadows and clouds, may lead you in an instant
Out from all footing? What thread of music, what word in
That frozen silence that drowns the noise of our living?
What is life, you answer,
But to extend life, press its limits farther
Into the uncolonized nothing we must prey on
For every hard-won thought, all new creation
Of stone bronze music words; only at life's limit
Can man reach through necessity and custom
And move self by self into the province
Of that unrealized nature that awaits him,
His own to enter. But there are none to guide
 Across the threshold, interpret the saying of perilous
Music or word struck from that quivering climate,
Whose white inquisitors in close attendance
Are pain and madness and annihilation.

xxx

Thistle, briar, thorn:
Dark sayings of an earth
Austere even in the joy
That gave them birth.

Sweet across snow, over rock,
Singing briar that sows
Mountain and desert with alms
Of poverty's rose;

Outlaw thistle, quick
Through wild and ploughed to run
With barbed defiant crest
Bowing to none;

And thorn, weaving in air
Thirsty nets of pain,
Pointed with seed-pearl flowers'
Compassionate rain—

How shall I read your tongue's
Gnomic economy,

To whom the muse of silence
Made the word free?

Be my companions still
With wind and star and stone
Till in your desert music
I hear my own.

Ambulando

i

In middle life when the skin slackens
Its loving clasp of our loose volumes,
When the bone tree stiffens and its well-jointed branches
Begin to creak, to droop a little,
May the spirit hold out no longer for
Old impossible terms, demanding
Rent-free futures where all, all is ripeness,
But cry pax to its equivocal nature and stretch
At ease with wry destiny,
Supple as wind bowing in every reed.

ii

Now that the young with interest no longer
Look on me as one of themselves
Whom they might wish to know or to touch,
Seeing merely another sapless greyhead,
The passport of that disguise conducts me
Through any company unquestioned,
In cool freedom to come and go
With mode and movement, wave and wind.

iii

Communicate with stones, trees, water
If you must vent a heart too full.
Who will hear you now, your words falling
As foreign as bird-tongue
On ears attuned to different vibrations?
Trees, water, stones:
Let these answer a gaze contemplative
Of all things that flow out from them
And back to enter them again.

iv

I do not know the shape of the world.
I cannot set boundaries to experience.
I know it may open out, enlarged suddenly,

In any direction, to unpredictable distance,
Subverting climate and cosmography,
And carrying me far from tried moorings
So that I see myself no more
Under some familiar guise
Resting static as in a photograph,
Nor move as I supposed I was moving
From fixed point to point;
But rock outwards like the last stars that signal
At the frontiers of light,
Fleeing the centre without destination.

Physics of Love

The mutual magnetism of love
Nullifies every other force
That acts upon two infected bodies.
Even gravity is weakened as
They leap obstacles, ride
On their commonest occasions
Six inches above the unbelieving ground.

No Reparation

To make reparation for love so blindly rejected—
How, Gods? how?
After the years have marked them, outward and inwardly,
And they who might have been one remain still two.

Ask pardon for blindness?—well, it argues
A saving recognition, self-knowledge at last,
Although too late to alter what's done, repair
The ravaging of grief, melt the heart's frost.

And that exultant blaze of power that should
Have brought them side to side in matched passion—
Has it gone underground for ever? or smouldered away
Feeding on sour blood for its sole portion?

Ask neither pardon nor forgetfulness,
Do not hope to explain, say no word;
Only be slower to judge now, readier to understand
Those who are not yet dead.

Cry Mercy

Getting older, I grow more personal,
Like more, dislike more
And more intensely than ever—
People, customs, the state,
The ghastly status quo,
And myself, black-hearted crow
In the canting off-white feathers.

Long ago I lost sight of
That famous objectivity,
That classic, godlike calm
For which the wise subdue
Their poisonous hot hearts,
Strength of arm and righteous
Tongue, right indignation.

To know all, to bear all
Quietly, without protest,
To bend never breaking,
To live on, live for another
Day, an equable morning—
Is that what men are born for?
Is that best of all?

To each his own way,
For each his particular end.
Judging one another
By inner, private lights
Fortuitous as ourselves,
We leave some other to judge
By impersonal sunlight

Objective, as we hope,
In the after-world, if any,
What we have made of ourselves,
How we have laid out
That miserly talent, gift
Bestowed on us at the start
For the problematical journey.

How shall I make excuse
That I am not with those
Who lost the loving word
In sumps of fear and hate,
Convicts, displaced persons,

Castaways even of hope?
On them too a sun rises:

Any of us may be hunted
Among them any day.
What certainties assure
Another dawn will wake me
Or the galaxy swim on?
To live is to remember
Remembering to forget.

I lay down no law
For myself or my neighbour.
I search for can and must
Along the broken flare-path,
Pitching left and right
Shaken by voices and thunders,
By other lights, by looms
Of chaos, and my self-shadow.

Liking and disliking,
Unloving and wanting love,
Nearer to, farther from
My cross-grained fellow mortals,
On my level days I cry mercy
And on my lofty days give thanks
For the bewildering rough party.

Wantword

You do not want for words
The words I want
But keep your end up
Easily, with the rest
Having an end to keep.
Words will not serve me so
It is I must run for them
To their ends, having no
End that is not theirs,
Personal affairs
Nor business in company.
You ask words of me
At the wrong hour, in the wrong
Wind, the wrong words.
But when you are not present
Words well up in me
Gesturing, calling

Not to you, not to me
But on my lips, wantword,
Solely to their task
Theirs, mine,
Word-task only.

Man Missing

Someone else, I see,
Will be having the last word about me,
Friend, enemy, or lover
Or gimlet-eyed professor.
Each will think he is true
To the man he thinks he knew
Or knows, he thinks, from the book.
Each will say, Look!
Here he is, to the life,
On my hook or knife;
And each, no doubt, having caught me
Will deal with me plainly, shortly
And as justly as he can
With such a slippery no-man.

Well, I'll be quite curious,
Watching among the dubious
Dead, to see what they make
Of this antique: Genuine, or Fake?
Myself, I've hardly a clue;
I know how I feel, what I do,
But how true my feelings are
And why I perform a particular
Act is quite beyond me,
Analyse and prod me
As I will, as they will,
Nothing quite fills the bill;
And the man writing this now
Is gone as he makes his bow.

Gone, for I never can bind
My seesaw will or mind
That keeps changing with the weather,
Not only from bad to better
And back, but changing aim
And course, myself still the same,
And looking everywhere
I find no centre anywhere,
No real self, only a sort

Of unthought self-conscious thought;
A house with no one at home,
Where any visitor is welcome
To name, try, spare or pan
A genuinely missing no-man.

Ergo Sum

Pretences, discontents—
Leaves of my raging tree,
Self-hate and self-deceit,
All shameful rancours that
Loathing cannot disown,
It is you keep me warm
In the chill fever of
Mood-modes I must try on,
Daily, hourly practising.

To make, unmake, remake,
Unmask and discover,
To cloak, bluff and confess,
These are the ritual
Twistings and contortions
That bedevil relations
Of one, two, and many
In self's game of self-will
In pursuit of its living.

Self scatters itself in
A swarm of witnesses
Against itself, and is
Stronger being scattered
In many that attest
By question, evasion,
Self-confirming doubt, all
Continuities that
Are covert forms of growing.

I die therefore I am:
Dying out of myself,
Dying into myself,
Sieved and sea-changed through
The calendar of roles,
Disguises, feints, black-outs,
Worn down by treadmill thoughts,
Torn by the harrow
And heartburn of becoming.

Who am I to command
A self and its leaf-selves
Living dispersed through all
With the salt grains of the sea?
I follow, obeying a word
That leads in whirling dance
Through the cloud of days
And the cries of living and dead
To the last leaf-burning.

Open the Heart

To run a thousand miles from a thousand men,
Flinching from every face indifferent or hostile,

Masks you cannot compose a mask to meet—
Doesn't it still leave you where you started,

Heart pounding because you could not endure
To catch your face naked in the mirror

And see heart, face, the whole quivering self
No more than a puff of wind

Raising the dust, settling into dust——?
No no no, that's mere

Decoration, rationalization, still running away—
Simply, you dare not stand, because

To speak out is more desperate than to keep silence,
To open the heart is to bleed to death surely.

Shoriken

I

Feel the edge of the knife
Cautiously—
Ice-keen
It lies against your cheek
Your heart
Will pierce at once if you should stir
Yet offers
A pillow loving to your head
A sword to cross the malevolent sea.

2

The wood of the world harbours
Lamb and lion, hawk and dove.
A world of lions alone
Or a world of doves—would it
Capture our headstrong devotion
Harness the wolf-pack of energies
That unsparing we spendthrift
Earning our lives till death?
Where in its white or black would be work for
    love?

3

The merciless strike with swords
With words
With silences
They have as many faces as the clouds
As many ruses as the heart
The fountains of their mercy never run dry.

4

In a world of prisoners
Who dare call himself free?

5

Every mark on your body
Is a sign of my love.
Inscribed by the years, you tell
Unwittingly
How we travelled together
Parted and met again
Fell out sometimes, then made peace.
Crowsfoot, scar, tremulous eyelid
Are not matters for shame
But passages of the book
We have been writing together.

6

Giver, you strip me of your gifts
That I may love them better.

7

To remember yesterday and the day before
To look for tomorrow
To walk the invisible bridge of the world
As a tightrope, a sword edge.

8

What wages are due to you
Unprofitable servant?
You come asking for wages?
Fifty years long you have breathed
My air, drunk my sweet waters
And have not been cut down.
Is it not a boon, living?
Do not your easy days mark
The huge forbearance of earth?

9

The bluntest stones on the road will be singing
If you listen closely
Like lilies or larks
Those that may stone you to death after.

10

Rising and setting stars
Burn with the same intensity
But one glows for the world's dark
One whitens into tedious day.

11

All yours that you made mine
Is made yours again.

12

To speak in your own words in your own
        voice—
How easy it sounds and how hard it is
When nothing that is yours is yours alone

To walk singly yourself who are thousands
Through all that made and makes you day by day
To be and to be nothing, not to own

Not owned, but lightly on the sword edge keep
A dancer's figure—that is the wind's art
With you who are blood and water, wind and stone.

13

One place is not better than another
Only more familiar
Dearer or more hateful
No better, only nearer.

14

He is earth, dying to earth.
The charge of life spends itself
Wears, wears out.
His sole enemy is the self
That cannot do otherwise
Than live itself to death
                    death
The desert sand
That dries all tears
                    death
Our rest and end.

15

Selfless, you sign
Your words mine.

16

To cross the sea is to submit to the sea
Once venture out and you belong to it
All you know is the sea
All you are the sea
And that sword edge itself a wave-crest of the
        sea.

Note. Shoriken is the Japanese name of one of the eight Taoist Immortals.
A kakemono by Motonobu in the British Museum shows him crossing
the sea, balanced on the edge of his sword.

World Without End

In all weathers? If imagination permit—
If imagination qualifies, then yes, in all.
Do you recall that day when the second war was ending
And from our sterile bureaux
We walked out into the green breath of the Park
Saying, 'Well, nothing more can happen now,
Nothing worse'? And it seemed so that day, that year.
How little we knew. There is always a worse and
        still worse
And no ending, though each in his turn is broken—
The will crumbled, the heart lost, mind given way,
And to humming hospital or knacker's yard
We are turned over, no longer master of our gates.
The end for each is no ending at all;
World persists, turning with us, in us,
Turned by us in all our weathers,
Intolerable to each, our common country.

from *Night Cries, Wakari Hospital*

Tempora Mutantur

Beautiful the strong man in his strength,
Happy the self-reliant.
I too rejoiced once
Walking the earth head high.

Farewell the careless days.
Now I enter another rule
Laboriously piecing together
The hard grammar of dependence.

Winter Anemones

The ruby and amethyst eyes of anemones
Glow through me, fiercer than stars.
Flambeaux of earth, their dyes
From age-lost generations burn
Black soil, branches and mosses into light
That does not fail, though winter grip the rocks
To adamant. See, they come now
To lamp me through inscrutable dusk
And down the catacombs of death.

Through a Glass, Darkly

Though spacious lands and oceans and far skies,
  My head sees from its five-feet-something shelf,
No matter how it tries
  It cannot clearly, wholly see itself;
And if it could, might hardly recognize,
  Since cameras and mirrors can tell lies.

So it may be with death, the pictured terror.
  That thronged, yet solitary frontier station
May, when the pilgrim turns discoverer,
  Bring such a revelation
As will unhide the hugeness of our error,
  Beyond life's luminous, distorting mirror.

Scything

All day I swing my level scythe,
  Slow-marching on the severed swath;
Content to know myself alone
  With grass, and leaves, and gusty sun.

The random handle that I hold,
  A strong lopped bough, bone-dry, and curled,
Is emblem of an ancient time
  When wandering man first dreamed of home.

Scared by my near blade's foreign hiss
  A lizard flickers where I pass
Like Adam stooping to the ground
  With a lost Eden in his mind.

Halfwit

He walks with shopping basket, and an air
  Of some tremendous secret in his keeping,
He dodges obstacles that are not there;
  Now checks his pace, and now goes skipping, leaping.
A noise frets in his head; he lets it loose
  And hears it flit about him like a bat;

Hoot of an owl, or trumpet of a goose:
   Then no one passes and he lifts his hat.
Shopping he goes, and might, with his poor head,
   Bring stones and scorpions for meat and bread.

Mushrooms

We went to look for stragglers on a ridge
Beyond the upland pasture, where the rough
Scrub country rolled away. But what we saw,
Or what I now remember was near home
Beside the neat green oatfield, a score or so
Mushrooms among the daisies and dandelions
And dewy wine-red sorrel, like a flock
Of sheep and lambs looked down on from a height;
Domes of old vellum, and buttons coy and small
White as new gloves; and scattered here and there
Some kicked by cows, showing their fleshy gills.
That morning we walked far and soaked our boots
Along the wet sheep-tracks, but now my thoughts
Stay in that mushroom paddock to recover
Childhood and all sweet mornings, dew, and grass.

The Trapped Hare

This morning I found a hare gaoled alive in a gin,
One red forepaw held bitten in clenched iron.
With ears laid back and large eyes full of woe
He crouched on the scoured floor of his open prison
Resting, poor creature, and gathering strength for his struggle.
Set him free, urged my heart, but my mind made excuse
As it will often at sight of familiar wrong.
My hollow sophistry said, End his pain—
Better to enter life maimed, pleaded those eyes.
So I dallied too long between thinking and doing
Until the practical farmer came without scruple.
Then the hoarse feminine scream and spinal blow
And the limp body dangling downward dishonoured;
Sagacity brought low and swiftness stilled
By braggart jaws set wicked in a gap.
There will be other hares, but never this one seen
Glad in his freedom some sweet evening
Skirting a boundary with easy idle stride,
Or squatting lord of his hundred-acre domain,
Hind legs like skis and tall ears up
And coat of ruddier brown than ripened corn.

No more, no more, this beauty and wild grace,
And I go sadly, troubled with grief and guilt
That I stood by, a dumb witness consenting
To the murder of an exquisite work of God.

The Unreturning Native

Above the sounds that echo eerily
　　Still in my mind
I hear those Valkyries of wild sea-wind,
　　Though now they blow more kind.

Of all lost faces one remains with me,
　　The downcast face
Of that dark, woebegone, uprooted race;
　　But now it haunts me less.

That raw harsh landscape in my memory
　　Once seemed hostile,
But tones more truthfully with human ill
　　Than gentle vale and hill.

Old friends beloved and loving faithfully
　　There yet abide,
To press their soft assault upon that pride
　　Which even from love would hide.

Still may that love, that land, and that blown sea,
　　Though never again
Present to prick my heart and eyes, remain
　　As constant as my pain.

CHARLES SPEAR

O Matre Pulchra . . .

When you whom Jules de Goncourt's prose
Had placed on shallow, leaf-strewn steps,
Against a tower, slate-roofed and rose,
When you gaze in your mirror's depths,

Dear worldling, do you understand
My seeing in those raffish eyes,
Instead of ladies of the land,
My landlord's fancy lady rise?

The Disinherited

They cared for nothing but the days and hours
Of freedom, and in silent scorn
Ignored the worldly watchers and the powers,
Left staples shattered and uptorn,
Filed window-bars and dynamited towers.

What was their wisdom whom no vice could hold?
Remote as any gipsy rover,
They stared along the cliffs, mauve fold on fold,
And watched the bees fly over.

From velvet hills, trees in the river-bed,
From glassy reefs in skeins of foam,
They reared the shell of vision and of words unsaid
To be their haunting and their earthly home.

Memoriter

Ovals of opal on dislustred seas,
Skyshine, and all that indolent afternoon
No clash of arms, no shouting on the breeze;
Only the reeds moaned soft or high their empty rune.

The paladins played chess and did not care,
The crocus pierced the turf with random dart.
Then twanged a cord. Through space, from Oultremer
That other arrow veered towards your heart.

Christoph

The wind blew strongly like the voice of fate
Through cheerless sunlight, and the black yawl strained
And creaked across the sullen slate
Of Zuider Zee. That night it rained;

The Hook of Holland drenched in diamonds lay
Far southward; but the exile coming home
Turns back to hours like golden tissues stacked away,
And sees no more the sulky, weltering foam,
But only roses, or white honey in the comb.

At a Danse Macabre

The glittering topaz in your glass
Was vintaged forty years ago;
Your emerald has seen eight kings pass,
A thousand thousand candles glow.

Watched in a jewel, the taper curls;
The royal men, the wine that flows
Are tints and crowns; the peerless girls
Are broken shadows of a rose.

Environs of Vanholt I

White and blue, an outspread fan,
The sea slopes to the Holmcliff, and the dawn
Spins vaporous spokes across the Broken Span
To light up Razor Drop and Winesael Yawn.

Beanpod sleeps out beside his malt-filled pot;
Behind him lies the still and silver land;
No atom bomb drops from a shapely hand,
But birds of boding in a greasy knot
Pick at the rusted corpse half-hid in sand.

The Prisoner

I walked along the winding road;
It was high summer; on one side
Behind pale foliage sinuously flowed
The hand-sown wheat in rustling pride.

Grey sprawling stone, before me towered the school;
I touched the chapel-corner through the hedge,
Traced dimly in the window's painted pool
Three mitres and the shield with rope and wedge.

Deep peace! Yet there was panic terror shut inside;
The bronze bells rolled and reeled in flowing tide.
Against that shock time buckled to resist,
And no sound pierced the loneliness, no voices cried;
Only the great towers trembled in the pouring mist.

Karl

Outside among the talking criss-cross reeds
The night of rain; then from the south
The whisper softly growing that none heeds
At first, till it comes weaving with a giant's mouth;

Till through the pass the hissing torches stream
Under the steely arrows of the rain,
And cavalry and foot and sweating team
Check at the ford and then surge on again.

The heralds in the Gothic Saxon blue
Come spurring, and the levelled trumpets sing.
Then in the courtyard clamour: cracked bells ring
Like waterfalls, and the exultant host pours through
The shattered hall to claim its exiled king.

News from Paris

Down through Venetian blinds the morning air
Sifts from a sky where peach and azure fuse;
Street noises enter too, and in a distant square
A regimental band plays *Sambre et Meuse*.

It is Felicity: she sits and reads once more
The Gothic script of the West-Easterly Divan;
Her silver shoe just touches the waxed floor,
And pot pourri transcends the vase from old Japan.

Animae Superstiti

Some leagues into that land I too have fared;
The diligence along the causeway sped,
While from the left a giant planet glared
Across the restless marsh with face of lead.

In number we were four: you, child, and I;
The swordsman next, who wore his mocking air
Of Papal Zouave, fencing master, spy,
And last the golliwog with vacant, saxe-blue stare.

Onward we whirled; you slept disturbed in mind,
And from your hand the English roses fell;
Europe by lamplight far behind,
We clove the white fog's shifting swell.

So for an hour, and then I must return,
And you with your creatures ply insensate flight.
Broken I stood beneath the frontier light,
Till through the endless marsh I could discern
No wheels, no sound, only the airs of night.

Scott-Moncrieff's Beowulf

In the curdled afterglow of night
The long ship leaves the cliff, the ness, the cave;
Unending arcs of icy light
Flicker about her on the climbing wave;

And coming close fierce warriors crowd
To shout across the Swan's Way. See! They pass.
She drives through trailing veils of cloud,
And time pours down like rain on weeping glass.

From a Book of Hours

Bearing white myrrh and incense, autumn melts
Through flower and fruit and combed blonde straw;
Thunder looms on the mountain forest-belt;
The winter firewood purrs beneath the saw.

Our garden scents upbillow like the veils
Of Solomon's Temple, shimmer in the rain,
And all is peace. Slowly the daylight fails,
And voice and lute bring back the stars again.

1894 in London

Like torn-up newsprint the nonchalant snow
Creaked down incessantly on Red Lion Square.
Clock chimes were deadbeats. Clang! Nowhere to go!
The cabbies drove with marble stare,
The snowed-up statues had a pensive air.

Inside the pub the spirits flowed,
And Sal and Kate the guardees' tanners shared;
Out in the dusk the newsboys crowed,
And to infinity the lamp-posts flared,
The gas-blue lilies of the Old Kent Road.

Old England's blue hour of unmeasured nips,
The Quiet Time for Dorian Gray,
The day off for the barmaid's hips,
Prayer-Book revision time down Lambeth way.

Karl

All day he stood at Weeping Cross,
While with its shot-ripped flags and battered train,
In full retreat, and stunned by loss,
The army came back through the freezing rain.

Behind, the rearguard seemed to swirl and drown,
As the gunsmoke curdled through the pass.
The slamming volleys switched the wet leaves down,
And scythed the dead upon the reddened grass.

Have done! Let none hereafter heed this cry
For the apostolic chivalry of time long past;
This prayer of all that smote the marble sky
Is least, and yet the proudest, for it is the last.

God Save the Stock

Dusk falters over shelf and chair,
Carnation webs of shadows hold
A symbol in that tranquil air,
A candle's hoop of uncoined gold.

He writes reports in sweet repose—
The Jews require new management;

Korea soothed with flowing prose,
He writes in charmed astonishment.

The horn-rimmed prefect on the primrose path
Commands success with lip upcurled.
Fare well, Commander of the Bath,
And good luck, playboy of the western world!

Balthasar

Hid near a lily-spangled stream,
The wild duck smooths his satin breast;
A league back, shattered hauberks gleam;
The wall no longer guards the West.

The crystal willow boughs of spring
Shimmer above on pearl-shell skies,
And Balthasar sets signet-ring
To war-dispatches full of lies.

Promised Land

Dispart the frost-white boughs, and lo!
The world of winter, mile on mile;
Wind-wavy seas of unplumbed snow,
Then endless peaks and one defile.

The high elect would fear to cross
Those wastes unconquerable, ideal:
There lies your path; count all as loss,
Cast armour by, lay down your steel;

For you shall walk the sheer gulf's brink,
Through glass-blue caves all brittle spars
And flaws. Thereafter you shall sink,
Snowblind in slush, beneath the stars.

Joachim of Flora

A swathe of violet at break of day,
Ribbon of glory for the opening reign;
And red and yellow like the flag of Spain
The fishing-boats at sea again
Through sheets of glitter drew away.

He left the sands by Dunkerque Lane
And watched the birds attend in solemn file
The ploughman as he clove with might and main
The path of honour and the line of style;

So putting by his craven doubt
He vowed to clasp and kiss the fleeting hour
While all the bells for joy rang out
Four-in-hand harmonies from spire and tower.

Escape

Against deep seas blue-black like mussel-shells
The island arched its bluffs and stony scarps,
Which, wave-rocked, tolled in winter time like bells,
Or chimed to spring as sweet as Irish harps.

Above, a fool's crown of canary cloud,
Moulded by mighty winds to dizzy height,
Leaned to the isle like press of sail o'erbowed,
And sunshine pierced the eyes with swords of light.

This have we chosen, far from friends and home,
This space of barren rock and crimson heath,
With cliffs of quaking honey-comb
And the tides of death in the galleries beneath.

Environs of Vanholt II

See! In the troubled glow of dawn
World rising—mountain to lowland smoothly laid,
River and hedgerow sharply drawn;
It is the continent of shade.

Sail into Stonecliff next; heraldic bronze
Chrysanthemums turn to the moody sea.
We call your name; there will be no response;
Only a dog barks in this land of memory.

Time

I am the nor'west air nosing among the pines
I am the water-race and the rust on railway lines
I am the mileage recorded on the yellow signs.

I am dust, I am distance, I am lupins along the beach
I am the sums the sole-charge teachers teach
I am cows called to milking and the magpie's screech.

I am nine o'clock in the morning when the office is clean
I am the slap of the belting and the smell of the machine
I am the place in the park where the lovers were seen.

I am recurrent music the children hear
I am level noises in the remembering ear
I am the sawmill and the passionate second gear.

I, Time, am all these yet these exist
Among my mountainous fabrics like a mist,
So do they the measurable world resist.

I, Time, call down, condense, confer
On the willing memory the shape these were:
I, more than your conscious carrier,

Am island, am sea, am father, farm, and friend;
Though I am here all things my coming attend;
I am, you have heard it, the Beginning and the End.

House and Land

Wasn't this the site, asked the historian,
Of the original homestead?
Couldn't tell you, said the cowman;
I just live here, he said,
Working for old Miss Wilson
Since the old man's been dead.

Moping under the bluegums
The dog trailed his chain
From the privy as far as the fowlhouse
And back to the privy again,

Feeling the stagnant afternoon
Quicken with the smell of rain.

There sat old Miss Wilson,
With her pictures on the wall,
The baronet uncle, mother's side,
And one she called The Hall;
Taking tea from a silver pot
For fear the house might fall.

People in the *colonies*, she said,
Can't quite understand . . .
Why, from Waiau to the mountains
It was all father's land.

She's all of eighty said the cowman,
Down at the milking-shed.
I'm leaving here next winter.
Too bloody quiet, he said.

The spirit of exile, wrote the historian,
Is strong in the people still.

He reminds me rather, said Miss Wilson,
Of Harriet's youngest, Will.

The cowman, home from the shed, went drinking
With the rabbiter home from the hill.

The sensitive nor'west afternoon
Collapsed, and the rain came;
The dog crept into his barrel
Looking lost and lame.
But you can't attribute to either
Awareness of what great gloom
Stands in a land of settlers
With never a soul at home.

The Unhistoric Story

Whaling for continents coveted deep in the south
The Dutchman envied the unknown, drew bold
Images of market-place, populous river-mouth,
The Land of Beach ignorant of the value of gold:
    Morning in Murderers' Bay,
    Blood drifted away.

It was something different, something
Nobody counted on.

Spider, clever and fragile, Cook showed how
To spring a trap for islands, turning from planets
His measuring mission, showed what the musket could do,
Made his Christmas goose of the wild gannets.
    Still as the collier steered
    No continent appeared;
    It was something different, something
Nobody counted on.

The roving tentacles touched, rested, clutched
Substantial earth, that is, accustomed haven
For the hungry whaler. Some inland, some hutched
Rudely in bays, the shaggy foreshore shaven,
    Lusted, preached as they knew;
    But as the children grew
    It was something different, something
Nobody counted on.

Green slashed with flags, pipeclay and boots in the bush,
Christ in canoes and the musketed Maori boast;
All a rubble-rattle at Time's glacial push:
Vogel and Seddon howling empire from an empty coast
    A vast ocean laughter
    Echoed unheard, and after
    All it was different, something
Nobody counted on.

The pilgrim dream pricked by a cold dawn died
Among the chemical farmers, the fresh towns; among
Miners, not husbandmen, who piercing the side
Let the land's life, found like all who had so long
    Bloodily or tenderly striven
    To rearrange the given,
    It was something different, something
Nobody counted on.

After all re-ordering of old elements
Time trips up all but the humblest of heart
Stumbling after the fire, not in the smoke of events;
For many are called, but many are left at the start,
    And whatever islands may be
    Under or over the sea,
    It is something different, something
Nobody counted on.

Wild Iron

Sea go dark, dark with wind,
Feet go heavy, heavy with sand,
Thoughts go wild, wild with the sound
Of iron on the old shed swinging, clanging:
Go dark, go heavy, go wild, go round,
    Dark with the wind,
    Heavy with the sand,
Wild with the iron that tears at the nail
And the foundering shriek of the gale.

Sailing or Drowning

In terms of some green myth, sailing or drowning,
Each day makes clear a statement to the next;
But to make out our tomorrow from its motives
Is pure guessing, yesterday's were so mixed.

Papa, Atea, parents of gods or islands,
Quickly forgave the treacherous beaches, none
So bloodily furrowed that the secret tides
Could not make the evening and the morning one.

Ambition has annulled that constitution;
In the solid sea and the space over the sea
Explosions of a complex origin
Shock, rock, and split the memory.

Sailing or drowning, the living and the dead,
Less than the gist of what has just been said.

Out of Sleep

Awake but not yet up, too early morning
Brings you like bells in matrix of mist
Noises the mind may finger, but no meaning.
Two blocks away a single car has crossed

Your intersection with the hour; each noise
A cough in the cathedral of your waking—
The cleaners have no souls, no sins—each does
Some job, Christ dying or the day breaking.

This you suppose is what goes on all day.
No one is allowed long to stop and listen,
But takes brief turns at it: now as you lie

Dead calm, a gust in the damp cedar hissing
Will have the mist right off in half a minute.
You will not grasp the meaning, you will be in it.

The Old Provincial Council Buildings, Christchurch

The steps are saucered in the trodden parts,
But that doesn't take long to happen here;
Two or three generations' traffic starts
In stone like this to make time's meaning clear.

Azaleas burn your gaze away below,
Corbel and finial tell you where to stop;
For present purposes, it does to know
Transport is licensed somewhere at the top.

Children of those who suffered a sea change
May wonder how much history was quarried
And carted, hoisted, carved; and find it strange
How shallow here their unworn age lies buried

Before its time, before their time, whose eyes
Get back from a stopped clock their own surprise.

The Skeleton of the Great Moa in the Canterbury Museum, Christchurch

The skeleton of the moa on iron crutches
Broods over no great waste; a private swamp
Was where this tree grew feathers once, that hatches
Its dusty clutch, and guards them from the damp.

Interesting failure to adapt on islands,
Taller but not more fallen than I, who come
Bone to his bone, peculiarly New Zealand's.
The eyes of children flicker round this tomb

Under the skylights, wonder at the huge egg
Found in a thousand pieces, pieced together

But with less patience than the bones that dug
In time deep shelter against ocean weather:

Not I, some child, born in a marvellous year,
Will learn the trick of standing upright here.

Landfall in Unknown Seas

*The 300th Anniversary of the Discovery of New Zealand
by Abel Tasman, 13 December 1642*

I

Simply by sailing in a new direction
You could enlarge the world.
                        You picked your captain,
Keen on discoveries, tough enough to make them,
Whatever vessels could be spared from other
More urgent service for a year's adventure;
Took stock of the more probable conjectures
About the Unknown to be traversed, all
Guesses at golden coasts and tales of monsters
To be digested into plain instructions
For likely and unlikely situations.

All this resolved and done, you launched the whole
On a fine morning, the best time of year,
Skies widening and the oceanic furies
Subdued by summer illumination; time
To go and to be gazed at going
On a fine morning, in the Name of God
Into the nameless waters of the world.

O you had estimated all the chances
Of business in those waters, the world's waters
Yet unexploited.
                        But more than the sea-empire's
Cannon, the dogs of bronze and iron barking
From Timor to the Straits, backed up the challenge.
Between you and the South an older enmity
Lodged in the searching mind, that would not tolerate
So huge a hegemony of ignorance.
There, where your Indies had already sprinkled
Their tribes like ocean rains, you aimed your voyage;
Like them invoked your God, gave seas to history
And islands to new hazardous tomorrows.

II

Suddenly exhilaration
Went off like a gun, the whole
Horizon, the long chase done,
Hove to. There was the seascape
Crammed with coast, surprising
As new lands will, the sailor
Moving on the face of the waters,
Watching the earth take shape
Round the unearthly summits, brighter
Than its emerging colour.

Yet this, no far fool's errand,
Was less than the heart desired,
In its old Indian dream
The glittering gulfs ascending
Past palaces and mountains
Making one architecture.
Here the uplifted structure,
Peak and pillar of cloud—
O splendour of desolation—reared
Tall from the pit of the swell,
With a shadow, a finger of wind, forbade
Hopes of a lucky landing.

Always to islanders danger
Is what comes over the sea;
Over the yellow sands and the clear
Shallows, the dull filament
Flickers, the blood of strangers:
Death discovered the Sailor
O in a flash, in a flat calm,
A clash of boats in the bay
And the day marred with murder.
The dead required no further
Warning to keep their distance;
The rest, noting the failure,
Pushed on with a reconnaissance
To the north; and sailed away.

III

Well, home is the Sailor, and that is a chapter
In a schoolbook, a relevant yesterday
We thought we knew all about, being much apter
        To profit, sure of our ground,
No murderers mooring in our Golden Bay.

But now there are no more islands to be found
And the eye scans risky horizons of its own
In unsettled weather, and murmurs of the drowned
    Haunt their familiar beaches—
Who navigates us towards what unknown

But not improbable provinces? Who reaches
A future down for us from the high shelf
Of spiritual daring? Not those speeches
    Pinning on the Past like a decoration
For merit that congratulates itself,

O not the self-important celebration
Or most painstaking history, can release
The current of a discoverer's elation
    And silence the voices saying,
'Here is the world's end where wonders cease.'

Only by a more faithful memory, laying
On him the half-light of a diffident glory,
The Sailor lives, and stands beside us, paying
    Out into our time's wave
The stain of blood that writes an island story.

Tomb of an Ancestor

In Memoriam, R.L.M.G.

The oldest of us burst into tears and cried
Let me go home, but she stayed, watching
At her staircase window ship after ship ride
Like birds her grieving sunsets; there sat stitching

Grandchildren's things. She died by the same sea.
High over it she led us in the steepening heat
To the yellow grave; her clay
Chose that way home: dismissed, our feet

Were seen to have stopped and turned again down hill;
The street fell like an ink-blue river
In the heat to the bay, the basking ships, this Isle
Of her oblivion, our broad day. Heaped over

So lightly, she stretched like time behind us, or
Graven in cloud, our farthest ancestor.

Self-portrait

The wistful camera caught this four-year-old
But could not stare him into wistfulness;
He holds the toy that he is given to hold:
A passionate failure or a staled success

Look back into their likeness while I look
With pity not self-pity at the plain
Mechanical image that I first mistook
For my own image; there, timid or vain,

Semblance of my own eyes my eyes discern
Casting on mine as I cast back on these
Regard not self-regard: till the toy turn
Into a lover clasped, into wide seas,

The salt or visionary wave, and the days heap
Sorrow upon sorrow for all he could not keep.

Eden Gate

The paper boat sank to the bottom of the garden
The train steamed in at the white wicked gate,
The old wind wished in the hedge, the sodden
Sack loved the yellow shoot;

And scampering children woke the world
Singing Happy Doomsday over all the green willows
That sprang like panic from the crotch of the cold
Sappy earth, and away in the withered hollows

A hand no warmer than a cloud rummaged
At the river's roots: up there in the sky
God's one blue eye looked down on the damaged
Boy tied by the string of a toy

And saw him off at the gate and the train
All over again.

Unhurt, There is No Help

When was it first they called each other mine?
Not in Donne's day: by then their love had grown
Or shrunk from Phoenix into spider, sign
Of sinner turned addict. Love, be your own

And stay the far side of that Tree
Whose seed struck earth between us; give again
A bite of apple; do not mind if He
Is somewhere in the garden, or that pain

Is frost or blight and the leaf blackens.
That is your birthright and redeeming sin.
Unhurt, there is no help for her who wakens
Puzzled, her sole power gone, in the obscene

Daffodil bed where the decrepit knees
Promised speech from heaven, and could barely please.

The Waking Bird Refutes

Rain's unassuaging fountains multiply
In air on earth and leaf. The Flood began
This way, listened to at windows by
The sleepless: one wept, one revolved a plan,

One died and rose again, one felt
That colder breath blow from the poles of lip
At love's meridian. This way now the spoilt
Firmament of the blood dissolves and drops;

The bright waste repossessive element
Beats barely audible, one sound imposing
Silence upon silence. This way I went
To pull our histories down, down, heavens accusing

Of rainbowed guile, whose penal rains descend.
But the waking bird refutes: world will not end.

To Forget Self and All

To forget self and all, forget foremost
This whimpering second unlicked self my country,
To go like nobody's fool an ungulled ghost
By unadorned midnight and the pitch of noon
Commanding at large everywhere his entry,
Unimaginable waterchinks, granular dark of a stone?
Why that'd be freedom heyday, hey
For freedom that'd be the day
And as good a dream as any to be damned for.

Then to patch it up with self and all and all
This tousled sunny-mouthed sandy-legged coast,
These painted and these rusted streets,

This heart so supple and small,
Blinding mountain, deafening river
And smooth anxious sheets,
And go like a sober lover like nobody's ghost?
Why that'd be freedom heyday, hey
Freedom! That'd be the day
And as good a dream as any to be damned to.

To sink both self and all why sink the whole
Phenomenal enterprise, colours shapes and sizes
Low like Lucifer's bolt from the cockshied roost
Of groundless paradise: peeled gold gull
Whom the cracked verb of his thoughts
Blew down blew up mid-air, where the sea's gorge rises,
The burning brain's nine feathering fathom doused
And prints with bubbles one grand row of noughts?
Why that'd be freedom heyday, hey
For freedom, that'd be the day
And as good a dream as any to be damned by.

Elegy on My Father

Tremayne Curnow, of Canterbury, New Zealand, 1880–1949

Spring in his death abounds among the lily islands,
There to bathe him for the grave antipodean snows
Fall floodlong, rivermouths all in bloom, and those
Fragile church timbers quiver
By the bourne of his burial where robed he goes
No journey at all. One sheet's enough to cover
My end of the world and his, and the same silence.

While in Paddington autumn is air-borne, earth-given,
Day's nimbus nearer staring, colder smoulders;
Breath of a death not my own bewilders
Dead calm with breathless choirs
O bird-creation singing where the world moulders!
God's poor, the crutched and stunted spires
Thumb heavenward humorously under the unriven

Marble November has nailed across their sky:
Up there, dank ceiling is the dazzling floor
All souls inhabit, the lilied seas, no shore
My tear-smudged map mislimned.
When did a wind of the extreme South before
Mix autumn, spring, and death? False maps are dimmed,
Lovingly they mock each other, image and eye.

The ends of the earth are folded in his grave
In sound of the Pacific and the hills he tramped singing,
God knows romantically or by what love bringing
Wine from a clay creek-bed,
Good bread; or by what glance the inane skies ringing
Lucidly round; or by what shuffle or tread
Warning the dirt of miracles. Still that nave
He knelt in puts off its poor planks, looms loftier
Lonelier than Losinga's that spells in stone
The Undivided Name. *Oh quickening bone*
Of the Mass-priest under grass
Green in my absent spring, sweet relic atone
To our earth's Lord for the pride of all our voyages,
That the salt winds which scattered us blow softer.

London, November 1949

The Eye is More or Less Satisfied with Seeing

Wholehearted he can't move
   From where he is, nor love

Wholehearted that place,
   Indigene janus-face,

Half mocking half,
   Neither caring to laugh.

Does true or false sun rise?
   Do both half eyes tell lies?

Cradle or grave, which view's
   The actual of the two?

Half eyes foretell, forget
   Sunrise, sunset,

Or closed a fraction's while
   Half eyes half smile

Upon light the spider lid
   Snares, holds hid

And holds him whole (between
   The split scarves of that scene)

Brimming astride a pulse
  Of moon-described eyeball's

Immobile plenitude—
  Flower of the slight stemmed flood.

Snap open! He's all eyes, wary,
  Darting both ways one query,

Whether the moonbeam glanced
  Upon half to whole enhanced,

Or wholly the soul's error
  And confederate mirror.

Keep in a Cool Place

A bee in a bloom on the long hand of a floral
Clock can't possibly tell the right time
And if it could whatever would the poor bee do with it
In insufferably hot weather like this?

Everything white looks washed, at the correct distance
And may be the correct distance. You could eat
Our biggest ship sweet as sugar and space can make her.
Every body's just unwrapped, one scrap of a shaving

Left for luck or the look, the maker's seal intact,
Glad to be genuine! The glassy seaside's
Exact to the last detail, tick of a tide,
Fluke of the wind, slant of a sail. The swimmers

On lawns and the athletes in cosy white beds have visitors
And more flowers. Poor bee! He can make up time
At frantic no speed, whether tick or tock,
Hour or minute hand's immaterial. That's

Exactly how it is now. It is. It is
Summer all over the striped humming-top of the morning
And what lovely balloons, prayer-filled (going up!) to fluke
For once and for all the right time, the correct distance.

Jack-in-the-Boat

is always ready to row across the bath or lake. Wind up the
motor, and watch him dip his blades like a true oarsman—
in, out, in, out—with never-tiring enthusiasm.

—LEGEND ON A TOY-MAKER'S PACKAGE

Children, children, come and look
Through the crack in the corner of the middle of the world
At the clockwork man in a cardboard house.
He's crying, children, crying.
   He's not true, really.

Once he was new like you, you see
Through the crack in the corner of the middle of the night,
The bright blue man on the wind-up sea,
Oh, he went so beautifully.
   He's not true, really.

O cruel was the pleasure-land they never should have painted
On the front and the back, the funny brand of weather,
For the crack in the corner of the middle of the picture
Let the colours leak away.
   He's not true, really.

One at a time, children, come and look
Through the crack in the corner in the middle of the day
At Jack-in-the-Boat where the light leaves float.
He's dying of a broken spring.
   He's not true, really.

Spectacular Blossom

Mock up again, summer, the sooty altars
Between the sweltering tides and the tin gardens,
All the colours of the stained bow windows.
Quick, she'll be dead on time, the single
Actress shuffling red petals to this music,
Percussive light! So many suns she harbours
And keeps them jigging, her puppet suns,
All over the dead hot calm impure
Blood noon tide of the breathless bay.

Are the victims always so beautiful?

Pearls pluck at her, she has tossed her girls
Breast-flowers for keepsakes now she is going
For ever and astray. I see her feet

Slip into the perfect fit the shallows make her
Purposefully, sure as she is the sea
Levels its lucent ruins underfoot
That were sharp dead white shells, that will be sands.
The shallows kiss like knives.

Always for this
They are chosen for their beauty.

Wristiest slaughterman December smooths
The temple bones and parts the grey-blown brows
With humid fingers. It is an ageless wind
That loves with knives, it knows our need, it flows
Justly, simply as water greets the blood,
And woody tumours burst in scarlet spray.
An old man's blood spills bright as a girl's
On beaches where the knees of light crash down.
These dying ejaculate their bloom.

Can anyone choose
And call it beauty?—The victims
Are always beautiful.

He Cracked a Word

He cracked a word to get at the inside
Of the inside, then the whole paper bag full
The man said were ripe and good.
The shrunken kernels
Like black tongues in dead mouths derided
The sillinesses of song and wagging wisdom:
These made a small dumb pile, the hopping shells
Froze to the floor, and those made patterns
Half-witted cameras glared at, finding as usual
Huge meteorites in mouseland.
What barefaced robbery!
He sat, sat, sat mechanically adding
To the small dumb pile, to the patterns on the floor,
Conscious of nothing but memories, wishes,
And a faint but unmistakable pricking of the thumbs,
The beginnings of his joy.

A Small Room with Large Windows

i

What it would look like if really there were only
One point of the compass not known illusory,
All other quarters proving nothing but quaint
Obsolete expressions of true north (would it be?),
And seeds, birds, children, loves, and thoughts bore down
The unwinding abiding beam from birth
To death! What a plan!
                              Or parabola.
You describe yours, I mine, simple as that,
With a pop and a puff of nonchalant stars up top,
Then down, dutiful dead stick, down
(True north all the way nevertheless).

One way to save space and a world of trouble.

A word on arrival, a word on departure.
A passage of proud verse, rightly construed.
An unerring pen to edit the ensuing silences
(That's more like it).

ii

                    Seven ageing pine trees hide
Their heads in air but, planted on bare knees,
Supplicate wind and tide. See if you can
See it (if this is it), half earth, half heaven,
Half land, half water, what you call a view
Strung out between the windows and the tree trunks;
Below sills a world moist with new making where
The mangrove race number their cheated floods.
Now in a field azure rapidly folding
Swells a cloud sable, a bad bitching squall
Thrashes the old pines, has them twitching
Root and branch, rumouring a Götterdämmerung.
Foreknowledge infects them to the heart.
                                        Comfortable
To creak in tune, comfortable to damn
Slime-suckled mangrove for its muddy truckling
With time and tide, knotted to the vein it leeches.

iii

In the interim, how the children should be educated,
Pending a decision, a question much debated
In our island realms. It being, as it is,
Out of the question merely to recognize
The whole three hundred and sixty degrees,

Which prudence if not propriety forbids,
It is necessary to avail oneself of aids
Like the Bible, or no Bible, free swimming tuition,
Art, sex, no sex and so on. Not to direct
So much as to normalize personality, protect
From all hazards of climate, parentage, diet,
Whatever it is exists. While, on the quiet,
It is understood there is a judgement preparing
Which finds the compass totally without bearing
And the present course correct beyond a doubt,
There being two points precisely, one in, one out.

iv

A kingfisher's naked arc alight
Upon a dead stick in the mud
A scarlet geranium wild on a wet bank
A man stepping it out in the near distance
With a dog and a bag
                on a spit of shell
On a wire in a mist
                a gannet impacting
Explode a dozen diverse dullnesses
Like a burst of accurate fire.

from *Trees, Effigies, Moving Objects*

I

Lone Kauri Road

The first time I looked seaward, westward,
it was looking back yellowly,
a dulling incandescence of the eye of day.
It was looking back over its raised hand.
Everything was backing away.

Read for a bit. It squinted between the lines.
Pages were backing away.
Print was busy with what print does,
trees with what trees do that time of day,
sun with what sun does, the sea
with one voice only, its own,
spoke no other language than that one.

There wasn't any track from which to hang
the black transparency that was travelling
south-away to the cold pole. It was cloud
browed over the yellow cornea which I called

an eyeball for want of another notion,
cloud above an ocean. It leaked.

Baldachin, black umbrella, bucket with a hole,
drizzled horizon, sleazy drape,
it hardly mattered which, or as much
what cometing bitchcraft, rocketed shitbags,
charred cherubim pocked and pitted the iceface
of space in time, the black traveller.
Everything was backing away.

The next time I looked seaward,
it was looking sooted red, a bloodshot cornea
browed with a shade that could be simulated
if the paint were thick enough, and audible,
to blow the coned noses of the young kauri,
the kettle spout sweating,
the hound snoring at my feet,
the taste of tobacco, the tacky fingers
on the pen, the paper from whose plane
the last time I looked seaward
would it be a mile, as the dust flies,
down the dulling valley, westward?
everything was backing away.

IX

A Dead Lamb

Never turn your back on the sea.
The mumble of the fall of time is continuous.

A billion billion broken waves deliver
a coloured glass globe at your feet, intact.

You say it is a Japanese fisherman's float.
It is a Japanese fisherman's float.

A king tide, a five o'clock low, is perfect
for picking mussels, picking at your ankle-bones.

The wind snaps at the yellow-scummed sea-froth,
so that an evanescence of irised bubbles occurs.

Simply, silverly the waves walk towards you.
A ship has changed position on the horizon.

The dog lifts a leg against a grass-clump
on a dune, for the count of three, wetting the sand.

There is standing room and much to be thankful for
in the present. Look, a dead lamb on the beach.

XVII

Lone Kauri Road

Too many splashes, too many gashes,
too big and too many holes in the west wall:
one by one the rectangles blazed and blacked where the
sun fell out of its frame, the time of the day
hung round at a loose end, lopsided.

It was getting desperate, even a fool could see,
it was feverish work, impossible to plug them all.
Even a fool, seeing the first mountain fall
out not into the sea or the smoking west but into
the places where these had been, could see the spider
brushed up, dusted, shovelled into the stove, and
how fast his legs moved, without the least surprise.

A tui clucked, shat, whistled thrice.
My gaze was directed where the branch had been.
An engine fell mute into the shadow of the valley
where the shadow had been.

Canst Thou Draw out Leviathan with an Hook?

I

An old Green River knife had to be scraped
of blood rust, scales, the dulled edge scrubbed
with a stone to the decisive whisper of steel
on the lips of the wooden grip.

You now have a cloud in your hand
hung blue dark over the waves and edgewise
luminous, made fast by the two brass rivets
keeping body and blade together, leaving
the other thumb free for feeling
how the belly will be slit and the spine severed.

The big kahawai had to swim close
to the rocks which kicked at the waves
which kept on coming steeply steaming,
wave overhanging wave
in a strong to gale offshore wind.

The rocks kicked angrily, the rocks
hurt only themselves, the seas without a scratch
made out to be storming and shattering,
but it was all an act that they ever broke
into breakers or even secretively
raged like the rocks, the wreckage of the land,
the vertigo, the self-lacerating
hurt of the land.
        Swimming closer
the kahawai drew down the steely cloud
and the lure, the line you cast
from cathedral rock, the thoughtful death
whispering to the thoughtless,

Will you be caught?

II

Never let them die of the air,
pick up your knife and drive it
through the gills with a twist,
let the blood run fast,
quick bleeding makes best eating.

III

An insult in the form of an apology
is the human answer to the inhuman
which rears up green roars down white,
and to the fish which is fearless:

if anyone knows a better it is a man
willing to abstain from his next breath,
who will not be found fishing from these rocks
but likeliest fished from the rip,

white belly to wetsuit black, swung copular
under the winching chopper's bubble,
too late for vomiting salt but fluent at last
in the languages of the sea.

IV

A rockpool catches the blood,
so that in a red cloud of itself
the kahawai lies white belly uppermost.

Scales will glue themselves to the rusting blade
of a cloud hand-uppermost in the rockpool.

Fingers and gobstick fail,
the hook's fast in the gullet,
the barb's behind the root
of the tongue and the tight
fibre is tearing the mouth
and you're caught, mate, you're caught,
the harder you pull it
the worse it hurts, and it makes
no sense whatever in the air
or the seas or the rocks
how you kick or cry, or sleeplessly
dream as you drown.

A big one! a big one!

A Balanced Bait in Handy Pellet Form

Fluent in all the languages dead or living,
the sun comes up with a word of worlds all spinning
in a world of words, the way the mountain answers
to its name and that's the east and the sea *das meer,*
la mer, il mare Pacifico, and I am on my way to school

barefoot in frost beside the metalled road
which is beside the railway beside the water-race,
all spinning into the sun and all exorbitantly
expecting the one and identical, the concentric,
as the road, the rail, the water, and the bare feet run

eccentric to each other. Torlesse, no less,
first mountain capable of ice, joined the pursuit,
at its own place revolved in a wintry blue
foot over summit, snow on each sunlit syllable,
taught speechless world-wide word-world's ABC.

Because light is manifest by what it lights,
ladder-fern, fingernail, the dracophyllums
have these differing opacities, translucencies;
mown grass diversely parched is a skinned 'soul'
which the sun sloughed; similarly the spectral purples

perplexing the drab of the dugover topsoil
explain themselves too well to be understood.
There's no warmth here. The heart pulsates
to a tune of its own, and if unisons happen
how does anybody know? Dead snails

have left shells, trails, baffled epigraphy
and excreta of such slow short lives,
cut shorter by the pellets I 'scatter freely',
quick acting, eccentric to exorbitant flourishes
of shells, pencillings, drab or sunlit things

dead as you please, or as the other poet says,
Our life is a false nature 'tis not in
the harmony of things. There we go again, worrying
the concentric, the one and identical, to the bone
that's none of ours, eccentric to each other.

Millions die miserably never before their time.
The news comes late. Compassion sings to itself.
I read the excreta of all species, I write
a world as good as its word, active ingredient
30 g/kg (3%) Metaldehyde, in the form of a pellet.

An Incorrigible Music

It ought to be impossible to be mistaken
about these herons, to begin with
you can count them, it's been done successfully
with swans daffodils blind mice, any number
of dead heroes and heavenly bodies.

Eleven herons are not baked in porcelain,
helpless to hatch the credulities of art
or to change places, e.g. number seven
counting from the left with number five,
or augment themselves by number twelve arriving
over the mangroves. Thirteen, fourteen, fifteen,
punctually the picture completes itself
and is never complete.

            The air
and the water being identically still,
each heron is four herons,
one right-side-up in the air,
one up-side-down in the tide,
and these two doubled by looking at.

The mudbacked mirrors in your head
multiply the possibilities of human
error, but what's the alternative?

The small wind instruments in the herons' throats
play an incorrigible music on a scale
incommensurate with hautboys and baroque wigs.

There's only one book in the world, and that's the one
everyone accurately misquotes.

A big one! A big one!

A Reliable Service

The world can end any time
it likes, say, 10.50 am
of a bright winter Saturday,

that's when the *Bay Belle*
casts off, the diesels are picking
up step, the boatmaster leans

to the wheel, the white water
shoves Paihia jetty back.
Nobody aboard but the two of us.

Fifteen minutes to Russell
was once upon a time
before, say, 10.50 am

The ketch slogging seaward
off Kororàreka Point,
the ensign arrested in

mid-flap, are printed and
pinned on a wall at the end
of the world. No lunch

over there either, the place
at the beach is closed. The *Bay
Belle* is painted bright

blue from stem to stern.
She lifts attentively. That
will be all, I suppose.

A Touch of the Hand

Look down the slope of the pavement
a couple of kilometres, to where it empties
its eyeful of the phantoms of passers-by

into mid-morning light which tops it up again
with downtown shadows. There has to be a city
down there and there is, and an 'arm of the sea',

a cloud to sprinkle the pavement, a wind
to toss your hair, otherwise your free hand
wouldn't brush it from your eyes, a welcome

touch of sincerity. As they pass down hill
away from you, their backs, and uphill towards you
their faces, the ages, the sexes, the ways

they are dressed, even one 'smile of recognition',
beg an assurance the malice of your mind
withholds. Look down, confess it's you or they:

so empty your eye and fill it again, with
the light, the shadow, the cloud, the other city,
the innocence of this being that it's the malice

of your mind must be the ingredient making
you possible, and the touch which brushes
the hair from your eyes on the slope of the pavement.

You Will Know When You Get There

Nobody comes up from the sea as late as this
in the day and the season, and nobody else goes down

the last steep kilometre, wet-metalled where
a shower passed shredding the light which keeps

pouring out of its tank in the sky, through summits,
trees, vapours thickening and thinning. Too

credibly by half celestial, the dammed
reservoir up there keeps emptying while the light lasts

over the sea, where it 'gathers the gold against
it'. The light is bits of crushed rock randomly

glinting underfoot, wetted by the short
shower, and down you go and so in its way does

the sun which gets there first. Boys, two of them,
turn campfirelit faces, a hesitancy to speak

is a hesitancy of the earth rolling back and away
behind this man going down to the sea with a bag

to pick mussels, having an arrangement with the tide,
the ocean to be shallowed three point seven metres,

one hour's light to be left and there's the excrescent
moon sponging off the last of it. A door

slams, a heavy wave, a door, the sea-floor shudders.
Down you go along, so late, into the surge-black fissure.

DENIS GLOVER

Holiday Piece

Now let my thoughts be like the Arrow, wherein was gold,
And purposeful like the Kawarau, but not so cold.

Let them sweep higher than the hawk ill-omened,
Higher than peaks perspective-piled beyond Ben Lomond;
Let them be like at evening an Otago sky
Where detonated clouds in calm confusion lie.

Let them be smooth and sweet as all those morning lakes,
Yet active and leaping, like fish the fisherman takes;
And strong as the dark deep-rooted hills, strong
As twilight hours over Lake Wakatipu are long;

And hardy, like the tenacious mountain tussock,
And spacious, like the Mackenzie plain, not narrow;
And numerous, as tourists in Queenstown;
And cheerfully busy, like the gleaning sparrow.

Lastly, that snowfield, visible from Wanaka,
Compound their patience—suns only brighten,
And no rains darken, a whiteness nothing could whiten.

The Magpies

When Tom and Elizabeth took the farm
    The bracken made their bed,
And *Quardle oodle ardle wardle doodle*
    The magpies said.

Tom's hand was strong to the plough
    Elizabeth's lips were red,
And *Quardle oodle ardle wardle doodle*
    The magpies said.

Year in year out they worked
    While the pines grew overhead,
And *Quardle oodle ardle wardle doodle*
    The magpies said.

But all the beautiful crops soon went
    To the mortgage-man instead,
And *Quardle oodle ardle wardle doodle*
    The magpies said.

Elizabeth is dead now (it's years ago)
    Old Tom went light in the head;
And *Quardle oodle ardle wardle doodle*
    The magpies said.

The farm's still there. Mortgage corporations
    Couldn't give it away.
And *Quardle oodle ardle wardle doodle*
    The magpies say.

Songs

I

These songs will not stand—
The wind and the sand will smother.

Not I but another
Will make songs worth the bother:

    The rimu or kauri he,
    I'm but the cabbage tree,

      Sings Harry to an old guitar.

II

If everywhere in the street
Is the indifferent, the accustomed eye
Nothing can elate,
It's nothing to do with me,
    Sings Harry in the wind-break.

To the north are islands like stars
In the blue water
And south, in that crystal air,
The ice-floes grind and mutter,
    Sings Harry in the wind-break.

At one flank old Tasman, the boar,
Slashes and tears,
And the other Pacific's sheer
Mountainous anger devours,
    Sings Harry in the wind-break.

From the cliff-top a boy
Felt that great motion,

And pupil to the horizon's eye
Grew wide with vision,
   Sings Harry in the wind-break.

But grew to own fences barbed
Like the words of a quarrel;
And the sea never disturbed
Him fat as a barrel,
   Sings Harry in the wind-break.

Who once would gather all Pacific
In a net wide as his heart
Soon is content to watch the traffic
Or lake waves breaking short,
   Sings Harry in the wind-break.

Once the Days

Once the days were clear
Like mountains in water,
The mountains were always there
And the mountain water;

And I was a fool leaving
Good land to moulder,
Leaving the fences sagging
And the old man older
To follow my wild thoughts
Away over the hill,
Where there is only the world
And the world's ill,
                    sings Harry.

The Casual Man

Come, mint me up the golden gorse,
Mine me the yellow clay
—There's no money in my purse
For a rainy day,
                    sings Harry.

My father left me his old coat,
Nothing more than that;
And will my head take hurt
In an old hat?
                    sings Harry.

They all concern themselves too much
With what a clock shows.
But does the casual man care
How the world goes?
                    sings Harry.

A little here, a little there—
Why should a man worry?
Let the world hurry by,
I'll not hurry,
                    sings Harry.

Thistledown

Once I followed horses
And once I followed whores,
And marched once with a banner
For some great cause,
                    sings Harry.
But that was thistledown planted on
    the wind.

And once I met a woman
All in her heart's spring,
But I was a headstrong fool
Heedless of everything,
                    sings Harry.
—I was thistledown planted on the
    wind.

Mustering is the life:
Freed of fears and hopes
I watch the sheep like a pestilence
Pouring over the slopes,
                    sings Harry.
And the past is thistledown planted
    on the wind.

Dream and doubt and the deed
Dissolve like a cloud
On the hills of time.
Be a man never so proud,
                    sings Harry,
He is only thistledown planted on
    the wind.

Themes

What shall we sing? sings Harry.

Sing truthful men? Where shall we find
The man who cares to speak his mind:
Truth's out of uniform, sings Harry,
That's her offence
Where lunacy parades as common sense.

Of lovers then? A sorry myth
To tickle tradesmen's palates with.
Production falls, wise men can prove,
When factory girls dream dreams of love.

Sing of our leaders? Like a pall
Proficiency descends on all
Pontific nobodies who make
Some high pronouncement every week.

Of poets then? How rarely they
Are more than summer shadow-play.
Like canvassers from door to door
The poets go, and gain no ear.

Sing of the fighters? Brave-of-Heart
Soon learns to play the coward's part,
And calls it, breaking solemn pacts,
Fair Compromise or Facing Facts.

Where all around us ancient ills
Devour like blackberry the hills
On every product of the time
Let fall a poisoned rain of rhyme,
                            sings Harry;
But praise St. Francis feeding crumbs
Into the empty mouths of guns.

What shall we sing? sings Harry.

Sing all things sweet or harsh upon
These islands in the Pacific sun,
The mountains whitened endlessly
And the white horses of the winter sea,
                            sings Harry.

A Woman Shopping

Beauty goes into the butcher's shop
Where blood taints the air;
The chopper comes down on the block
And she pats her hair.

Death's gallery hangs ready
Naked of hair and hide,
But she has clothes on her body
And a heart inside.

What's death to the lady, pray?
Even shopping's a bore.
—The carcasses gently sway
As she goes out the door.

But death goes with her on the way:
In her basket along the street
Rolls heavily against her thigh
The blood-red bud of the meat.

from *Arawata Bill*

The Scene

Mountains nuzzle mountains
White-bearded rock-fronted
In perpetual drizzle.

Rivers swell and twist
Like a torturer's fist
Where the maidenhair
Falls of the waterfall
Sail through the air.

The mountains send below
Their cold tribute of snow
And the birch makes brown
The rivulets running down.

Rock, air, and water meet
Where crags debate
The dividing cloud.

In the dominion of the thorn
The delicate cloud is born,

And golden nuggets bloom
In the womb of the storm.

The Search

What unknown affinity
Lies between mountain and sea
In country crumpled like an unmade bed
Whose crumbs may be nuggets as big as your head
And it's all snow-sheeted, storm-cloud fed?
    Far behind is the blue Pacific,
    And the Tasman somewhere ahead.

Wet or dry, low or high,
Somewhere in a blanketfold of the land
Lies the golden strand.
        Mountain spells may bind it,
        But the marrow in the bone
        The itch in the palm
        The Chinaman's talisman
        To save from harm,
        All tell me I shall find it.

These mountains never stir
In the still or turbulent air.
Only the stones thaw-loosened
Leap from the precipice
Into shrapnel snow-cushioned.

    An egg-timer shingle-fan
    Dribbles into the pan
    And the river sluices with many voices.
        The best pan is an old pan
        —The grains cling to the rust,
        And a few will come from each panning,
        The rust brown, and golden the dust.
But where is the amethyst sky and the high
Mountain of pure gold?

A Prayer

Mother of God, in this brazen sun
Lead me down from the arid heights
Before my strength is done.
Give me the rain
That not long since I cursed in vain.
Lead me to the river, the life-giver.

The River Crossing

The river was announcing
An ominous crossing
With the boulders knocking.

'You can do it and make a fight of it,
Always taking the hard way
For the hell and delight of it.

But there comes the day
When you watch the spate of it,
And camp till the moon's down
—Then find the easy way
Across in the dawn,
Waiting till that swollen vein
Of a river subsides again.'

And Bill set up his camp and watched
His young self, river-cold and scratched,
Struggling across, and up the wrong ridge,
And turning back, temper on edge.

Camp Site

Earth and sky black,
And an old fire's sodden ashes
Were puddled in porridge clay
On that bleak day.

An old coat lay
Like a burst bag, worn
Out in the tussle with thorn.
Water ran
Through a hole in the rusted can.

The pass was wrapped
In a blanket of mist,
And the rain came again,
And the wind whipped.

The climbers had been there camping
Watching the sky
With a weatherwise eye.
And Paradise Pete
Scrabbling a hole in the sleet
When the cloud smote and waters roared
Had scrawled on a piece of board
RIVERS TOO DEEP.

Wata Bill stuck his shovel there
And hung his hat on the handle,
Cutting scrub for a shelter,
Lighting wet wood with a candle.

To The Coast

I

There's no horse this time,
Going's too rough.
It's a man with an eighty-pound pack,
And that's more than enough.

> *Always the colour, in quartz or the river,*
> *Never the nuggets as large as a liver.*

Five years ago I tried this route
Taking the left branch. Now try the right.
It'll mean tramping half the night
Before the weather breaks, turning
Tarns into lakes.

> *The colour is elusive, like streaks*
> *Of wind-cloud. Gold dust must*
> *Come from somewhere. But where?*

Neither river nor mountain speaks.

III

Jacksons Bay on the Tasman, the end
Of many a search round many a bend.

Does the terminus of the sea
Contain my mystery,
Throwing back on the beach
Grains of gold
I have followed from sea to sea
Thirty times and again
Since I was thirty years old?

> *A seaboot full of gold, tempest tossed,*
> *They hid somewhere on the coast*
> *When their ship was lost.*

But back to the mountains!
I know
The fire of gold
Lies under that cold snow.

Soliloquies

III

When God made this place
He made mountains and fissures
Hostile, vicious, and turned
Away His face.

Did He mean me to burn out my heart
In a forty-year search
In this wilderness
Of snow and black birch,
With only a horse for company
Beating on a white tympany?

Is this some penance
For a sin I never knew,
Or does my grail
Still lie in the snow or hail?

Yet it might be His purpose to plant
The immaculate metal
Where the stoutest hearts quail.

IV

They'll not laugh this time
When I come home
With something in my poke.
They've been saying too long
That Arawata Bill's just a joke.

The fools! There's more gold beneath
These rivers and mountains
Than in all their clattering teeth.

The Crystallized Waves

Snow is frozen cloud
Tumbled to the ravine,
The mist and the mountain-top
Lying between.

The cloud turns to snow or mist,
The mist to the stream,
The stream seeks out the ocean
All in a geographer's dream.

What are the mountains on high
But the crystallized waves of the sea,

And what is the white-topped wave
But a mountain that liquidly weaves?

The water belongs to the mountain,
Belongs to the deep;
The mountain beneath the water
Suckles oceans in sleep.

How are the tops in the dawn?

The End

It got you at last, Bill,
The razor-edge that cut you down
Not in the gullies nor on the pass
But in a bed in town.

R.I.P. where no gold lies
But in your own questing soul
Rich in faith and a wild surmise.

You should have been told
Only in you was the gold:
Mountain and river paid you no fee,
Mountain melting to the river,
River to the sea.

PAUL HENDERSON

Object Lesson

A hill you may say is a hill; take a hill,
Or a group of them forming an island,
Range, or peninsula. Here's the benign
Slope, thrust of deceptive hand
Green-gloved over the strong racked bones
Of earth assaulting sky. Follow the up,
The flow, the final burst in the sun;
Measure the cone; a hill, you perceive, is a hill.
A man you may say is a man; but when
He's extended himself to the hill, included
The spur and the curve in the light of his
Knowing how this was formed; pondered if
Time, place, thought and strewn heaven
Matter a tinker's curse; noticed the blue
Haze hills absorb from the sea, clouds
Cumbering the island; known the slight
Fear of far hills, and the sweet solace
Of these, being home; then we consider again
Well, what is a hill? Is it a hill,
Or a hill through the eyes of one human?

Return Journey

Wellington again slaps the face with wind
So well remembered; and now the mind
Leaps; all sea, all tossed hills, all white-
Edged air poured in tides over the tight
Town. Bleached bones of houses are hard
To distinguish, at some distance, from a graveyard.

But do not consider death; we have tucked
Too snugly into the valleys; we have mucked
With the rake of time over the tamed
Foreshore. Battering trams; Lambton, lamed
With concrete, has only a hint of ghost waters
On the Quay stranded among elevators.

There is no need to remember swamp-grass,
Or how the first women (let the rain pass,
They had prayed) wept when the hills reared up
Through the mist, and they were trapped

Between sea and cliffed forest. No ship could be
More prisoning than the grey beach at Petone.

No need to consider (here where we have shut
The tiger tight behind iron and concrete)
How we might yet drown deep under the wind;
And the wind die too; and an insect find
(Columbus of his day) the little graveyard town
Set in a still landscape like porcelain.

Elegy

I

Morning after death on the bar was calm;
There was no difficulty in looking for the boy's body.
The boat had been found in the dark, overturned,
And at dawn the men went out again
To search the beaches and sweep, in the boats, offshore.
The mountains to the north stood up like sepulchres
Rising white-boned out of a black sea.
The flat hymnal of light lay asleep in the sky
And sang morning in a minor key
To wake the wheeling flights of birds
That, curious, mark down all drifting wrack
And disabled drowned bodies.

2

He should not have attempted the bar, of course;
The tide was ebbing but he was making for home.
On the wide sea with night falling,
Only the open, small yacht to uplift him,
He must have felt, well, try it.

Moments make miniature green globes in the mind;
Light flaring on dark from house windows
As the lifeboat slid out on the ways;
Searchlight like an awed moon at sea
Probing the black night and white breakers,
A drawn will of the anxious, twining a tight knot
In the shadows of Shag Rock; car lights
A stereoscopic, too brutal revelation of tears.

The shocked boy saying that his friend was gone;
That they'd found the boat, turned turtle,
But that Jack was lost, they couldn't find him.

O weep all night for this drowned youth,
Waiting in the rock's black arms for the foreseen time
Of lifeboat returning, lonely, in the small hours;
Of certainty frozen in the immutable shape of hands;
Of a boy's boat is no bond, nor even a safe coffin.

Get some sleep, if you can; by now he's dead,
The water is too cold, it is almost winter.

3

Yet at dawn they were searching the beaches.
In the immense dawn distances the groups of men
Walked like little pins over the sandspits
And the morning light broke bitterly like snowflakes

On the sun-dazed self-conscious sea
That tight-lipped along the beaches hides
Its dreadful truths, its doused, its double-drowned boys
Lying like Jonahs in a beast's belly.

The sun rose on a silver-lidded sea that lapped
Over the sandbanks like turning shillings,
Making enormous shadows which, when reached,
Were nothing at all. In such confusion
Of light and lazing sand-pipers and lumps of seaweed
How find in this vast soul of silver and of sand
All that is left of one boy?

Yet at noon the beast opened its lips,
Or perhaps it was just that, with the sun higher,
The light was no longer tricky, but anyway
The boy was spewed up, and the body was seen
Floating face down, in a life-jacket, beyond the surf.

So is the sea-god fed, and one more sacrifice
Strewn on the waves. No fairer limbs
Are demanded, their separate toll will delay
Disaster in the mind's millennial time and kiss
The countless bare noons where there are no shadows.

It was easy enough then to go out on surf-skis,
Into the light that by afternoon would be blue,
And bring in the boy's body, for a calmer burial.

I Think of Those

Sometimes I think of those whose lives touch mine
Too briefly; who, by a look or word, show me
A little of what lies beneath, but, leaving then,
Because we are trained to silence, they are shut away.

How shall I tell one friend from casual passer
Who am walled also in self; and cannot say
Do not hesitate; here is a love without fear;
The mind in its lonely prison forfeits today

As well as its yesterdays; and black tomorrows
Are chained with the hooded falcon on time's wrist
Unknowing and therefore unenvious of ecstatic arrow
Flight when the dark bird is released.

Yet I come to you in these words as surely
As though you were here surprised again at my eyes,
Though if this be all, if there is never any
If there is never between us more, no such awakening dies.

M. K. JOSEPH

Off Cape Leeuwen

Leviathan the ocean, spiked and mailed,
Scalloped with imbricated scales,
With clots of granite clawed and tailed
(His parasites are wandering whales)

Hails in Behemoth the ship
A creature of the self-same mould
Nonchalantly in iron grip
Bearing its passengers embowelled.

Leviathan's somnolent shoulder nudges
Behemoth's ridged and riveted flank,
Who majestically heaving, sideways budges
Flounders and skids like a mudded tank,

Poises straddling, wavers and heels,
Peers at the moon with squinted face,
Then hip and shoulder to Leviathan reels
In a solemn brotherly drunken embrace.

Above them in sky's spinning dome
Stars bloom to meteors at each roll—
These tipsy monsters reeling home
Between Australia and the Pole.

Nurse's Song

It's better not to ask, not to deny
But soothe the baby with a lullaby
Nor hint his legacy of grace and grief
Of state and sorrow, bearing and belief.

The palace duties and the palace joys;
The Dauphin howling at his emerald toys
The Infanta in a grape-skin velvet dressed
Low cut to show the glamour of her breast;

The ebony and ivory of the table
In circled candle-light; the hand scarce able
To lift the monstrous amethyst, which afar
Shines to its trembling like a dancing star;

The polished galleries on a summer night
Ablaze like rivers in the thunderous light
(Still and unwinking stood the halberdiers
As the cloaked figure passed with sound of tears);

The chapel where, by chantry screen, there sings
A youth leading responses to the king's
Obsequies, whose lineaments he bore.
He sings in sweet soprano evermore.

Distilled Water

From Blenheim's clocktower a cheerful bell bangs out
The hour, and time hangs humming in the wind.
Time and the honoured dead. What else? The odd
Remote and shabby peace of a provincial town.
Blenkinsopp's gun? the Wairau massacre?
Squabbles in a remote part of empire.
Some history. Some history, but not much.

Consider now the nature of distilled
Water which has boiled and left behind
In the retort rewarding sediment
Of salts and toxins. Chemically pure of course
(No foreign bodies here) but to the taste
Tasteless and flat. Let it spill on the ground,
Leach out its salts, accumulate its algae,
Be living: the savour's in impurity.
Is that what we are? something that boiled away
In the steaming flask of nineteenth-century Europe?
Innocuous until now, or just beginning
To make its own impression on the tongue.

And through the Tory Channel naked hills
Gully and slip pass by, monotonously dramatic
Like bad blank verse, till one cries out for
Enjambement, equivalence, modulation,
The studied accent of the human voice,
Or the passage opening through the windy headlands
Where the snowed Kaikouras hang in the air like mirage
And the nation of gulls assembles on the waters
Of the salt sea that walks about the world.

Mercury Bay Eclogue

I

The child's castle crumbles; hot air shimmers
Like water working over empty sand.
Summer noon is long and the brown swimmers
For fear of outward currents, lie on land.
With tumbleweed and seashells in its hand
The wind walks, a vigorous noonday ghost
Bearing gifts for an expected guest.

Hull down on horizon, island and yacht
Vanish into blue leaving no trace;
Above my head the nebulae retreat
Dizzily sliding round the bend of space
Winking a last red signal of distress.
Each galaxy or archipelago
Plunges away into the sky or sea.

In the dry noon are all things whirling away?
They are whirling away, but look—the gull's flight,
Stonefall towards the rainbows of the spray
Skim swim and glide on wing up to the light
And in this airy gesture of delight
See wind and sky transformed to bless and warn,
The dance, the transfiguration, the return.

The turning wheels swing the star to harbour
And rock the homing yacht in a deep lull,
Bring children to their tea beneath the arbour,
Domesticate the wind's ghost and pull
Islands to anchor, softly drop the gull
Into his nest of burnished stones and lead
The yachtsmen and the swimmers to their bed.

II

A shepherd on a bicycle
Breaks the pose of pastoral
   But will suffice to keep
   The innocence of sheep.

Ringing his bell he drives the flock
From sleepy field and wind-scarred rock
   To where the creaming seas
   Wash shoreward like a fleece.

The farmer and his wife emerge
All golden from the ocean-surge

Their limbs and children speak
The legend of the Greek.

The shadowy tents beneath the pines
The surfboards and the fishing-lines
    Tell that our life might be
    One of simplicity.

The wind strums aeolian lyres
Inshore among the telephone wires
    Linking each to each.
    The city and the beach.

For sunburnt sleepers would not come
If inland factories did not hum
    And this Arcadian state
    Is built on butterfat.

So children burn the seastained wood
And tell the present as a good
    Knowing that bonfires are
    Important as a star.

And on his gibbet the swordfish raised
With bloody beak and eye glazed
    Glares down into the tide
    Astonishment and pride.

Machine once muscled with delight
He merges now in primitive night;
    The mild and wondering crowd
    Admire the dying god
    Where Kupe and where Cook have trod.

III

Over the sea lie Europe and Asia
    The dead moulded in snow
The persecution of nuns and intellectuals
    The clever and the gentle
The political trials and punishment camps
    The perversion of children
Men withering away with fear of the end.

Fifteen years of a bad conscience
    Over Spain and Poland
Vienna Berlin Israel Korea
    Orphans and prostitutes
Unburied the dead and homeless living

We looked on ruined cities
Saying, These are our people.

We sat in the sun enduring good luck
   Like the stain of original sin
Trying to be as God, to shoulder
   The world's great sorrow
Too shaken to see that we hadn't the talent
   That the clenching heart is a fist
And a man's grasp the reach of his arm.

Be still and know: the passionate intellect
   Prepares great labours
Building of bridges, practice of medicine.
   Still there are cows to be milked
Students to teach, traffic direction
   Ships unloading at wharves
And the composition of symphonies.

IV

The poets standing on the shelf
Excavate the buried self
Freud's injunction they obey
Where id was, let ego be.

Yeats who from his tower sees
The interlocking vortices
Of the present and the past,
Shall find the centre hold at last.

Eliot whose early taste
Was for the cenobitic waste
Now finds the promise of a pardon
Through children's laughter in the locked garden.

Pound in his barbed-wire cage
Prodded into stuttering rage
Still earns reverence from each
Because he purified our speech.

Cavalier or toreador
Is Campbell expert to explore
The truthful moment when we face
The black bull in the arid place.

And Auden who has seen too much
Of the wound weeping for the healer's touch

A surgeon in his rubber gloves
Now cauterizes where he loves.

The summer landscape understood
The morning news, the poet's mood,
By their imperatives are defined
Converging patterns in the mind.

V

Come fleet Mercury, messenger of gods and men
Skim with your winged sandal the resounding surf
Quickly come bearing to all things human
Celestial medicine for their tongueless grief.
Heaven's thief and merchant, here is your port
Lave with your gifts of healing and of speech
All mortals who shall ever print with foot
These silent hills and this forsaken beach.

Come sweet Venus, mother of men and beasts
While meteors fall across the yellow moon
Above the hills herded like sleeping beasts,
Gently come lady, and with hand serene
Plant fruits of peace where by this mariner's mark
The torrents of your sea-begetting roar
And trouble in their dreams of glowing dark
These sleeping hills and this forbidden shore.

Come swift ship and welcome navigators
Link and line with your instruments this earth
To heaven under the propitious stars,
Show forth the joined and fortune-bearing birth
And set this fallen stone a meteorite
Where Mercury and Venus hand in hand
Walk on the waters this auspicious night
And touch to swift love this forgotten strand.

Girl, Boy, Flower, Bicycle

This girl
Waits at the corner for
This boy
Freewheeling on his bicycle.
She holds
A flower in her hand
A gold flower
In her hands she holds
The sun.

With power between his thighs
The boy
Comes smiling to her
He rides
A bicycle that glitters like
The wind.
This boy this girl
They walk
In step with the wind
Arm in arm
They climb the level street
To where
Laid on the glittering handlebars
The flower
Is round and shining as
The sun.

from *The Tourist in Seat 29*

Granada the Last City

. . . thinking of the tall triumphant horsemen
Boabdil in tears, the tired army
Winding through this valley
How the Caliphate ended
How in a way America began, here.

Now see where it lies empty splendid and resonant
Where the colours fade grain by grain from the carved stucco
Where the mosaics retain their gilt and azure
And only the sunlight dances gravely among the courts
Where the rectangular water shines green between the myrtles
And the carved lions guard their silent fountain.
Here the red hill once raised up a life
Of civilized luxury and rottenness.
How has time transfigured it.
Caliphs and janissaries eunuchs and odalisques fall
And turn to glittering fish in the green pool.

There is blood in the fountain of the lions.

Outside (it is years ago but) still
Lorca and the rest are passing by
To their grey anonymous death
The hoarse voice of lorries climbs the hill
The gears angrily clash
The wheels swing away to the Sierras
Folded like cerecloths over the far valleys

Over the pinetrees
                    (sprig of green pine . . .
green I desire you green . . .
Can't you see the wound I carry
across the throat and chest? . . .)
And all those years away the volleys begin
And the goldfish turns away with the flick of a fin.

There is blood on the palisade of green pine.

Now the guitars drum out and the singing
The evening stars together singing the highpitched
Mo rish lament of love, bending above the stone terrace
Where the gitanas gather. The rouged evening sky
Swirls her tawdry flounces and instantly
Cuts out upon the amber air images
Of stone flowers. Now he who honoured them
Dreams afar off visions of the fierce gipsies
Of how their pride towers out of the dust.
Their chocolate eyes contemn the Leicas
And the white bespectacled faces. Because of pride
They are not poor; they do not beg but command
Like exiled princes. Over there on the red hill
The honeycomb walls of Alhambra drip and run
With the slow inconsolable golden blood of the sun.

Epilogue to a Poetry Reading

Ladies and gentlemen, that is the end of the programme.
You may think you have been entertained (we hope you have)
But don't be deceived, you have also been – 'got at'.
For the poet is like a kindly children's physician
Dazzling the young patients' eyes with baubles and vanishing
        coins
And just when you least expect it, *in* goes the hypodermic;
For Apollo the god of medicine is also the lord of verse
(Keeping the Muses nine in a kind of platonic harem)
And the poet is also a doctor, a mountebank if you like,
Or bluntly, a quack. Though his nostrums won't always cure
He has an infallible knack of diagnosis.

Or since we are met in a picture-gallery, let's change the
        metaphor
Saying with Horace that poems resemble pictures—
An old and fallacious belief, yet true since the poet
Is also Madam Zaza, the figure with the crystal ball
In which can be seen the past, the present, the future,

Three scenes in which you, we, everyone, have a part.
Think then of a kind of triptych, three tall panels
In each of which there is something of each of us, somewhere.

On the left, the past, small and clear like an old monk's missal—

The swarthy ploughman in his green hood pushes his plough
Behind two round-eyed oxen, and bent to labour
He ignores the swifts who tumble away in a cold breeze
Towards the white castle from whose gate emerges a procession
Of horsemen in blue and crimson, and seigneurs and ladies
Canter across the watermeadows into the woods,
Where horns are winding and dogs bell-mouthed give tongue
At running boars, and a tall stag bears a gold
Cross between his antlers. Yet for none will he stand
At gaze until the hunter-prince shall turn hermit.

The main panel, the largest and least composed, is the present—

In our centre, the shaft of day moves like a spotlight
Leaping across continents in whose bays the entrails of ocean-
Liners are rummaged by cranes, and whose angular mountains
Are threaded by the steel tape of railways, and whose skies are
        eyed
By the lenses of telescopes, and whose air trembles with the echoes
Of radios and the mutter of motors and the nightglare of towns.
Here a policevan gongs down empty streets
And here the frenzied fans mob a popstar,
Here are barbed wire and machineguns, and here are parliaments
And powerhouses, ballets and bookshops, and mothers walking
Their children in sunlit parks. All clocks are striking
Noon together, as three jetplanes slide
Across the air, toward the city of windowed monoliths.

On the right, split clear down the middle, an attempt
To present insoluble enigmas in human terms, the future—

All things are possible on this plateau, where at one side
A forest blazes, and on the other, glaciers splinter
Into icebergs and between are the terraced hills crowned
With strange towers and crowded with simple but un-
Intelligible machines, for here are earthquake and famine,
Plague and buried cities, yet here are men
And women standing in gentle light, absorbed
In unknown activities of mathematics intricate
As dreams and starships of unusual design. From the clouds
Two hands offer lightning or music, but not both.

GLORIA RAWLINSON

The Islands Where I was Born

I

Fragrances that like a wind disturb
The child's pacific dry in suburban shell
And send it murmuring through time's bony curb
Have caught me in the glassbright thoroughfare:
Pineapples oranges limes, their island smell
A catspaw rocking heart to hoist and dare
The long remembrance. Heart, if you would mime
Journeys to where a child blinked half the truth
Let points of origin be fixed where time
May be measured for a meaningful azimuth;
Your flowery isles are masked in Medusa's blood
And the sapphiry elements wear a darker hood.

II

There was no Pacific then, reef-broken spray
Flared on extremities of childish vision,
Under the mango tree's dim acre, at play
In sunflower groves I lived my changeless season.

When insular hours with morning steps unfurled
Chickens and coconuts, bronze fisherboy,
And old deaf Ka Ngutu's wagon howled
Past the tree of flying foxes it seemed that joy

Was born like my shadow in the sun's presence
With fuming orange in hand and the everywhere
Odour steaming from copra's oily crescents
Soothed and smoothed the least rebellious air.

Then foster speech of my Friendly Islands tongue
Could wag its music, the Ofa Atu sworn
With a white smile and all sweet change sung
For trade or gift or guile where I was born.

And I didn't believe in that realm of banished fairies
The Graveyard of Disobedient Children and hushed
Sleepers who once ran hatless, ate tapu'd berries
Or cut their feet on coral and never confessed.

For then I thought we lived on the only route,
In the apple of a heavenly eye, the fond
Providence of flowery oils and fruit,
Kingdom of Joy and Enjoy to the farthest frond.

It was out of all reckoning one last Steamer Day
When I saw the Pacific skyward beyond our coral;
Farewells fluttered . . . palm-trees turned away
And cool on my cheeks the wind from a new littoral.

III

The key was your clear maternal voice
In stories drolled like a deepsea shell
Except they smacked of human salt
And fancy that your witty mind
Spun from the long-fetched tale,
But colour was counted less than fault
Since truth was nearest to be found
In the swift light of your humorous eyes.

Friends at our fireside listened and laughed.
I blazed with private wonder.
You spoke of places I knew when small
But Oh how far may living stretch?
How many fathoms does heart fall under?
And mind grows—how many mountains tall?
The world's wild wisdom sang out of reach
Till one had learned its tortuous craft.

IV

They were our legends, we flagged them on our lives;
Though tattered with telling I wouldn't haul them down!
Sometimes you remembered the two days' journey
'—in a boat rigged with twine, leaking at every seam.
When a tall sea rushed upon us
Thrust the roaring tongue-tip of its swell
Under the boozing timbers, how they groaned, staggered
    down!
One small rusty tin was our bailer
And this I scooped in the settling weight of our death
While the Tongan crew prayed and sang for mercy of our
    lives.
And how we survived, by craft or prayer or bailer
Seems crazy now, and the last thing to be dreamed
That land's relief humped on the reddening west.'
    'Jiali was the girl from Nukualofa
Swam forty miles from where a boat went down.
Through the sun-beaten, shark-schooled waters
Armed with a high heart swam the long day home;
When, her hair snatched on coral, the foaming breakers
Shelved her torn and screaming on the reef,
    She said a spirit wouldn't let her drown.'
'Hunting one brilliant midnight by calm lagoon

And burning copra to range the wild pigs near,
No grunting, no scuffle we heard, no sound
But where our horses pulled on their tethered reins
And the inward step by step of mounting fear.
Then smashing mirrored light with gulching waves
Lunged to the shoregrass out of the lagoon
A huge sea-beast, ball-eyed, long-necked, frill-maned.
Leaping to horse we saw with twisted glance
That image, unforgettable, reared at the moon.'

    'Once on an island voyage
A mating of whales, the thing most rarely seen;
How she, pale belly up, lay still on the moving blue,
And was the centre of the circling bull;
How whorling out to the rim of the sky he turned
And shirring a leaguelong wake flashed for his centre.
And they at the clash stood up like two enormous columns,
Fell with splashing thunder, rolled over and under,
Down through the sealight's fathoms, into the ocean's
    night.'

    'Eua Iki! Quite lacking in mementoes
And I never thought to bring back seeds and cuttings.
Rips, foam-fierce, guarded the narrow entry,
Bucking between the reefs you were cannoned ashore.
They were silks of sand one stepped on, warm and shining
As the island's phantasy. No one would believe . . .
Flowers, but I can't name them,
Stemmed perhaps from that oldest and richest of gardens.
    We skipped on ropes of orchids
In moist rock-hollows hung with trumpeting vines;
    Roamed little valleys
Where grass like green mice meadowed tiny ponies;
    Bathed in crystal—
Clear sweet fathoms, watching jewels of fish in the coral-
    trees—
(They matched I thought the giant butterflies in the sun's
    gleam.)
    Slept at last to the island's
Soft Ariel untragic sigh of a futureless dream.
Sometimes I wonder was it really so.'
Years later you remembered
'Eua Iki lies on the edge of the Tongan Deep.'

V

The stars that sing for recollective sails
With no iron pulling at the point of pleasure
Are child and dreamer exulting in fabled isles
That Maui fished out of the dolphined azure.

'The goldless age where gold disturbs no dreams',
So Byron burning for a south could sigh
With lovesweet oil of his romantic themes
Drawn from the leaves of Mariner and Bligh.

Perhaps that goldless age is the fruit-full sense
Of the islands where I was born, when servitor
Of earthly wishes the sun spreads an immense
Glitter over the Deep's unfathomable sore.

The Tongan Deep! Like death's gut or time's cleft
One grinding yard for dug-out galleon schooner,
Husking bones and bells to pelagic drift,
Repelling our brightest reason, the quick lunar

Tides of our laughter and grief with a quietest mouth.
Thereover we blue-weather-wise would sail
Leaving the wounded day unturned for truth
But mind hears soundings, haulnets a dragon's scale

And must pursue beyond the serving sun
Its utter depth; as Oh, wild-fire-west hurled
To the cod of the track its vast hurricane
Of gilded dreams across the nescient world.

But old as man the island ghosts that rise
From sacrificial stones, purgations of history,
Rinse with undying rains our turnaway eyes
Till the coiled mountain sombres the sapphire sea.

Fear we to know these things? The changing wind
Itself must halt before the Royal Tombs,
Old Lord Tortoise wanders battered and blind
Who shielded his sleep against a thousand dooms;

So in the metropolis panged by the day's alarms
Sail for that strength of witness you recall
By heart to the Friendly Kingdom, its crooked palms
Shall say what pacific hands environ all.

VI

Who is the dancer
Sways at her anchorage
By the salt grave?
The palmtree our sister
Of Adam's red clay;
Slantset by hurricane
Stripped to bone courage

She claps like a scaredevil
Through the moon's and sun's day.

Who are the singers
With timebeat and palmclap
Shake the green grave?
Brown lass, brown lad,
Of sweet banqueting heart:
Earth's night is long
But laughing they clip
Hibiscus and jasmine
In their hair, in their song.

Merry-go-round

All day where Megaphone
the gala tyrant booms
twelve painted animals
wind up the clockwise dreams

of mounted cherubs with
brave eyes and comet curls,
while groundlings wait their turn
scuffing impatient heels.

Whirled like a stars' cavalcade
they spin on a glittering core,
pumped by the hot serenade
their young blood could pirouette for—
ever and ever and ever and ever

O children ride the swan,
ride the zebra, ride
the only tiger you
are really safe upon.

For time will halt the rounds,
silence and moonlight share
your popcorn bags, your cones,
and grinning melonrinds.

The Hare in the Snow

Afraid and trackless between storm and storm
Runs the mountain hare blinded with snow,
Digs in its dazzle her last desperate form
But seeks a refuge not a death below.

What shall our utmost clarity unlock?

Where she had rooted for her darkened hope
Time, immense, unhumbled, turns with the sun
Stripping snows down to adamantine rock:
All that's left of grief on the bright slope
Discover now—a small crouched skeleton.

RUTH DALLAS

Deserted Beach

If there had been one bird, if there had been
One gull to circle through the wild salt wind
Or cry above the breaking of the waves,
One footprint or one feather on the sand,
Then the great rocks leaning from the hills
Might have been the ruins of great walls.

Because no bird flew there, because there was
Nothing on that beach that called or sang,
The rocks leaned out towards the sea and watched
As women watch beside the sea day-long,
Shut within themselves like flowers in rain,
For men and ships that will not come again.

Of that warm moment when they rang with song,
Threw back the clink of sharpened stone on stone,
When firelight dimmed the stars, and when they heard
Above the lonely sea-sound, creak and groan
Of keels on shingle, nothing now remained
But oven-stones, and mounds of shells and sand.

If there had been one bird—but no; as once
For pillar, pyramid, and lion, all
Rock waited, still the great rocks waited, watched;
No cry of child or gull above the fall
Of waves on stones. Only the sea moved there,
And weeds within the waves like floating hair.

Grandmother and Child

The waves that danced about the rock have gone,
The tide has stolen the rock as time has stolen
The quiet old lady who waited beneath the trees
That moved with a sad sea-sound in the summer wind.

When death was as near as the wind among the leaves,
Troubling the waking fear in the heart of the child
As the wind was troubling the shadows on the sunlit lawn,
The grandmother seemed as frail as the frailest leaf.

But she sat so still in the shade of the summer trees
With the wind of death on her cheeks and her folded hands,

Her strength seemed large and cool, as the rock in the sea
Seemed large and cool in the green and restless waves.

As the rock remains in the sea, deep down and strong,
The rock-like strength of the lady beneath the trees
Remains in the mind of the child, more real than death,
To challenge the child's strength in the hour of fear.

A Striped Shell

Not for us this shell grew like a lily,
Is striped outside and ivory within,
Too many flower-like shells have been washed up
And crushed and scattered on these wild beaches,
Spin and glint along the blowing sand.

A shell must have some shape, but you would think
That any shape would serve, any colour;
And then the way they break through all that seems
Dark and threatening in the sea, as strangely
Easily as snowdrops through dead leaves.

It is the same with every beautiful thing
Perhaps that breaks through darkness or decay,
But here where we walk warily, at times
In places where no man has been before,
These things are startling held against the silence.

If it is not a striped and rounded shell
Found unharmed among sharp rocks or under
Yellow snakes of weed, it is a fern
That seems too delicate to touch uncurling
In the gloom of some deep forest glade.

Behind a shell that fills and cups the hand,
Ferns that shine like sunlight through dark trees,
Must lie innumerable shells and ferns
No man has seen, shells like this, and ferns
As delicate as any we have found.

If only one could learn to accept this shell
For what it is; but there is something in
Its shape and colour, something in its breaking
Like a flower from the sea, that makes one
Turn it over in the hand, and over.

The Boy

Miraculously in the autumn twilight, out of
The wet-grass smell of the apple, out of the cold
Smooth feel of it against his shrunken fingers,
He made the boy; he was not there before,
A boy in the trailing apple branches hiding,
Surprising us like the cobwebs hung with rain
That suddenly shone from the darkness under the leaves.

Out of the apple he made the boy, the apple
So pensively turned and turned in the rainy twilight,
Cold yellow apple out of his childhood heavy
Again in his hand. So quietly he stood,
Under dark leaves, shoulders and grey head bent,
Cupped fingers gnarled and knotty as old twigs,
He seemed at first another apple tree.

Then he made the boy, the boy who still
In autumn twilight shakes, when no wind stirs,
The yellow apples from the trees, or swings
On the oldest boughs; but he was not the boy;
We could in a moment see the tight-skinned apple
Fall and open into roots and leaves,
But never the hands grow into the boy's young hands.

A Tea-shop

If in the scent of violets there came
The moment only, then how warm the spring
And even the little flower-shops would seem
With their forced winter blooms; but violets bring
A rush of uninvited details, two
Great tattered leaves, deep wrinkled and dull green,
That almost hide the tiny flowers, blue
As far-off hills before the fall of rain;
They bring the grey light in the tea-shop, sound
Of people in the street, their wooden-heeled
Quick stepping through the chill September wind;
And clear as the cups of tea that have grown cold,
    The face of an old sad woman sitting near,
    Side on, with a large bright ear-ring in her ear.

from *Letter to a Chinese Poet*

Beating the Drum

Warming a set of new bones
In the old fire of the sun, in the fashion
Of all men, and lions, and blackbirds,
Finding myself upon the planet earth,
Abroad on a short journey
Equipped with heart and lungs to last
Not as long as a house, or a peony rose,
Travelling in the midst of a multitude
Of soft and breathing creatures
In skins of various colours, feathers, fur,
A tender population
For a hard ball spinning
Indifferently through light and dark,
I turn to an old poem,
Fresh as this morning's rose,
Though a thousand summers have shed their blooms
Since the bones that guided brush or pen
Were dust upon the wind.

So men turned to a carved stick
That held the lonely history of the tribe.

Round the sun and round the sun and round.

We have left the tree and waterhole
For a wilderness of stars.

Round the sun and round the sun and round.

I sing the carvers of sticks and the makers of poems,
This man who worked on ivory,
That one who shaped a fine jar,
And the man who painted a cave wall
By the light of fire.
   Reminded in the noon hour
    With the sun warm upon the bone
  Under the canopy of the climbing rose,
That man is cut down like a flower,
I sing the makers
Of all things true and fair that stand
When the wind has parted
The warm and obedient bones of the hand;
All those I sing,
And among them name your name,
Who left the earth richer than when they came.

The rose is shaken in the wind,
    Round the sun
        The petals fall
           And round the sun and round.

Among Old Houses

In every second back yard
Maimed and rheumaticky branches swell
And break
        violently
Into shell-clear petals calm as porcelain,

Or foam afloat behind a travelling wave.

No yard made hideous by discarded oil-drums,
Rusted scrap-iron, crates, collapsing sheds,
That is not visited by madcap Spring;
It's not just one old tree that glitters forth,
Not two, but tree on blossoming tree—
A fairytale procession, like the arrival
Of twenty sisters ready for a ball,
Or mermaids, voluptuous, glistening from the sea.

Over the pates of the old men thawing
Their cold limbs in the spring sun,
Over the leaping children, over wheels
Still bound and netted with last year's straws,
On angel and sinner, on all, on all,
                    like rice,
Like a gift, like a blessing,
        The immaculate petals fall.

Shadow Show

Watch, now.
From this black paper,
If I cut a silhouette,
Hands blown sideways by unceasing winds,
Shoulders bowed under a burden,
Knees bent,
A birdsclaw foothold on the earth,
You could say that I made a tree,
Storm twisted.

Or a woman, or a man.

HUBERT WITHEFORD

Elegy in the Orongorongo Valley

Sundered from this beauty is its fond lover
Who wandered in boredom over far oceans
Again and again remembering, till the day
When decks split in flame and the sea choked him.

Did his despairing salt-water stormed eye-balls
Search, as they broke, for these streams sprawling
Over high places, the mountains of springtime,
Out of the world on a lost morning?

Did death's lightning show him this shadowed valley
Burning through oceans, green beyond time?
Was this the river he felt closing over
Islands of pain and over his life?

Here and in exile and in last anguish
He found no frenzy to win him this wanton—
In his full failure glistens the wild bush
Too long remembered, too long forgotten.

The Waters, Indeed, are to the Palate, Bitter

Half my life has passed me by
In my island washed around
By desert seas and void security—
Each year my heart becomes more dry.

Through nerveless fingers life like rice
In slow storm runs to the ground;
Not distance nor insentience provides
Cuirass against that mild fatality.

And slowly, slowly, our life flows
To the proud blaring of the Tramways Band
By postered walls of corrugated iron
And past abominable bungalows.

Slow though that blast, its taste of failure stings
As the salt spray from out the seething waste
Scalds, on the naked headland, human lips.
Let me fathom that sheer taste.

The Cactuses

It is the orange flower on dark-flushed stem
Or the small spines to guard the so sleek flesh,
Amid dry sand and stone,
That waken an almost malicious love
For the mild cunning of the old creation.
Unblurred by virtue's or by sin's delusion
Out of the inert debris of disaster
It rose among the thinning atmosphere.
We cannot emulate. But, as across the aeons
Our later sense accosts these presences,
A sting of freshness runs from skull to heel
And, on the palate, sparkling waters fleet.

At the Discharge of Cannon Rise the Drowned

One forfeit more from life the current claimed
While, on the horizon, rose white-sheeted spars;
Bare of their canvas when the morning came
They rode the bay that held its prisoner.

Some days then, by our time, of windless rain
That poured and ebbed to shroud or almost show
The unpeopled decks, the looming guardian
On the phantasmal world where no clock marks
Duration of the cold abandonments
And weird acceptances that lead man hence.

Till from the flickering scene one stark vignette
Glares in ambiguous hues of hope and death—
Out of a port-hole bursts a smear of flame,
A blast of thunder from the flood rebounds.
With gliding leap, impelled by answering fire,
Lazarus rises from his restless couch.

Now his corrupted life is as the charge
Exploded in the cannon's narrow depth.
Native no longer of the earth, he springs,
Breaking the waters he surrendered in
And, as he leaves the limbo of vague dream,
Out of the wash and weed he plucks his death.

Back, then, from harbour to the mounting storm,
Into the gale that blows from their high port,
Back from mortality the vast sails slide.

King of Kings

The Emperor (you've heard?) went by this road.
Ahead, police, postillions, cuirassiers;
Behind, ambassadors, air-marshals, equerries,
And, all around, this mild, unjubilant crowd.
I saw the Emperor?
Well, no. It seemed important to be there.
I'd travelled far. Spent my life's savings, too.
But, while I looked at the half-witted horsemens' plumes
And thought of some of what was wrong with me,
I saw his back, receding down new streets.

Snow

You like those images of snow that ask emotion,
Or press their chromium blade against the skin
Or trick the little surface of the brain.

You do not want
The dazzling, *naïf*, still descending one.

Cloud Burst

The fuchsia and I seem happy now.
Up from the sun-hard soil the rain is bouncing
And lightning bursts out of the afternoon.
The radio
Crackles with anger much more lively than the dim
Threats of peace-loving statesmen that it drowns.
Closer
Reverberations. Flower-pots overflow.
Even the heart
Has burst its calyx of anxieties;
The spouting
Cascades superbly into two brown shoes
Put carefully—by someone else—out in the yard.
The lightning makes a difference to the room.

The Displacement

How can I look at my unhappiness
As it puts its hand over the side
Of the crumbling old well
And hooks itself up?

I know without opening my eyes
It is ugly,
It is mine.
It is really not unhappiness at all,
Who is to tell what it is?
It is something pressing up toward the light;
I call it ugly but feel only it is obscene,
A native, perhaps beautiful, of the vasty deep.

Barbarossa

Addiction to the exceptional event—
That flaw
In something like *My Childhood Days in X*,
And fault-line—as from the Aleutians
Down the Pacific to where I was when
It opened wide one day when I was ten.

The town-hall whistle blows. It's five
To twelve. Now homewards, slow,
Turning a legend like a stone, sea-worn,
Red-streaked. The bearded Emperor in the German cave
Sits in his armour; when will he wake and go
Clanking into the light to lead his hordes?

The gutters heave.
                Upon the rumbling ground
I balance. I sit down.
A stop to stories of the death of kings.
I watch the telegraph
Poles. A great hand plucks the strings.

Upon the other coast Napier, too, sways
Most irrecoverably: flames. Looters are shot
By landing-parties near the gutted shops.
Half a hill
Spilt on the coast-road; squashed in their ancient Fords
The burghers sit there still.

Bondage

Watching the lightning
On the Basin d'Arcachon
Link the sea to the sky,
Atlantic with Gironde,

I sit, and there might be
Just the cold glass in my hand,
Far storm, the tropic breeze,
The *plage*—neon-lit, abandoned.

But flashing in my skull
I feel that other chain
From cell to clattering cell
Saying

'You have been here too long' and 'Go
Back. Tell her to come.'
Blaze, forked conjunctions,
Who dares to stand alone?

The Arena

The life drains out. In drops and spurts it flows
And, as it runs, I move. In stops and goes.
Lurching, spasmodic, I draw nearer to
The obscure centre I have turned around,
My forty years—say 'God', say 'sex',
But know the sensual bound
While strength leaks
Out, of life within, the race against the wheel
Spun faster every month, each month more fell.

A wound takes time and resurrection more.
Slowly I cross this room,
What will have died before I reach a door?

White Goddess

When will she come again—

The milk-white muse,
Whose wings, spread sheer, close in
Over the nightmare and the activeness?
'Like any living orgasm'
As the man stranded there,
At the bright-bottled bar,
Anxiously says of his roses.

They, too, are in question.

KEITH SINCLAIR

Memorial to a Missionary

*Thomas Kendall, 1778–1832, first resident missionary in
New Zealand, author of* The New Zealanders' First Book
(1815), grandfather of the Australian poet, H. C. Kendall.

Instructed to speak of God with emphasis
On sin and its consequence, to cannibals
Of the evil of sin, he came from father's farm,
The virtuous home, the comfortable chapel,
The village school, so inadequately armed,
His mail of morals tested in drawing-rooms,
Not war, to teach his obscure and pitied pupils.

There were cheers in Clapham, prayers in Lincolnshire,
Psalms on the beaches, praise, O hope above.
Angels sang as he built the south's first school,
For Augustine had landed with the love
Of God at the Bay; he would speak for his aims were full
Of Cranmer, Calvin; would teach for he brought the world
Of wisdom, dreamed of the countless souls to save.

But though he cried with a voice of bells none heard,
For who was to find salvation in the sounds
Of English words? The scurrilous sailors spoke
More clearly with rum and lusting, so he turned
To the native vowels for symbols, sought to make
The Word of God anew, in the tribes' first book
Laying in Christ's advance a path of nouns.

Seeking the Maori name for sin, for hell,
Teacher turned scholar he sat at Hongi's feet
And guns were the coin he paid for revelation.
To the south men died when Hongi spent his fees.
Wrestling with meanings that defied translation,
Christian in seeking truth found sorcery,
Pilgrim encountered sex in philosophy.

A dreaming hour he spent at that mast of a tree,
And apple of his eye his mother withheld was that love,
The night of feeling, was pure and mooned for man,
Woman was made of earth and earth for wife.
In following their minds he found the men
And reached for a vision past his mother-land,
Converted by heathen he had come to save.

He drank the waters of the underworld
Lying all day in the unconverted flesh,
Entangled in old time, before Christ's birth,
Beyond redemption, found what a nest of bliss,
A hot and mushroom love lay fair in the fern
To suck from his soul the lineaments of desire,
And leave despair, O damned undreamed of pleasures.

To cure the sick at soul the little doctor
Sought out an ardent tonic far too hot,
Though not forbidden, for his infirmity.
With the south on his tongue and sweet he had forgotten
His mission, thirsted for infinities
Of the secret cider and its thick voice in the throat,
Bringing the sun all a-blossom to his blood.

But as sudden and in between such dawns his conscience
Sharpened his sins to prick his heart like nails.
The hell the Christian fears to name was heaven
To his fierce remorse and heaven and hell
Were the day and night in his life and wasted him
With their swift circling passions, until he cursed
In prayers but hated the flush of his concupiscence.

Did he fall through pride of spirit, through arrogance
Or through humility, not scorning the prayers
Of savages and their intricate pantheon?
He lacked the confident pity of his brethren.
To understand he had to sympathize,
Then felt, and feeling, fell, one man a breath
In the human gale of a culture's thousand years.

The unfaithful shepherd was sent from the farm of souls
To live, a disgraceful name in the Christian's ear,
A breathing sin among the more tolerant chiefs.
An outcaste there, or preaching where he fled
To Valparaiso from devils and reproof,
Or coasting logs round Sydney, still he strove
To find the life in the words his past had said.

Drowning off Jervis Bay, O the pain,
For death is a virgin rich in maidenheads
And memories, trees two hundred feet and tall.
The sea is a savage maiden, in her legs
Sharp pangs no missionary drank before,
And the immortality that Maui sought.
O move to Hawaiki, to the shadow of Io's breath.

No man had died such a death of dreams and storms,
For drowning with memories came that expected devil.
He was racked on the waves and spirit wrecked he wept
For his living sins, each tear-drop swimming with evil.
O soul be chang'd into little water drops
And fall into the ocean ne'er be found!
Dying he shrank from that chief who would seize him for ever.

But there no tohunga met him, angels flew
To draw his frightened soul quivering to heaven,
Bright there, bright in the open life of light.
Trying to speak known words that the unbelievers
Might know what was said and bring their ears to Christ,
He had sung with the spirit, prayed with the understanding,
Thus saved the soul he had paid to save the heathen.

His was the plough, he turned the sacred soil
Where others reaped, a pioneer in Christ's
New clearing, strove with unswerving will
Amidst the roots, the rotting stumps and compost
Of the mind to make a bed where the gospel
Might lie down in the breeding sun and grow
A crucifix of leaves, O flowers of crosses.

Immortal in our mouths, and known in heaven,
Yet as we praise we wish him greater—left
On our fractured limb of time, not yet possessed,
Where north will not meet south, of the south's lost gift.
Taught of the sinful flesh he never sensed
That to reach for truth was to reach for God, nor found
God immanent in the cannibals' beliefs.

Father he left us a legacy of guilt,
Half that time owed us, who came from the north, was given:
We know St Paul, but what in that dreaming hour,
In that night when the ends of time were tied—and severed
Again and so ever—did he learn from the south?
He could not turn to teach his countrymen,
And lost, (our sorrow), lost our birthright for ever.

The Parakeet

Shadows of bars suggest perhaps,
If memory slumbers behind
Those jewelled eyes, eucalypts
Festooned with bark strips, ribboned
With light. But his scream echoes
From farther than Bimberi Peak

Before a word or thought arose
To sing or check the slash of beak.
Clapper in a wire bell, voice
Of a demon in a nun's dream,
Chiming, enticing, then raucous
With a mad, a mindless glee;
His glaze was baked in a volcanic kiln.
Was his the first loudness to rage
Glittering over a slow, reptilian
Earth? Anachronism caged
He sits, a focus of unease—
As though, a sailor's pet, he might
Spout blasphemies to greet the visitors.
Perhaps (his own augur) it is not the light
Of past that keeps him spry: he wakes
Us to an instant's fear that this
May be the sunrise he awaits,
His inheritance of flame, a citrus
Strip in smoking morning, wing-slashed,
And Sydney a screeching desert.

The Young Chess Player

So Orpheus stared, on passing the dog of hell,
Foreseeing milky limbs and cruel, deaf shades;
Or the general, hearing a nightingale while shells
Fell harmlessly, defences well-prepared;
Or Maui, thoughtful, when he felt our weight
Tug from time on his legendary line.
Abstracted, Botticelli-eyed, his sight
Unseeing, he makes in his abstract delight
A future form, where hieroglyphic stars
Wheel to a music singing in his ears.
But these are onlookers' orbits, not the seer's
Awakened images. Perhaps his pure
Designs take flesh or the ghostly form of flesh:
A Persian Queen assaults a Knight with zeal,
But falls before his white, deceptive thrust;
A midnight Bishop slants across a field;
The fainting King surrenders still unhurt;
And all his art is breathless, bleeding action—
His art all struggle, this struggle all his art.
There is only one mystery, a thousand visions—
Who can say (in each man's heavy dream)
If Einstein's incommunicable One
(As each stares blind into his paradigm)
Or this small boy's exact, exacting patterns
Differ from Mallarmé's ice-throttled swan?

KENDRICK SMITHYMAN

Simple Ode

My woman weeping under a bush of stars
twelve points of compass and twelve winds
    I name you
beneath whose halcyon gesture moving now
you may stand like a flower tall over
      an earth, a hatred.

To have been a signal flame in time of
desert, the Moses' burning through way through
    torrid exile
    I name you
bird, being loved, whom distance attends on
that flying is light for miles and burning
      bush is the flame
      a fire puts out.

Across these centuries of hostile miles I send
from summer into autumn all my meaning
    with windy approach of leaves
    from a harvest, when armour
    I name you
between the political seasons of danger and
destroying, the days of the weeping woman
between the terror of love and the tremor
history shakes in a bride bed, is making
yet more token of you in your continent yet
not united but in some sad glory trailing
      over my reasonable page
      your fury your story.

Die Bauernhochzeit

He is the victim whom the lean predict
wearing his sad importance on parade
whose special virtue is the awkward stance
who may be led but cannot ever lead.
For Brueghel he made music. Understood
by that old master history commits
his anonymous canvas like a word
which may be said when needed most somewhere
and time assures someone will need to hear.

There with his pipes he watches, slightly drunk
filled with the giggling bawdry of the bedding.
Acquitted of the guilt of those who think
his innocence assumes his painter's sins
and wears them out. His are the neutral lines
subserving pain or power. Does Brueghel
devise with these a text? Is the reading
true sees more than marriage in the bridal?

The piper questions and the indifferent
waiter replies while Brueghel stands behind:
'What is it simply that these people want?'

For all the wind falls on, the suffering
finding daily a surprising light like snow
banked clean on each household after rain,
for the thin trees, strict fingers offering
stringency, for the smooth signal swan,
for all those things which, being, have been,
comets and weddings and admitted pain;
the thrust and the humour and the show
of meaning that was familiar to their homes
they ask evasive morning shall contain.

Anzac Ceremony

That bird that bears our branchy future flies
suddenly from his thicket, and the saddest clown
turning to tell his message of too much grief
puts up his hand for the charity of one leaf,
pleading affection. No one hears or replies.
Will there be never or ever where he may lie down?

I drove my brother bleeding away from my porch.
I, sated, cursed my sister afraid and hungry away.
She took up strength from the blood he gave;
she bound his wound; she brought water to lave
a hurt now healed in them bleeds my reproach.
What difficult word is there which I must say?

Who can forgive me, now being still and alone
with the touch of power, a saintly healing touch?
At their scarred and brothel kiss I cannot balk.
I must walk with the beggar and with the idiot talk;
abandon my goods; my warm bed give to the clown,
that my sister's loss be redeemed as I learn to mumble
    my brother's speech.

Inheritance

Tree, paddock, river: plan
landscape for a child
who will inherit all,
and grow, to be a man—
but when does manhood's wild
ordinance of downfall
first rack him? What the mild
pronouncing deciding year?
five, seven, twenty-one?
How high against the wall
standing knows love and fear
measure him, then undone?
Plan paddock, river, and tree.
The witless agents scan
their amicable sky
but mark fair weather there
where lark and harsh gull fly.
His shadow dulls a stone
outcrop below the track.
A harkaway runs the ridge;
his ewes drift out while clear
morning covers the flat,
pattering feet in the dust.
What morning does he hear
first running at his back
(his heeler, his black bitch)
his silent sedulous pair:
his love, his lovely fear?

from *Considerations*

'High in the Afternoon the Dove'

High in the afternoon the dove
winds melancholy to his mate
a thread of music, monotone
upon the languid afternoon.
The language of his simple love
spills phrases, breaking through the heat.

Heraldic and primeval birds
reflect from their neglected tree
the clemency we did not know,
the charity we could not say,
who kept behind our uncouth words
a terrifying privacy.

Returned to memory they wind
ingenuously, note under note,
our pain commingled with their song,
the pain of music which must hang
like heat stiff on a lazy wind,
stabbing our history to the heart.

After

Put your man down somewhere
in a good lasting soil.
Do not think, bitterly, there
goes the sum of love and toil.

He was so part of you:
you bred him from your fall
into his own; today you endow
your life with his burial.

What was he, this manchild
childman? A doll of stone,
a sop for whatever ailed
you once, a weakness outgrown.

To be Absent Without Leave

Time, sweeping, desolates
your best hours and your hand
stays, short of miracle. You need
look neither far nor hard—the State's
drab agents there demand
your man again to arms;
he's sworn to serve, but not to bleed.

Easterlies cramp the pines,
gorse runs mad on the hill.
Remember me. The game is played
not to be won, but who designs
loss as his aim? I tell
you nothing new; I know
only we are, in time, dismayed.

A Thing Remembered

A thing remembered from some forgotten war,
a trivial thing (which the campaign had bowled
beyond reminiscence, a stuporous earth mould
out of sight for a hundred years) wearing
its yet telltale brain-searing scar
cleaved above the frontal bone—a skull,
purely anonymous, its pure cavity full
only with dirt; distasteful, but enduring.

What is it, to endure? To revive a name
among the unmentionably profane
who inherit us, gene by decrepit gene?
It is nothing, or less, or else should damn
our potency and be our shame.
Brown bone jigged from a conqueror's oven,
it is yours, is it my misgiving unforgiven
I hear whistle sharply while these days cram

rye, wattle, hawthorn, and blackberry
with the sour fruit of merest survival?
Be black, and buried in the pit where charnel
imagining, moping, squats sullen.
Let the imprudent worms marry
in the brain's tenement, their prolix
issue amply use the dome, their colonies wax
fatly fine another century's dissembling:

and then a day. Ghost and shade may we meet
(so fine, they will be seen through at a glance)
at this same funeral ground, the haws' intense
scarlet along the embattled hedge,
that I may pick an armful fit
to show I loved you, knowing that in love
we have compounded faiths our wit will not forgive . . .
This crabbed hawthorn, that was once my clansmen's badge.

Waikato Railstop

Two suicides, not in the one season
    exactly, as we count what is materially
a season: principally I remember for
this railstop a so ordinary quality,
    so neutral, it may be
        distinguished for,

by, what was unusual there, as though
       intensely they cut peepholes through February's
smoke and haze revealing, instantaneous and all-
summing, purest motives, marrying perdition
       with action. Do not, please,
              misrepresent

the hamlet as an enthusiasm
       for the mortuary-minded in a death-centred
democracy. That certain young women should find
themselves unseasonably with child is to be
       understood and even
              an interest

to those on outlying farms. There was also
       an engineer who built an aircraft in his backyard,
which he could not fly; ambition was not licensed
to go soaring. Such an ascent measures most days'
       custom of being flat.
              You may set off

one day from another if you wish or
       if you can, skirting their outlook in the sandy
pinebelts while the Highway on the slight ridge above
consigns traffic elsewhere and a rake of coal-cars
       retreating south does not
              hurry, clacking

into the crossing and out, nor disturbs
       mynahs and bulbuls from their squabbling. Let orchard
and vineyard tally freights of purpose; you do well
or wither and rot where, to entertain your summer
       listening, the child's play
              musketry of

gorsepods fusillades at no target big
       enough to miss. Admiring does not get you far.
Wattleseeds crushed underfoot stink as from a knoll
you track farther across the swamp ravelling out
       and winding mazily
              acres of peat

smoke their signals, but no one, slouching hot,
       cares to separate smoke hulk from thundery cumulus.
Noon massed above blackens cloudland and a cuckold
below, seething skein by skein impartially.
       Outside the billiard room
              a truck backfires.

Parable of Two Talents

Somewhere I read how, long since oh very
Long ago a certain Knight (most certain
In his faith) fought with the Beast
Who was his unbelief, his lack-faith contrary
In all contrarieties; but again,
    Again the Beast would hoist
Himself up from injudiciously being dead
    And not done with
    However he bled,
Stank or staggered, a corrupt patch-pelt
Scurfy verminous draggletail, caricature
    Of piety's detestably impure
Other. And the Knight—how was it he felt?

Variously he felt, variously. There was his pride
Going triumphantly before his fall
With his humility, taxed
Excessive—the Beast was, and could not be, denied.
He felt this way and that while temporal
    Lords, lords spiritual passed
Before him deferential. So he retired
    To a wilderness
    Where his absurd
Pitying servile victim followed him,
His handy monster who sustained him in that place.
    There in his hour Beast washed his tired face,
Digged deep, and chose to die, a lasting whim.

Man and a Brute lie proper in one pit,
Whom warring could not sunder: how deep should
We read the tale? I give it
No commentary, but wonder (an autumn night
Dropping dropping leaves from a dying wood)
    What medieval wit
Intended how far, how much is left unsaid;
    And sit, your virtue's
    Beast, my day not played
Wholly away or so far undone
That I cannot see marriage and this parable
    Could have some truck: you, admirable
And chaste vowed to your Brute. And how alone

Should either face the wilderness who have
So much together fought, so much one mind,
So little understanding,
So much need? Flaunt handsome on your high horse and brave

My scruffy riots; they will again down, bend
    Their craggy knee, commending
Their deathly due the tax of a humbled blood
    night of autumn,
    moonshine pricking the wood
that is a wilderness as I trick
No one (you less than any) with this metaphor
    In which I hide what I should declare
Plainly, a debt that needs no rhetoric.

A Note on the Social Arts

A poem quietly goes aside to weep.
The sulky poet draws his beer and fills
one corner of the bar with flying words
whose wings beat irritable silence in
being birds. Each beak holds a tear
delicious as the christian pearl, yet sullen.
They cry, the birds? but no cry comes.
The pearls roll down. The poet drinks.

My love is a bag of nails, is a bag,
is waiting for me, watching me, is there
outside the street *the barman groans.*
Soon she will tire of me, call Time, she'll move
in step with needless clocks
about the dial of her love to ring
no pressure, then no beer. She pouts, must go
somewhere apart from me to wind her hair
out of another's window till she fall.
I shall be old, dreading to climb and stare.

Round round around the noisy fan glows.
The writer tries his craft. An empty glass.
In a corner stands a poem weeping yet.
The words have talked themselves up to a perch
erratic on a stag's head; where, let pass,
their shades discountenance what mirrors search.
They loom like Furies as the beer goes down.

Someone is singing in the urinal.

Hint for the Incomplete Angler

Not too far north from where I write set dawn
Before your bow precisely. Out there, cast
The kingfish from his feeding while you prey.

Smug blue worms will peck at your neat craft's side.
Show due respect then while you steal the tide.

There was a fisherman once who did things right.

For more than forty years he pulled fish out.
By line, net or pot God's plenty hauled to pout
And puff on the bottomboards, to smack
Themselves silly and die, else were tossed back
Until they swelled a right size for the pan
He kept on the wall by his sink. That man
Had long outgrown the truth of simple tales
Which said if he stroked his arm he showered scales,
That said for years he nourished an old mermaid
All to himself in his bach. Friend, he was staid,
Ordinary, and (it may be) none too bright,
But who could come godlike home with that high light
Morning on morning, to be sane as we
Would claim we are? Yet he did fittingly
More than we'd dream, and with more dignity.

For when he couldn't heave any more at the net,
When the old man snapper clung too hard, he set
His nose to the sea away out east of the Head
To give what was due from good years to the tide.

Watch for the worms as you go, at your dinghy's side.

Blackleg

Careering on a downslope from the bail,
it was myself, in part it was myself
committed to the pothole, steep
sickening rumbledumble with a fly's
lewd concert at the end. Such a close
to round one only summer, and be dung
or even less than dung: a dissolution
of the parts corporal, their incorporeal arts.

In the holding yard where the calves guzzled
tippling skim milk, pattering, I bawled
that he was found the missing one,
him offered to arbitrary summer
where one by one or squadrons at a whim
thistles discharged their flights.
Gauze in a fine wearing, but the yard
unhallowed; he must have been lying

all through the day near the trough
coarsening—you know how the eyes are,
looking past seeing and not looking,
his near forequarter swollen blackly.
Or the tongue, although it is not
detail which quickens remembering,
the masculine pouch prematurely
unrealized, the not-meditative horns.

While wood pigeons grossly fed on
karaka berries, exulting appetite,
I looped a chain about the hindlegs,
the Thing in his unbecoming I dragged
down the slope to a pothole which had
been abandoned by the Forest stream,
there resigned him
to be forgotten. And washed my hands
where the pool blinks with native trout.

It was February in nineteen thirty-nine.
I was old enough and too young to know
that exceptions breed like flies,
but what is to be imported
in a commonplace? The younger bulls
in their simplicity sported the paddock.

Night-Piece

Late, of a late summer night, almost white
with being still, highway sounds remote
like assurance of land looming not quite seen
which surrounds a lake where you go
as though stalking the water, and the lawn is
dew damp, the air is leaning into autumn
a shade more than cool less than cold.

Light among trees there, a neighbour's tenor
strangled in his shower box, an irrelevant
dialogue of the insects of our darkness.
It is too soon to go to bed. The crickets scratch
meticulously at what your moon makes smooth.

To be alone is what you pay for peace.
It is too soon to try for sleep, but staying
awake is lying at the mercy of darkness
in a room of many faces, heavy-eyed.
We are blamed in our generation.
All I have learned is how to fail differently.

Building Programme

Man never is; yet here are men
who walk about on the skyline to fire
the edge of a disc into some precision,
making streams of blue sparks fall from their fingers
which burn whitely down upon a finite distance
lately bright as cold, a winter in being.

Man never is, but always is to be
and is to be superseded. A saffron crane-arm
lifts out in benediction or to mean goodbye
over those who walk shining
around their circle in the sky.
The machine is docile. Competent, it does
not know about man fallen; claims no sin
in its origin; is neither wilful nor free
of this brilliant unnatural calm morning in July.

They are changing the way of my city.
The skyline is not what it was. Nor are we.

Colville

That sort of place where you stop
long enough to fill the tank, buy plums,
    perhaps, and an icecream thing on a stick
while somebody local comes
    in, leans on the counter, takes a good look
        but does not like what he sees of you,

intangible as menace,
a monotone with a name, as place
    it is an aspect of human spirit
(by which shaped), mean, wind-worn. Face
    outwards, over the saltings: with what merit
        the bay, wise as contrition, shallow

as their hold on small repute,
good for dragging nets which men are doing
    through channels, disproportioned in the blaze
of hot afternoon's down-going
    to a far fire-hard tide's rise
        upon the vague where time is distance?

It could be plainly simple
pleasure, but these have another tone

or quality, something aboriginal,
reductive as soil itself—bone
   must get close here, final
      yet unrefined at all. They endure.

A school, a War Memorial
Hall, the store, neighbourhood of salt
      and hills. The road goes through to somewhere else.
Not a geologic fault
   line only scars textures of experience.
      Defined, plotted; which maps do not speak.

In Our Manner of Speaking

Land without presence. We stand
in light. In our manner of speaking,
we throw no shadow to quiet morning
where, steeped in light so much blue,
a habit of wind waits for a wave
to ride midday's most bland surf over
cocksfoot or hillside bents and grey
white manuka flowering. The bees imply
more than we say: they imply history.

Here, echo only dies. From hot rocks
voices return not heightened. Echo
only dies, where the bees' murmuring
minutely underscores our burden,
of innocence, and a theme, our lack
in tradition of being guilty.

At the horizon are banded some heavy
lanes of cumulus, not wise, not omened.
Olives have not clustered in these gullies.
Few eat the octopus. Few make offering.
To lack a family guilt is being deprived.
Our singers' voices are wanting overtones.
We tenant lands, without presence,
we are at home while the light continues
profoundly to reconcile us, assuaging
in its wonder what we do not need
to make.
            Except tomorrow. We exist
in terms of tomorrow as we break a fig
or spread with honey a recovered bread.
Below, a small surf cracks and hisses
where a shearwater bursts from her cliff,

where red crabs clatter among crevices,
reefs depend, fish gather at weedbanks —
soon we too shall gather, oiling skins,
stretching on sand or soft rock shelves
not apprehensive of a water's boiling
as her doves furiously describe
arrivals of the Maiden to a foamfoot.
But briefly, we shall be content.

Underwater Pieces

Gulls sprinted for harbour
to scatter the news: boats were coming,
loaded. Gulls followed feathering
diesels, quick to be in at the kill.

The skippers wanted to unload fast,
take on ice and get out again
straightaway. They'd struck it rich,
on crayfish tails.

Nothing like it, in their experience.
This wide where they netted, that long
on the chart. Unpredicted.
They weren't even looking for crays.
Miles of them, they said,
fishermen told each other it could happen,
there must be miles of them.

Crayfish migrating, from where to where?
Below winds, below tides, trekking,
thousands, thousands of them,
their rickety armour clicking,
plodding gullies and uplands,
going. Just going.

2

Sea elephants when their term comes
for bearing pups and mating
haul out on beaches of Guadalupe.
Pups, in that press, lose their mothers.
They starve, or suffocate.
Some drown close to the shingle.

A little offshore Cousteau's divers slid
through a canyon almost motionless.
From superficial levels into

depth, variably aged
corpses variously buoyant,
stationed. Old wives' story,
graveyard of the elephants,
perversely comes true, in a wrong ocean,
like a maladroit novelist's
gothic frenzy, a not so capable
designer's set for submarine *Scandals*
of Nineteen-Thirty, outlandish as

bins of matchless shoes, miscounted
pairs of spectacles, tons of human hair.

Idyll

Adam and Eve, without serpent
or guile, all night the river *duetto*,
voices that were steps and stairs.
Those smallest rapids in the gorge
spelled out sleep for jittery timbers,
lulling coves and sandbars.
Sang, right through the night, just loud
enough to tell they kept their distance
from your doorstep which was
a pair of honeysuckle trees,
Adam and Eve left and right by the path
which you took, to rinse a bucket of washing,
where we lifted any bucket of water.
We drank the last light.

And sank the last of the whisky,
letting the fire go blank.
Indefinite as smoke upstream,
a stag roared. Nightfall,
a truckload of kids cruised the road
spotting for possums with a .22,
but went off before long,
maybe to tickle trout.

We also, we were illicit, apart from
our eiron's habitual domain,
vulnerable. Whatever anyone means by
life is not in our hands. You are lived
by. Most of twenty-four hours
of each/any/every day,
when the little white faithful pills work
as quietly as the sisters

at the hospital of Mater Misericordiae
where they shot you full of gold
salts, copper salts, salts of tears
not without failing.
How, elementary, is your will free?

The malformed path ended at
those honeysuckle trees, rewarewa.
The river's name rightly is Waiata.
Vulnerable, we could not
distinguish good from evil. Our
sin was original. It was content.

The Last Moriori

Reputedly last of his kind,
quite surely one of the last
not crossbred but (as They said) pure
as pure goes, a Chatham Island Moriori
taken for a slave when a boy, taken
again in some other raiding, passed
from band to band, from place to place
until he washed up on the River.
That was the story, anyway, which is
as may be. He was

very old, he did not belong,
some chunk of totara which lay too long
    in acid swamp.
He was kumara left on the pit's floor,
    sweetness dried, its hull drawn small.
He was what you found in caves but did not
    mention, travesty gone
beyond human. A tatty topcoat, bowler hat,
blanket which seemed to look your way
without seeing you from the stoop of a hut
at the Pa. A few weak hungers,
he survived. He endured,

already myth, beyond legends of his kind,
a poor fact. But the fact was, and the myth
was, and they endure together.

This is written particularly to you.
Remembering, I shiver again as on that day
taking small comfort from our day as it is.

Closedown

We who do not belong in and from
our distance watched while the town aged,
not promised to any Indian Summer.
From age, to ailing,
                    however seawinds freshen
their houses are unbraced, their shops
more stocked with memories than current
goods. Everything was staked on
the Works, unjustified.
                    The Works allowed
to run down at last closed. A ghost town
in the making? It's not comfortable,
delaying.

What have we ever known about it?
    A couple of rightwing local Members we didn't
    think much of.
    One young novelist of then promise set his first
    novel up and down the slope: troubled faith,
                            unrecovered innocence.
    Years as a river port, fifteen wrecks,
    all fairly humdrum.
    A Constabulary post, frontier fashion, freighting base,
    another name in the second Taranaki campaign.
The main street is the main highway.
An oldest business looks out grimly,
    McSomething or other and Hunger, Est. 1878.

Waitomo

Guides ask for silence, and have
no difficulty in getting their parties
to go quiet. At a dollar a head, nations
file underground. All shapes of age bow
their heads, step carefully after.
Go deep, go down to silence.

Bridal Chamber, and Cathedral,
play of fancy which wants to discover
limestone making metaphors, shadow likenesses
and shadow play. Here is Dog, there is
Camel. We call this the Modern Art
gallery, but go down
further, one more, a couple more flights.

A boat at a landing stage idles,
another will carry us, silently
animated through the grotto
where cannibal worms hunt, breed, age,
consume their partners, are consumed.

How this would have pleased Coleridge,
riding a verbless river, the dome,
darkness, glowworm haven
generously imitating, freely outdoing, stars.

I have been here before, without words.
After their climax of love people lie thus,
as though drifting dark waters, caverned.
If you speak, all the lights will go out.
Say nothing. She reaches for his hand,
he presses her finger. The boat slides
curving back to its landing.

A guide at the stage sweeps his lamp
over a pool. What is he looking for?

Te Rangi Hiroa/Buck

Te Rangi Hiroa is sleeping
at Oroki, outside Urenui.
There he and Pomare were boys.

Offsea winds arrive to make their blades keen;
every so often they need to come, to sharpen.
They rub on the canoe's prow, perhaps
they have questions.

Buck had questions. Wherever he went
he mightn't ask outright — he knew how to behave —
of this one and that one, or of this one and that knew
alright to say directly 'Tell me . . . Show me'.
Said 'Show me how they tie a knot and I'll tell you
something worth knowing about these people.'
Looking down the land to Petrocorp,
it makes you wonder, doesn't it?

He went up and down dividing the North Island.
Later, he went up and down in many islands.
Knew this, getting to know that. He liked knowing.
Knowing today, knowing only something about yesterday.

Once he dreamed a long, very detailed, dream
about a marae on Nukuhiva (he wasn't half-Irish for nothing)
where he hadn't been. A voice said
'To ha'afiti ia Te 'Ani Hi'oa. This share for
        Te Rangi Hiroa.'
That was his share. Can we, he wrote, ever
see the throbbing past except in dreams?

So there he is, only ashes, but dreaming in his sleeping.
Catching up with, all that he didn't get to know.
Somebody robbed the gravegoods.

Buck hadn't been to the Marquesas.
All he had were Linton's diagrams. 'I do not wish
to awake, for when I do, I will see but a line drawing
in a book that conjures up a lone terrace overgrown
with exotic weeds, and sad stone walls crumbling to
    decay.'
He did not mean, to refer to Petrocorp.

Think not, O Children of the Earth, our parents' love
    is dead.

HONE TUWHARE

Lament [1]

In that strident summer of battle
    when cannon grape and ball
    tore down the pointed walls
    and women snarled as men
    and blood boiled in the eyes:
    in the proud winter of defeat
    he stood unweary
    and a god among men.

He it was whom death looked hotly on
    whilst I in adoration
    brought timid fuel to his fire:
    of all things manly he partook

yet did it plummet down like a bird
    engulfing him as he headlong
    rushed towards the night:
    the long night
    where no dawn wakes to pale
    the quaking stars: farewell

Farewell companion of laughter and light
    who warmed the nights with the
    croaking chants of olden times: hear
    me now sing poorly sing harshly. . . .

At dawn's light I looked for you
    at the land's end where two oceans froth
    but you had gone without leaving a sign
    or a whispered message to the gnarled
    tree's feet or the grass or the inscrutable
    rock face. Even the innocent day-dreaming
    moon could not explain the wind's wry mirth.

To you it seems I am nothing—
    a nobody and of little worth
    whom the disdainful years
    neither praise nor decry
    but shall abandon to fat
    and the vast delight of worms: farewell

[1] Suggested by a tangi in Sir George Grey's *Nga Moteatea.*

Farewell farewell
    Let the heavens mumble and stutter
    Let them acknowledge your leaving us
    Mine is the lone gull's cry in the night
    Let my grief hide the moon's face
    Let alien gods salute thee
    with flashing knives cut open
    the dark belly of the sky.

I feel rain spit in my face

I bear no malice, let none stain my valedictions
For I am at one with the wind
the clouds' heave and the slapping rain
the tattered sky and the wild solitude
of the sea and the streaming earth
which I kneel to kiss. . . .

Burial

In a splendid sheath
of polished wood and glass
with shiny appurtenances
lay he fitly blue-knuckled
and serene:

hurry rain and trail him
to the bottom of the grave

Flowers beyond budding
will not soften the gavel's
beat of solemn words
and hard sod thudding:

hurry rain and seek him
at the bottom of the grave

Through a broken window
inanely looks he up;
his face glass-gouged and bloodless
his mouth engorging clay
for all the world uncaring. . . .

Cover him quickly, earth!
Let the inexorable seep of rain
finger his greening bones, deftly.

The Old Place

No one comes
by way of the doughy track
through straggly tea tree bush
and gorse, past the hidden spring
and bitter cress.

Under the chill moon's light
no one cares to look upon
the drunken fence-posts
and the gate white with moss.

No one except the wind
saw the old place
make her final curtsy
to the sky and earth:

and in no protesting sense
did iron and barbed wire
ease to the rust's invasion
nor twang more tautly
to the wind's slap and scream.

On the cream-lorry
or morning paper van
no one comes,
for no one will ever leave
the golden city on the fussy train;
and there will be no more waiting
on the hill beside the quiet tree
where the old place falters
because no one comes any more

no one.

The Girl in the Park

The girl in the park
    saw a nonchalant sky
    shrug into a blue-dark
    denim coat.

The girl in the park
    did not reach up to touch
    the cold steel buttons.

The girl in the park
    saw the moon glide
    into a dead tree's arms
    and felt the vast night
    pressing.
    How huge it seems,
    and the trees are big she said.

    The stars heard her
    and swooped down perching
    on tree-top and branch
    owl-like and unblinking.

The grave trees,
    as muscular as her lover
    leaned darkly down to catch
    the moonrise and madness
    in her eyes:
    the moon is big, it is very big
    she said with velvet in her throat.

    An owl hooted.
    The trees scraped and nudged
    each other and the stars
    carried the helpless
    one-ribbed moon away. . . .

The girl in the park
    does not care: her body swaying
    to the dark-edged chant
    of storms.

Muscle and Bone of Song

And of trees and the river
no more say
that these alone are sources
for the deft song and the sad:
nor from wave-curl and the sun
cross moon wind and hail
calm and storm come.

Joyously I sing
to the young girl's hip-knock
and taunt: swing-cheerful breasts
shape my hands
to eternal begging-bowls.

Rain

I can hear you making
small holes in the silence
rain

If I were deaf
the pores of my skin
would open to you
and shut

And I should know you
by the lick of you
if I were blind:

the steady drum-roll
sound you make
when the wind drops

the something
special smell of you
when the sun cakes
the ground

But if I should not
hear
smell or feel or see you

you would still
define me
disperse me
wash over me
rain

Time and the Child

Tree earth and sky
reel to the noontide beat
of sun and the old man
hobbling down the road.
Cadence—

of the sun-drowned cicada
in a child's voice shrilling:
... are you going man?

Where are you going man where
The old man is deaf
to the child.

His stick makes deep
holes in the ground.
His eyes burn to a distant point

where all roads converge....
The child has left his toys
and hobbles after the old
man calling: funny man funny man

funny old man funny
Overhead the sun paces
and buds pop and flare.

Tangi

I did not meet her
on the bordered path
nor detect her fragrance
in the frolic of violets
and carnations.

She did not stroll riverward
to sun-splash and shadows
to willows trailing garlands
of green pathos.

Death was not hiding in the cold rags
of a broken dirge:
nor could I find her
in the cruel laughter of children,
the curdled whimper of a dog.

But I heard her with the wind
crooning in the hung wires
and caught her beauty by the coffin
muted to a softer pain—
in the calm vigil of hands
in the green-leaved anguish
of the bowed heads
of old women.

Not by Wind Ravaged

Deep scarred
        not by wind ravaged nor rain
        nor the brawling stream:

stripped of all save the brief finery
of gorse and broom; and standing
sentinel to your bleak loneliness
the tussock grass—

O voiceless land, let me echo your desolation.
The mana of my house has fled,
the maraae is but a paddock of thistle.
I come to you with a bitterness
that only your dull folds can soothe
for I know, I know
my melancholy chants shall be lost
to the wind's shriek about the rotting eaves.

Distribute my nakedness—
Unadorned I come with no priceless
offering of jade and bone curio: yet
to the wild berry shall I give
a tart piquancy; enhance for a deathless
space the fragile blush of manuka. . . .

You shall bear all and not heed.
In your huge compassion embrace
those who know no feeling other
than greed:
of this I lament my satisfaction
for it is as full as a beggar's cup:
no less shall the dust of avaricious men
succour exquisite blooms with
moist lips parting
to the morning sun.

No Ordinary Sun

Tree let your arms fall:
raise them not sharply in supplication
to the bright enhaloed cloud.
Let your arms lack toughness and
resilience for this is no mere axe
to blunt, nor fire to smother.

Your sap shall not rise again
to the moon's pull.
No more incline a deferential head
to the wind's talk, or stir
to the tickle of coursing rain.

Your former shagginess shall not be
wreathed with the delightful flight
of birds nor shield
nor cool the ardour of unheeding
lovers from the monstrous sun.

Tree let your naked arms fall
nor extend vain entreaties to the radiant ball.
This is no gallant monsoon's flash,
no dashing trade wind's blast.
The fading green of your magic
emanations shall not make pure again
these polluted skies... for this
is no ordinary sun.

O tree
in the shadowless mountains
the white plains and
the drab sea floor
your end at last is written.

To a Maori Figure Cast in Bronze outside
the Chief Post Office, Auckland

I hate being stuck up here, glaciated, hard all over
and with my guts removed: my old lady is not going
to like it.

I've seen more efficient scare-crows in seed-bed
nurseries. Hell, I can't even shoo the pigeons off.

Me: all hollow inside with longing for the *marae* on
the cliff at Kohimarama, where you can watch the ships
come in curling their white moustaches.

Why didn't they stick me next to Mickey Savage?
Now then, he was a good bloke.
Maybe it was a Tory City Council that put me here.

They never consulted me about naming the square.
It's a wonder they never called it: Hori-in-the-gorge-at-
bottom-of-Hill. Because it is like that: a gorge,
with the sun blocked out, the wind whistling around
your balls (your balls mate). And at night, how I
feel for the beatle-girls with their long-haired
boy-friends licking their frozen finger-chippy lips
hopefully. And me again beetling

my tent eye-brows forever, like a brass monkey with
real worries: I mean, how the hell can you welcome
the Overseas Dollar, if you can't open your mouth
to poke your tongue out, eh?

If I could only move from this bloody pedestal I'd
show the long-hairs how to knock out a tune on the
souped-up guitar, my *mere* quivering, my *taiaha* held
at the high port. And I'd fix the ripe *kotiros* too
with their mini-*piupiu*-ed bums twinkling: yeah!

Somebody give me a drink: I can't stand it.

A Fall of Rain at Miti-Miti

Drifting on the wind, and through
the broken window of the long house
where you lie, incantatory chant
of surf breaking, and the Mass
and the mountain talking.

At your feet two candles puff the
stained faces of the *whanau*, the vigil
of the bright madonna. See, sand-whipped
the toy church does not flinch.

E moe, e te whaea: wahine rangimarie

Mountain, why do you loom over us like
that, hands on massive hips? Simply
by hooking your finger to the sea,
rain-squalls swoop like a hawk, suddenly.
Illumined speeches darken, fade to metallic
drum-taps on the roof.

Aanei nga roimata o Rangipapa.

Flat, incomprehensible faces: lips moving
only to oratorical rhythms of the rain:

quiet please, I can't hear the words.

And the rain steadying: black sky leaning
against the long house. Sand, wind-sifted
eddying lazily across the beach.

And to a dark song lulling: *e te whaea, sleep.*

LOUIS JOHNSON

Magpie and Pines

That dandy black-and-white gentleman doodling notes
on fragrant pinetops over the breakfast morning,
has been known to drop through mists of bacon-fat,
with a gleaming eye, to the road where a child stood, screaming.

And in the dark park—the secretive trees—have boys
harboured their ghosts, built huts, and buried treasure,
and lovers made from metallic kisses alloys
more precious, and driven the dark from pleasure.

A child was told that bird as his guardian angel
reported daily on actions contrived to displease;
stands petrified in the sound of wings, a strangle
of screams knotting his throat beneath the winter leaves.

Look back and laugh on the lovers whose white mating
made magpie of dark; whose doodling fingers swore
various fidelities and fates. They found the world waiting,
and broke the silence. A raven croaks 'Nevermore'

to their progenitive midnight. The guardian is aloof
on his roof of the small world, composing against morning
a new, ironic ballad. The lover has found small truth
in the broken silence, in faith, or the fate-bird moaning.

New Worlds for Old

'New worlds for old,' sings the golden-fisted youth
Smashing the morning into a myriad stars
To wind in his girl's dark hair, pin on her mouth
In lightning kisses set to glimmer there.

New worlds for old he promises, and takes
The blind blank windows of her life and fills
The garden with dreamseed, shocks and shakes
Fruit from the tree—forbidden, so it thrills.

And looking out, she will not recognize
The formal pattern under the new leaves,
But think that flame of flowers the true size
Of his earthshaking manhood: so she believes

His shape and slogan as he grows and sings
'New worlds for old!' And true, it's changing fast.
There is a thickness in the voice that wings
With less abandon among echoes past.

'Old worlds for new!' the note is tremolo.
The old man quavering is grey with tears.
Is it his voice, or a youth beneath the window
Smashing the morning with promise that he hears?

Here Together Met

I praise Saint Everyman, his house and home
    In every paint-bright gardened suburb shining
With all the age's verities and welcome
        Medalled upon him in contentment dining;
                And toast with gin and bitters
                The Muse of baby-sitters.

I sing Dame Everyone's whose milky breast
    Suckles the neighbourhood with pins and plans
Adding new rooms to their eternal rest,
        The next night's meat already in the pan:
                And toast with whisky and ice,
                The Goddess who keeps things nice.

I honour Maid Anybody's whose dreams are shaping
    Lusts in her heart down the teasing garden-path
Where she stops in time as she must at the gaping
        Graveyard of Hell and rescues her girlish laugh:
                And toast in rum and cloves
                The course of balanced love.

I drink to Son Mostpeople's whose honourable pride
    In things being what they are will not let him run,
But who keeps things going even after he has died
        In a distant desert clutching an empty gun:
                And toast in brandy and lime
                The defenders of our great good time.

from *Four Poems from the Strontium Age*

I

Before the Day of Wrath

There were cities here in the hills
In my great-grandfather's youth
Where now are only blackened bricks and walls
Devoured in the year of wrath.

And in the desert where none of us
Dare venture, hearing tell
Of fabulous, dangerous monsters, flowers
Were said to emerge when rare rain fell.

Today the rain draws blood; the winds
Burn out our eyes; the barbarous
Plants tear flesh that never mends:
Sweet water-holes turn suddenly poisonous.

It must have been a lovely country once,
Populous and inventive—a golden age
Wherein the young knew laughter, loved to dance,
Even grew old. Daylight as bright as courage

Existed for many hours at a time, we're told.
But these, perhaps, are fables meant to inspire
Us now in the darkness helping us to hold
Something to cherish crouched by the guttering fire.

3

Spring

All day the black rain has fallen
And now, in the hour of light
The livid river and the lake are swollen;
The range of hills that were bright

And red with their carpet of dust
Are dissolving away. Soon there will be
No shelter: again we must
Pack and move in search of kinder country.

Then will begin again that dread migration
Through sightless deserts, and the silent land
Reflecting sickness into our eyes, starvation
Bloating the children with its grotesque hand.

And never knowing which way is the best
To set the foot because the perils met there
Can never be foreseen nor wholly guessed,
For who can tell what colour of the air

Harbours most pain? Surely the Spring
Is the most bitter season of suffering.

4

Haven

We have come to a quiet valley in the hills
Where a road, this time unbroken, runs
Right back to the desert fringe. It fills
Us with a dreaming hope. The sun's

Mild light is clean; about and above
The slopes are grassy. In our ears
The little river sings a song like love.
In the old country, for two thousand years

There ruled a king called God, the story goes.
It seems impossible, but here is a place
Where one might trust to fable. Flowers grow
And trees stand straight beside the watercourse.

Let us not be afraid. After two days and nights
In such a haven, we fear that we may have brought
With us those breeding poisons of the world's blight
That will blacken the earth here and pollute the light.

And already the leaders confer in the common interest,
And it's rumoured that they plan to eliminate
The sickliest and those of us who are least
Like men should be. Oh, may we all grow straight

In this place of the sun. Let me not think of these
Cruel facts of life in this valley of green trees.

Bread and a Pension

It was not our duty to question but to guard,
maintaining order; see that none escaped
who may be required for questioning by the State.
The price was bread and a pension and not a hard
life on the whole. Some even scraped
enough on the side to build up a fairish estate

for the day of retirement. I never could
understand the complaints of the restless ones
who found the hours long, time dragging;
it always does. The old hands knew how good
the guardroom fire could be, the guns
gleaming against the wall and the nagging

wind like a wife—outside. There were cards
for such occasions and good companions
who truly were more than home since they shared
one's working life without difference or hard words,
aimed at much the same thing, and shared opinions
on news they read. If they cared

much it was for the quiet life. You cannot hold
that against them, since it's roundly human
and any decent man would want it the same.
For these were decent: did as they were told,
fed prisoners, buried the dead, and, on occasion
loaded the deathcart with those who were sent to the flames.

Matter of Urgency

Most prefer not to know, proceed by faith and chance
Between one day and the next; but he
Had been given his passport—had one year to live—
And could not afford the casual, passing glance
In the face of that journey. Each activity
Now must count, each minute be made to give.

There was nothing stoical in the face he turned
To hail the morning, but a measured welcome
Like Midas counting his money, and reaching out
To transform another deliberate rose. The bond
Between his hand and each object became
So strong he could give nothing up, nor surrender to doubt.

He became obsessed by minutiae; would sit
By the hour observing flies at their rituals,
Noting the motes in sunbeams, but could not bring
His forces down on what once had seemed important—
To tidy his papers, enter up all the journals
And leave his desk in order for his going.

Disorder was, in fact, a thing he'd survived,
And he could not bear to appear uncharacteristic;
There were always others to edit, care for such matters

More expert and better paid than himself. He thrived
In his final idleness: shaved daily, enjoyed breakfast
And took out the scraps and crumbs to feed to the sparrows.

He Smelt the Smell of Death Within the Marrow

Waking one morning, he was alarmed to find
he had a different odour, riper and more
unpleasant than he had ever noticed before;
bodily or a characteristic of mind
he could not be sure though he tried
to trace the spot exactly. It did not seem
to bother others unduly: it was the dream
of himself, he found, that died
and added to his disgust. And even though
he walked more finically, washed more often,
took greater pains all round it would not soften
the fact. It was like learning to live with a blow
that landed and stunned one every seventh minute;
and then—it scarcely surprised him—he did not appear
to wear the same face any more but one vaguer
as though he were copying something and within it
tried to maintain an act prescribed by someone
he was no longer in touch with. Gradually
this indefinition began to appear as an ally—
giving him less to dislike—allowing the run
of the luck to change. Again he could stand
and assess the claims of the passing girls though he did
not fully believe that act any more and hid
his fear under many conquests, birds in the hand
meaning more than hopes in the hush of himself.
He saw God as a deodorant on a completely immaculate shelf.

What his friends noticed most was an indrawn air
pinching the nostrils; he did not laugh so much
as they remembered; and there was a touch
of distance about him.
                        He was more mature,
they consoled themselves, and never sensed the throes
he went through daily under their very noses.

The Birthday

The old man is a greyer stone this year
the morning of his fifty-seventh birthday:
a sputtering gaiety among defining
clocks, the blessing fingers of grandchildren:

and it's a small score in the accountancy
of history: simply a private matter
with little jokes, familiar knives and cups
and the same circle of faces to testify:

the tokens are scarcely a harvest—rather
a minor festival of little people poised
between the murder of years in time
like a wave at the ends of worlds

that will rise, engulf them, drown
eyes, hands, around the table of smiles,
same cups and knives and faces saying
(in spite of skies that fall) our father.

The Perfect Symbol

I remember reading as a boy, Giotto,
Asked for a picture fit for a Pope's wall,
Picked up a brush, painted a perfect circle,
And offered this as prize to the puzzled pontiff
Whose shocked reaction was a dark reproof.
'No, sir,' the painter answered, 'Nothing less
Than this would be apt gift for your great grace.
This line is endless and begins nowhere.
It contains all the truth a man might know
And is a barrier excluding dross.
Or, it's a world, and outside it, the heavens
And every aspiration worthy of him.
I made it with one stroke: you cannot tell
Where I began it, only that, through grace,
Patience, the pain of all my craft,
I made what Nature does not make—the circle,
The thing enclosed, entire, perfection's symbol.'

Humbled, his master gave it pride of place
Upon the palace wall, and no doubt gave
Much thought as well to what might burn within
A peasant breast that beat beyond itself
In realms of contemplation learning strove for
Without, always, the same degrees of insight.
Then let Giotto's circle stand for those
Who see beyond the lines and shapes of things,
The orders, and the ordering of men's lives,
And all the passing show, to what might be
Ultimate truths contained in a simple act,
The maker's hand unveiling what is hidden

From understanding by what's understood,
And what is real surprisingly revealed,
Hard, simple, whole, something to stand for ever.

Wellington
1 9 6 8

From Brooklyn Hill, ours is a doll-size city;
A formal structure of handpicked squares and bricks
Apprehensible as a child's construction
Signifying community. I look
From the rain-blurred window down on the toy cranes,
Funnels of let's-pretend ships at the waterfront,
And the dark strips of reclamation fingering
Into the blue of the painted harbour, beckoning
Somes Island to swim ashore and join the gang,
Aware that compactness speaks a language
Encouraging broad and human views. We belong,
In the fact of the polar wind, to a conception
That does not defy comprehension through sheer size.
How many capitals are so human? Here, you must
Get down to detail, get down among the noise
And see the child's-brick buildings take on stature—
Tower into actual clouds—to know
The total is more than illusion. Some who live here
Have been hurt as much as any; loved as much,
Died their own deaths, and wished they could live forever—
Rulers, perhaps, of just such a kingdom a child
In his perfect and simple building might have planned.

New Guinea Time

Time is mainly a fiction here. There are
Two seasons — and that is near enough —
One for growing, and one for taking stock.
Between them, things gradually disappear.

No feature of the landscape looms as permanent,
And no man stable. Talking of change, we mean
Stages of dermatitis, rust and heat
Etching the native and his habitat.

Near enough is too close: if things get done
Or merely overgrown, who is to blame?
Whom to congratulate? Out of the warm
And septic seas Death grows its territory

Gradually as an atoll in the mind
Might form itself of bone and alcohol
Or failing medication. What stands, skeletal,
Is rock, or the pulse of water, the tale

Of time so quietly running down it tells
Not what one seeks to know, naming the minute,
Placing the day or the week. Things get done
By the season and life goes finish.

What Became of the Family?

This father, mother and son, trapped in the lens
Of a spent, Edwardian day, had no idea
They would be so dispossessed, or end up here
Unwanted against a couch in the auction-room.
Her curved white neck is still a delicacy
Emerging with some candour, for her day,
From the suggestions of a low-cut blouse.
His hand upon her knee has an owner's air,
The twirled moustache its pride. None separates;
Nothing can come between, is what his style,
Her eagerness, imply. Not even the son
Spun of their loving in the webfoot dark
When, breasting tides of sleep, they sank,
Moaning into their harbouring dream, and woke
shaken and sure that something new would come
from such incredulous intensity.
The boy sits by her at the end of the seat;
Knows he is shared, but cannot interrupt,
Frighten them into love, or a new arrangement
Centered upon himself, by a word of warning
Of how he will die on a hill called Vimy Ridge,
Still separate, and still so far to fall
Into this cast-off day. The death of a house
Echoes under the hammer. A world has gone
Like a dream, or a photograph of no-one
Known now at all. I can give them no name;
Guess only their griefs and the terror
Of who hides under the hood of every camera
Mocking with permanence what must fade and fall
And end anonymous. It will not help to ask
Why we are here? What happened to their family?

The Mouse

I heard the snap of the trap from the hot-water-cupboard
While I was reading about the balance of nature.
There were sounds of wind and rain outside,
The vague disturbances that one accepts,
Like the whirr of the fridge, the burning of the air
Heartbeats consume. All became one
Except for that metallic clack
Pronouncing doom: and, curious,
Sensing the event, I took a stool
To stand on while I peered into that room-
in-miniature housing the water-tank
Where I'd set the snare, with bacon baited.
Twitched in last throes the hind legs of the mouse.
A small and delicate thing—a matter of fur and faeces—
But mainly faeces. These were what caused complaint,
And were the evidence that, in our house,
Came uninvited guests who knew no more
Than crapping on clean clothes set by to dry
In the air of warmth our wealth and labours paid for.
What was removed was the merest soft-haired corner
Of a life we were not prepared to afford.
And the children reveal all possible attitudes.
"A dear little mouse," they say next morning, knowing
How little a murder it is when I empty the trap
In readiness for another midnight assault.
That mouse is dead to me and them. Their words
Convey a world of size that is belied
By the unnatural light in their small, hard eyes.

There Was Something Wrong With My Life . . .

An emptiness: something lacking: I couldn't
Put my finger on it, and though
There was plenty to do, what with my husband,
Two kids, the home, and part-time teaching,
Something there at the centre didn't connect.
I said to him, to my husband, you don't
Need me anymore, you don't pay me
The same attention and he said: Right
I Will: but it didn't work and the more
I wanted the more he said He Would,
But didn't, and then I knew I was driving him
Away and what could I do but chase?
And when I followed him there to those other
Women I never knew what went on because

When I knocked the houses would disappear and I'd
Be standing under a tree on an empty allotment,
Wind in my hair and the rain crying over me.
Or I'd knock, and the door would open
On a deserted house and I'd think: For him
To have come here it must have been very secret,
Serious; but when I looked he wouldn't be there.
Going home, I'd say, Why did you do it?
And he'd say: Do What? My God I Don't
Know Anymore. And next time I tried to follow
The street would close up on me or a wall
Suddenly rear up and stop me. I'd cry,
Don't leave me, and find I was standing
Under a vacant tree in a windy space
Beating my hands on the bark with the blood
Crying over me, and he wouldn't be there,
Nor on the road 1 took back to the house,
Nor in the kitchen when I took the knife
From the drawer to go and attend to the children.

Coming and Going

If love is what would make one offer himself
to bear the pains of another, there is so much
the baby does not understand I would gladly
stand in her stead for. But you cannot take
the pang for another or teach
pain quicker than the piercing thorn
any more than explain to the blind
the colour of blood or a bird.

Through glass of the kitchen door she watches
me return through the burning light of the day
and the indescribable sunset; her arms
suddenly wild signalling welcome.
What she makes of my comings and goings
I cannot guess or begin to explain.
Here one minute, gone another: small wonder
children find fathers incomprehensible
shadows, moon-ruled like tides, undependable.

Which is not why I pick her up from the floor—
but to secure for myself the fact of return
and the weight of the welcome. My fifty-odd
years are closer to a last departure
I know I should have thought harder
about such a new beginning. I tell myself

that love is quite as extreme as any entrance
or exit, and does not come too late. Its colour
glows in the room where I have closed the door.

At Large in the Eighties

The hotels are quieter this year: the merest
peppering at the tables tonight, and all of them
eating alone. They do not look about or wish
to talk. A finger stabs the menu: a pencil
records with the faint whisper of grass
in a small breeze. Behind the palms
a faceless music registers dismay from its can
as neutrally as maybe. In the lounge
the news has the air of having been suppressed
and is as quickly forgotten. And so
to bed. There will be nothing here
for a diary entry. A cigarette in the dark
ripens its one dangerous fruit.

Uneasy Resident

You could say I came home to the hooley,
met up with the Maoritanga and found
everything up the booai. It hasn't
been easy to learn to relive the language.

Or to rethink the position, or any one
of the sixty-nine that used to add up to love:
something sickens in the social stewpot:
the prices are up and everyone has to pay.

Outside the electric fences a few talk barter,
know there is wind, trees, but that there was never
much evidence of active nature—a thriving
animal life—nothing larger than vermin, drab birds.

Not a country for people. Everyone here is
a migrant spat from another climate of failure
to feed on roots or look for them. To make
clearings in the undergrowth, proselytize innocence.

All of these factors seem to tell us something
of a rough message like an ad-man's jingle:
A great place to raise children—but we cannot

easily let them grow to full stature, laugh, fart,

stand. Lately we have begun to tear more of it
down to rebuild. We erect the age of plastic
towers and the glassy stare. A new law shaping
intends the roads shall be safer for heavy traffic.

Wherever you go you take yourself. Returning,
I sense the drift is not movement so much
as a running-on-the-spot as in those younger dreams:
you were always running away but never moving

while the hot breath of pursuit pounded behind
nearer and nearer with a tongue like a stopwatch.

Elephant

Miranda, as usual, indefatiguable
(curiosity unspooling like a firehose
or endless rope for her disappearing trick),
has gone on ahead to the top of the hill
to interview giraffes.
                    But after an hour
of painted birds and jigsaw monkeys angular
in their dance and fitting together, her smaller brother
has had it. Retired, slumped in the pushchair
near collapse, I wheel him along the central path
when ahead, I see the great shape approaching;
and, as he catches it at the edge of the eye—
the world wheeling before him—the sharp intake
of breath. Awe. A stillness cloaking him, intent
as the quiet mass fills the whole of his vision:
an avalanche closing the freeway.

"What is it?" whispered, followed by memory—
"Elephant!" so soft you know his voice has found God
and is hushed by the language of size. Grey,
tusked and house-high, wrinkled walls and roof
are on the move to another climate or street.
Snails can carry their own—but here is proof
the whole lived-in world could be gipsy. Kamala,
I tell him, and he whispers that one too.
A name for everything, and the sound is worship.

JANET FRAME

Yet Another Poem About a Dying Child

Poets and parents say he cannot die
so young, so tied to trees and stars.
Their word across his mouth obscures
and cures his murmuring good-bye.
He babbles, *they say*, of spring flowers,

who for six months has lain
his flesh at a touch bruised violet,
his face pale, his hate clearer
than milky love that would smooth over
the pebbles of diseased bone.

Pain spangles him like the sun,
He cries and cannot say why.
His blood blossoms like a pear tree.
He does not want to eat or keep
its ugly windfall fruit.

He does not want to spend or share
the engraved penny of light
that birth put in his hand
telling him to hold it tight.
Will parents and poets not understand?

He must sleep, rocking the web of pain
till the kind furred spider will come
with the night-lamp eyes and soft tread
to wrap him warm and carry him home
to a dark place, and eat him.

At Evans Street

I came one day upon a cream-painted wooden house
with a white bargeboard, a red roof, two gates,
two kinds of japonica bushes, one gooseberry bush,
one apple tree lately in blossom; and thus I counted
my fortune in gates and flowers, even in the white
bargeboard and the fallen roofbeam crying religiously
                to the carpenter,
Raise me high! and in this part of the city that would
                be
high indeed for here my head is level with hills and sky.

It is not unusual to want somewhere to live but the
        impulse
bears thinking about seriously and it is wise
never to forget the permanent impermanence of the
        grave,
its clay floor, the molten centre of the earth, its untiled
roof, the rain and sunbeams arrowing through slit
windows and doors too narrow to escape through,
locked by the remote control of death-bed convulsions
in a warm room in a cream-painted wooden house with
a red roof, a white bargeboard, fallen roofbeam . . .
                        no, it is not unusual
to nest at my time of year and life only it is wisest
to keep the spare room always for that unexpected guest,
        mortality,
whose tall stories, growing taller, tell
of the sea-gull dwelling on bare cliffs, of eagles high
where the bailiff mountain wind removes all furniture
        (had eagles known the need
for chairs by the fireside—what fire but the sun?) and
        strips the hangings
from the trees; and the men, also, camouflaged as trees,
        who climb the rock
face and of the skylark
from whose frenzied point of view harvest is hurricane
and when
except in the world of men
did hurricanes provide shelter and food?

In my house I eat bread and wish the guest would go.

The Clown

His face is streaked with prepared tears.
I, with others, applaud him, knowing it
is fashionable to approve when a clown cries
and to disapprove when a persistent sourface
does whether or not his tears are paint.

It is also fashionable, between wars,
to say that hate is love and love is hate,
to make out everything is more complex than we dreamed
and then to say we did not dream it,
we knew it all along and are wise.

Dear crying clown dear childlike old man
dear kind murderer dear innocent guilty

dear simplicity I hate you for making me pretend
there are several worlds to one truth when
I know, I know there are not. Dear people like you and me
whose breaths are bad, who sleep in and rumble
their bowels and control it until
they get home into the empty house or among the family
dear family, dear lonely man in torn world of nobody,
is it for this waste that we have hoarded words over so many
million years since the first, groan,
and look up at the stars. Oh oh the sky is too wide to sleep under!

Rain on the Roof

My nephew sleeping in a basement room
has put a sheet of iron outside his window
to recapture the sound of rain falling on the roof.

I do not say to him, The heart has its own comfort for grief.
A sheet of iron repairs roofs only. As yet unhurt by the demand
that change and difference never show, he is still able
to mend damages by creating the loved rain-sound
he thinks he knew in early childhood.

Nor do I say, In the travelling life of loss
iron is a burden, that one day he must find
within himself in total darkness and silence
the iron that will hold not only the lost sound of the rain
but the sun, the voices of the dead, and all else that has gone.

Wet Morning

Though earthworms are so cunningly contrived
without an opposing north and south wind
to blow the bones of Yes apart from the flesh of No,
yet in speech they are dumbly overturning,
in morning flood they are always drowned.

This morning they are trapped under the apple tree
by rain as wet as washing-day is wet and dry.
An abject way for the resilient anchorage of trees,
the official précis of woman and man,
the mobile pillarbox of history, to die!

When the Sun Shines More Years Than Fear

When the sun shines more years than fear
when birds fly more miles than anger
when sky holds more bird
sails more cloud
shines more sun
than the palm of love carries hate,
even then shall I in this weary
seventy-year banquet say, Sunwaiter,
Birdwaiter, Skywaiter,
I have no hunger,
remove my plate.

LAURIS EDMOND

August, Ohakune

All night in winter the dogs howled
up the hill in the mad woman's house—
she had forty living inside,
half starved, truculent, snarling
at all who came; but only kids
would creep along the derelict track:
half choked with fear they stalked phantoms,
found their nightmare, an ancient stag,
eyeless, ghastly holes gouged
by rats, above the blackened door.
They smothered screams—and went back,
in daylight only....
                                    Further off
we could hear the river
intermittently tapping its menacing morse
and the morepork call through the dark;
at last the frost hunted us in
to take shelter in a cold uneasy sleep.

Over all was the mountain, Snow Queen
of an old tale, brilliant and deadly, brooding
on the fate of frozen villages.

Before a Funeral

The great bright leaves have fallen
outside your window
they lie about
torn by the season from
the beggared cherry trees.
In your room, alone,
I fold and hide away
absurd, unnecessary things—
your books, still ready and alert,
it seems, for understanding,
clothes, dry and cold,
surprised in holding still
to hairs upon the collars,
handkerchiefs in pockets,
socks, awry, not ready for
the queer neglect of death.

Mechanically useful, I make
preparations for some possible
impossible journey no one
will ever take; work will help
they tell me, and indeed
your room is now nothing
but things, and tidy.
I have put away your life.

Out in the autumn garden
a sharp rapacious wind
snatches the brilliant booty
of the leaves. The blackened branches
grown. They knot, and hold.
And yet the cold will come.

Two Birth Poems

1. A Shift of Emphasis

Do not come too close, nor touch
the swollen knot
that tightens round
my multiplicities of pain;
that scream that flies about the room
is mine. I allowed it out.
Keep off. Join the mice in nice
white uniforms running about
with their routines.

It happens here. All my eyes glare,
a thousand fists fight
in the raging darkness of my body—
this smothered yell
comes to kill.
Look out! It cracks me open, it is
the axe that splits the skull—

the knot of blood is cut.
I am broken, scattered,
fragments of me melt and flow—
I am not here; gravity's red centre
has slipped; off course, I roll about
like wind-blown eggshells.

Cradled in the world's lap lies instead
a tiny grey-faced rag of flesh

with a cry as thin as muslin,
and all the power to possess the earth
curled up behind the blindness of its eyes.

2. Zero Population Growth

It was the anonymity I noticed first—
the flowers and I both languishing
in unlit corridors,
banished for recalcitrant
behaviour, minor problems
for the management.

A kind carnation said
'Your water's leaking dear,
you'll have your baby long before the morning.'
But still the teacups chattered
while a yellow string of light remained in place
between the supper cups
and our disgrace.

Then a big pain bowled me,
I reeled, sprawled—
Heavens! it would not do!
A flock of nurses flew
to peck protestingly
at a wavering whale
impaled on a lino square.
Even the flowers disdained to smile.

I became incorrigibly plural—
there seemed no end to limbs and things
I could produce; the refuse disposal squad
briskly dismantled, finally towed away
the remains, still seething;
beside me a strange animal
in a basket, breathing.

Later I noticed a small sardonic smile
on the curtain, having a swing;
it chirped 'You've done it.
You clever thing.'

The Third Person

I do not know how to describe the third person but
on days when the doves came hurtling over the city
flung upwards in great purring armfuls outside your window

and fell, piling like black hail on ledges of buildings
across the street, he came in, he was there—let us
call him a man. He preened his purple feathers.

His eyes were brilliant, unblinking; he became
servant, interpreter, master and miracle-maker,
intricate designer of harmony out of
our broken fragments of love and confusion; I thought
you had summoned him for me, understanding
my weakness. I found him beautiful.

I came to you one cold evening in April,
the summer doves had flown, you were busy;
in the hard blue light the third person was very tall
and sharpened his steely claws meticulously.
When I showed my fear you moved slowly to stand beside him
and stared at me calmly without recognition.

The Names

Six o'clock, the morning still and
the moon up, cool profile of the night;
time small and flat as an envelope—
see, you slip out easily: do I know you?
Your names have still their old power,
they sing softly like voices across water.

Virginia Frances Martin Rachel Stephanie
Katherine—the sounds blend and chant
in some closed chamber of the ear, poised
in the early air before echoes formed.
Suddenly a door flies open, the music
breaks into a roar, it is everywhere;

now it's laughter and screaming, the crack
of a branch in the plum tree, the gasping
and blood on the ground; it is sea-surge
and summer, 'Watch me!' sucked under
the breakers; the hum of the lupins, through
sleepy popping of pods the saying of names.

And all the time the wind that creaked in
the black macrocarpas and whined in the wires
was waiting to sweep us away; my children who
were my blood and breathing I do not know you:
we are friends, we write often, there are
occasions, news from abroad. One of you is dead.

I do not listen fearfully for you in the night,
exasperating you with my concern,
I scarcely call this old habit love—
yet you have come to me this white morning,
and remind me that to name a child is brave,
or foolhardy; even now it shakes me.

The small opaque moon, wafer of light,
grows fainter and disappears; but
the names will never leave me, I hear
them calling like boatmen far over
the harbour at first light. They will sound
in the dreams of your children's children.

Going to Moscow

The raspberries they gave us for dessert
were delicious, sharp-tasting and furry,
served in tiny white bowls; you spooned cream
on to mine explaining I'd find it sour.
The waitress with huge eyes and a tuft
of hair pinched like a kewpie so wanted
to please us she dropped two plates as
she swooped through the kitchen door.
No one could reassure her. Snow was falling;
when you spoke, across the narrow white
cloth I could scarcely hear for the distance
nor see you through floating drifts.

Then the tall aunt brought out her dog,
a small prickly sprig like a toy; we put on
our coats and in the doomed silence Chekhov
the old master nodded at us from the wings.
At the last my frozen lips would not
kiss you, I could do nothing but talk
to the terrible little dog: but you
stood still, your polished shoes swelling up
like farm boots. There are always some
who must stay in the country when others
are going to Moscow. Your eyes were
a dark lake bruised by the winter trees.

To an Old Rebel

Feel how the round world rolls
in its rind of mountains and seas,

how we cling like flies to the morning
as we move from the shadowed arc of sleep
—oh Galileo, what adventuring that was,
what sternness, what gall, to push off
in your creaky reckonings from the level
earth into a nightmare of stars! Was it
heaven, though, phosphorescent through
the small telescope, or merely Jupiter's
moons? It's the question still; atoms
or Immanence, it curls an undying freshness
around our infections; the white fire
still draws us, and burns, and blinds.

The Henri Rousseau Style

Waking at this broad window I discover
every morning's green; the massed pohutukawas

sketch a sky as bright as malachite
the rain has lit a spider's web

with emerald reflections. It's
a Rousseau forest, the glass preserving

all that weird precision; only the beast
is lacking, murderous behind the leaves.

I turn away. Morning's for voices
lazy, low-toned, messing about

with tea and sugar spoons, recalling trifles
for 'perhaps' and 'mm—' for 'did I say...?'

equivocations soft and slack
as tumbled bedclothes. To live alone

is to choose a static pageantry—
this silence that stares from corners

with its feral eyes and shows through
tawny fur the tips of predatory claws.

Tristesse d'animal

Here, yes, I am here—
don't you see my hand at the window, waving?

It's all still the same,
tremulous water lifting its face
to the wind, a clock calling over the city

light late on the hills—
and I'm alone, as before.

Where are you, companions
who promised to come
to the very door of the grave

—where did you turn back?
Are you dancing somewhere nearby

or is that only the neighbours?
I might call you
but what language is there for it

—the blood-smear we were born in
the gasp of that strong bitter oxygen
the first taste, the last we shall have.

The Sums

Somewhere you are always going home
some shred of the rag of events
is for ever being torn off and kept
in an inside pocket or creased satchel
like the crayon drawing, blurred now,
you frowned over once in a desk

—it's kept for the moment when you go
mooching along the verandah and through
the back door, brass-handled, always ajar,
to where the floured apron stands monumental
above veined legs in a cloud of savoury steam,
mince, onions, the smell of childhood's July's;

there again you are quick-flounced and shrill
shrieking on a high stool the answers
to sums—multiplication, addition, subtraction
all the mysteries known as 'Mental'—alchemy
that could transmute 48 + 17 (when you got it,
yelling) to a burst of fire in the blood—

it is still there, still finding its
incorruptible useless answers,
your life's ruined verandah, the apron
the disfigured legs that with a stolid
magnificence used to hold up the world.

The Noh Plays

'Three months,' they said in July
but it is November and you are here still
gaunt on the pillow, your eyes
following us, pleading not so much for us
to settle your question but to know
how a man might give up his asking.

For us too the time is defined—
this is the last act: we cannot afford
a single careless gesture.
In your room at given positions
we are poised in a watchful patience.
The white window dare not close its eye.

In the Noh plays of Japan death is not
mentioned, but a character speaks
as a ghost bearing the soul of a man
—one who has endured his torment
in the Three Worlds of nature
and earned his release;

he plays out his suffering, his folly,
his search for wisdom; at last
his voice dims. Out of the silence
a young man begins to recount
new and remarkable exploits. But these are
the first words of another cycle.

The Ghost Moth

Once we lived so close to the bush
each day wore the beech trees' rangy profile,
all night the creek purred, brushing
the antennae of our sleep; in the evening
moths came pouring into the lamplight,
some small, blue-sheened, as though it was
light itself combed to dust on their wings

or a ghost moth stared from the doorway
sheathed in its gentle shallow gaze;
and we ourselves seemed diffused like
the light, and would wander away
past the moths to the leaf-shivering trees
as though summoned in secret
by the morepork's comfortless cry.

That earthy unearthly life is over now
but sometimes still when you come in
from the purposeful street and hesitate,
blinking, I think of the moths
how they wheeled into the lamp's bright
aureole and turned and turned, dazzled
by something they never really saw.

Camellias

2 Working

A rough morning, wind thumping the house
and all about it these bustling bodies
shoulders sawing up sunlight in chunks
hands scrabbling and beating the clay
of my lumpy hillside: three young men
I have asked to conceive it as garden
their flung shouts whirling
along the corridors of the wind.

Older, I stay inside (besides, I am
paying) here where camellias are stuck
in a pot and Wilhelmina, young too
and inextinguishably cheerful, is cleaning
my windows. What a season is spring—
raw, hyperactive, blatantly kind
reeking like sweat of the future:
did I too once take the season full on

like a fist, like a kiss, like
a drowning...? Look, the flowers
have fallen, they lie like pink
crumpled skin on the floor, but the leaves,
the unyielding bright leaves, are
making a stand. I likewise turn back
to my desk, to this page, to you,
to hear how my poem tells you.

ALISTAIR CAMPBELL

from *Elegy*

2

Now he is Dead

Now he is dead, who talked
Of wild places and skies
Inhabited by the hawk;

Of the hunted hare that flies
Down bare parapets of stone,
And there closes its eyes;

Of trees fast-rooted in stone
Winds bend but cannot break;
Of the low terrible moan

That dead thorn trees make
On a windy desolate knoll;
Of the storm-blackened lake

Where heavy breakers roll
Out of the snow-bred mist,
When the glittering air is cold;

Of the Lion Rock that lifts
Out of the whale-backed waves
Its black sky-battering cliffs;

Of the waterfall that raves
Down the dark mountain side,
And into a white cauldron dives.

8

The Laid-out Body

Now grace, strength and pride
Have flown like the hawk;
The mind like the spring tide,

Beautiful and calm; the talk;
The brilliance of eye and hand;
The feet that no longer walk.

All is new, and all strange—
Terrible as a dusty gorge
Where a great river sang.

Daisy Pinks

O catch Miss Daisy Pinks
Undressing behind her hair;
She slides open like a drawer
Oiled miraculously by a stare.

O the long cool limbs,
The ecstatic shot of hair,
And untroubled eyes
With their thousand mile stare.

Her eyes are round as marigolds,
Her navel drips with honey,
Her pulse is even, and her laugh
Crackles like paper money.

Hut Near Desolated Pines

Cobwebs and dust have long
Deadened an old man's agony.
The choked fireplace, the chair
On its side on the mud floor,
May have warmed an old man's
Bones or propped them upright
While his great head nodded;
Fantastical images may have stirred
His mind when the wind moaned
And sparks leapt up the chimney
With a roar. But what great gust
Of the imagination threw wide
The door and smashed the lamp
And overturned both table and chair . . .?
A rabbiter found him sprawled
By the door—no violence, nothing
To explain, but the hungry rats
That scurried over the fouled straw.
A foolish lonely old man
With his whiskers matted with dung.
Since when birds have stuffed the chimney
With straw, and a breeze flapped
Continually through the sack window;
And all the while the deft spiders
Doodled away at their obituaries,
And the thin dust fell from the rafters . . .
Nothing but cobwebs and dust
Sheeting an old man's agony.

At a Fishing Settlement

October, and a rain-blurred face,
And all the anguish of that bitter place.
It was a bare sea-battered town,
With its one street leading down
On to a shingly beach. Sea winds
Had long picked the dark hills clean
Of everything but tussock and stones
And pines that dropped small brittle cones
On to a soured soil. And old houses flanking
The street hung poised like driftwood planking
Blown together and could not outlast
The next window-shuddering blast
From the storm-whitened sea.
It was bitterly cold; I could see
Where muffled against gusty spray
She walked the clinking shingle; a stray
Dog whimpered and pushed a small
Wet nose into my hand—that is all.
Yet I am haunted by that face,
That dog, and that bare bitter place.

Aunt Lucrezia

A Portrait

Yes. Such were the eyes through which in rage and pain
Coiled the spent zodiac of her spirit;
And skin that tarnished where a finger rubbed it,
And jewelled boneless hand that stroked a ferret.

And mark the enamelled mouth, the ears laid back
Bitch-like against a head whose pride appalled
(Despite the coiffeur's art) my uncles most of all:
The head beneath the wig rose clear and bald.

The approving eye unerringly alights
On formal trees as fine as maidenhair,
Takes in a tower, moves upwards to interrogate
A hawk and pigeon circling in the air

Behind her. A day as lucid as the brows
For which ironic loves expend their breath,
Brandy behind their ears, brandy on their breath—
O subtle miniaturist in violent death!

—As I remarked, the head was bald . . . as glass,
And was especially odious to my uncles
To whom all forms of glass breathed and were evil;
The eye inhales the jug, dilates and rankles

Where Lucrezia's hand, boneless as a mollusc,
Slips in a phial, winks, and disappears,
As do my uncles and all their heirs . . .
The jewelled hands play with the ferret's ears.

Looking at Kapiti

Sleep, Leviathan, shouldering the Asian
Night sombre with fear, kindled by one star
Smouldering through fog, while the goaded ocean
Recalls the fury of Te Rauparaha.

Massive, remote, familiar, hung with spray,
You seem to guard our coast, sanctuary
To our lost faith, as if against the day
Invisible danger drifts across the sea.

And yet in the growing darkness you lose
Your friendly contours, taking on the shape
Of the destroyer—dread Moby Dick whose
Domain is the mind, uncharted, without hope.

Without hope I watch the dark envelop
You and like a light on a foundering ship's
Masthead the star go out, while shoreward gallop
The Four Horsemen of the Apocalypse.

My Mother

Rebellion was in her character.
Sullenly beautiful, of *ariki*
Descent, childbearing utterly wrecked her,
So that she died young in Tahiti
Where she was buried. (There's a snapshot
Of her flower-strewn grave, with my sister,
Morose with grief, beside it.) I forgot
To cry, being puzzled, but later missed her.

Sleepless tonight in hospital I search
My memory, but I can find no trace
Of that rebellion, yet like a damp torch

It smouldered in her, lighting up her face
With unearthly beauty. What was its name
If not tuberculosis of the womb?

Wild Honey

Stuart's gallantry . . . I recall how once
he beat a bully who had called his girl
some mildly offensive name . . . *Wild honey*.

Margaret's passion . . . She danced a hula once,
for a Director of Education,
on a cluttered supper board . . . *Wild honey*.

Lilburn's solitude . . . Alone he paces
an empty beach, creating in his head
bare harmonies of sand and wave . . . *Wild honey*.

Meg's loveliness . . . In that absurd boatshed
how it glowed, while the tide chuckled and slapped
below us—God, how she glowed! . . . *Wild honey*.

These things: gallantry, passion, solitude,
and loveliness—how they glow! . . . *Wild honey*.

The Return

And again I see the long pouring headland,
And smoking coast with the sea high on the rocks,
The gulls flung from the sea, the dark wooded hills
Swarming with mist, and mist low on the sea.

And on the surf-loud beach the long spent hulks,
The mats and splintered masts, the fires kindled
On the wet sand, and men moving between the fires,
Standing or crouching with backs to the sea.

Their heads finely shrunken to a skull, small
And delicate, with small black rounded beaks;
Their antique bird-like chatter bringing to mind
Wild locusts, bees, and trees filled with wild honey—

And, sweet as incense-clouds, the smoke rising, the fire
Spitting with rain, and mist low with rain—
Their great eyes glowing, their rain-jewelled, leaf-green
Bodies leaning and talking with the sea behind them,

Plant gods, tree gods, gods of the middle world . . . Face down-
      ward
And in a small creek mouth all unperceived,
The drowned Dionysus, sand in his eyes and mouth,
In the dim tide lolling—beautiful, and with the last harsh

Glare of divinity from lip and broad brow ebbing . . .
The long-awaited! And the gulls passing over with shrill cries;
And the fires going out on the thundering sand;
And the mist, and the mist moving over the land.

Bitter Harvest

The big farm girl with the dumb prophetic body
And shoulders plump and white as a skinned peach
Goes singing through the propped-up apple boughs.

Behind her steps an ancient Jersey cow
With bones like tent-poles and udder swinging.

And last a hairy boy who with a fishing-pole
Drives youth and age before him, flanked by boulders
More yielding than his love. O bitter harvest

When drought affirms and plenitude denies!
Well, let them pass. Assuredly the boy
Will drop his worm into a dusty hole

And fish up . . . death, and the ancient cow
On which so much depends will clear the moon.

Blue Rain

Blue rain from a clear sky.
Our world a cube of sunlight—
but to the south
the violet admonition
of thunder.

Innocent as flowers,
your eyes with their thick lashes
open in green surprise.

What have we to fear?
Frost and a sharp wind
reproach us,

and a tall sky pelts the roof
with blue flowers.

You and I in bed, my love,
heads leaning together,
merry as thieves
eating stolen honey—
what have we to fear
but a borrowed world
collapsing all about us
in blue ruins?

Why Don't You Talk to Me?

Why do I post my love letters
in a hollow log?
Why put my lips to a knothole in a tree
and whisper your name?

The spiders spread their nets
and catch the sun,
and by my foot in the dry grass
ants rebuild a broken city.
Butterflies pair in the wind,
and the yellow bee,
his holsters packed with bread,
rides the blue air like a drunken cowboy.

More and more I find myself
talking to the sea.
I am alone with my footsteps.
I watch the tide recede,
and I am left with miles of shining sand.

Why don't you talk to me?

Gathering Mushrooms

Dried thistles hide his face.
Look closely—
that's your enemy.
Ants carry away his flesh,
but still he grins.
You know him by his thumbs,
round and white,
breaking the earth like mushrooms,
coated with fine sand.

A bony finger flicks a bird
into your face,
daisies snap at your heels,
nostrils
flare in the ground
that you believed was solid—
and a dark wind rides
the whinnying tussock up the hillside.

Gather your mushrooms then,
and, if you dare,
ignore the thin cries of the damned
issuing through the gills.

Sick of running away,
you drop in the soaking grass.
Through tears
you watch a snail climbing a straw
that creaks and bends
under its weight,
and note how tenderly it lifts
upon its shoulder
the fallen weight of the sky.

Purple Chaos

'Chaos is purple,' you said.
'A painter's phrase,' I said,
disagreeing.
'Chaos is a colourless force
tossing up stars, flowers
and children,
and has no beginning
and no end.'

But lying in bed,
washed up,
I know you are right.
You were talking of something else—
You were talking of death.
Purple chaos has surged through me,
leaving me stranded—
a husk,
an empty shell
on a long white swerving beach.

Something has died,
something precious has died.
It may have been a flower,
a star,
it may have been a child—
but whatever it was, my love,
it seems to have died.

The Gunfighter

You will see him any day in Te Kuiti
or Cannons Creek,
immaculate in black
and triggered like a panther on the prowl.

Conscious of all eyes,
but indifferent to all except the heroine
watching from behind lace curtains,
doom walks the main street of a small town.

Is it fear or admiration that widens
those lovely eyes?
He knows her eyes are on him,
but gives no sign he knows—
he has a job to do.

The sun has reached high noon.
The shadows stand with flattened palms
against the walls of buildings,
or shrink back into doorways.
the heroine lets fall the curtain.
She has fallen—
drilled clean through the heart with love.

Now he stands alone
in the pool of his own shadow,
his wrists flexible as a dancing girl's,
his palms hovering like butterflies
over the blazing butts of his sixguns.

The streets are cleared,
the township holds its breath—
for the gunfighter, the terrible gunfighter
is in town.

Memo to Mr Auden, 29/8/66

Re your 'Musée des Beaux Arts', Mr Auden,
The Old Masters may have never been wrong,
But we regret that you were often wrong,
Sometimes appallingly, as in 'Miss Gee'.
As Mother's little boy with close-set eyes,
You might have thrown fewer stones at birds
And more at Mother who may have been to blame.
Suffering is a personal thing, but we believe
You see it rather as a spectacle—a public thing.
Suffering is a small girl screaming to her mother
That the torturer's horse has run her sister down.
As to the children skating on the pond,
One cry of anguish from the girl in labour
Will stop them all—excepting Mother's boy
Who will skate on . . . Mr Auden, not all the agèd
Reverently, passionately await the miraculous birth.
Some may have been stone-throwers in their youth,
And that same cry will pierce them with cruel delight.
The Old Masters knew that. You must have known that.
But you chose to write of doggy dogs and a horse
With an innocent behind—mere stage props, Mr Auden.
And as to that dreadful martyrdom, admit you willed it
Into happening so you could write about it.
Mr Auden, you are the ploughman in Bruegel's 'Icarus'
Following a stage prop. You are the delicate
Expensive ship that sees something amazing, perhaps
Even tragic—a boy falling out of the sky,
But you have a poem to finish and sail calmly on.

Waiting for the Pakeha

Here we are assembled on the bank,
a hundred souls—the remnant of our tribe—
decked out in mats and bearing greenery
to welcome to the pa our Pakeha.

And there's our chief, his club held ready
to give the signal for the show to start,
a sudden blink as of the moon through cloud
the only sign of life on his carved face.

Behind him, with bowed head, her pointed breasts
parting her long black hair, stands his daughter—
an offering to the Pakeha. . . Surely
such loveliness will fetch a crate of muskets.

The scouts we sent to meet the Pakeha
grin at us from the opposite bank,
their heads impaled on stakes. Our enemies
grow bolder every day, and they have guns.

But where is he? Where is the Pakeha?
The elders in their fly-blown dog-skin mats
yearn for their smoky whares—the womb
of Mother Night. Dogs whimper and the children

dream fearfully of ovens as they burrow
into the warmth of their mothers' bodies . . .
The enemy guns are growing more insistent:
we shall not wait again for the Pakeha.

Dreams, Yellow Lions

When I was young
I used to dream of girls
and mountains.

Now it is water I dream of,
placid among trees, or lifting
casually on a shore

where yellow lions come out
in the early morning
and stare out to sea.

The Dark Lord of Savaiki

I am the one in your dreams,
        master of passion,
                favourite child
of Tumu and Papauri.
                Te Ara o Tumu

        I   Under the Tamanu Tree

Who, who and who?
Who is the dark Lord of Savaiki?
        Crab castings,
                convulsions under the house
where the landcrabs
        tell their grievances
to the roots of the tamanu tree.

Agitation of the leaves,
        the palm trees clash
                their fronds,
and the wind hurries past
        clutching in its fingers
the leaf-wrapped souls
        of children torn
                from the eyelids
of despairing mothers.
                        Hung
on spiderwebs for safekeeping,
        they will dangle there,
until the spirits come
                and eat them.

III   Teu

Mother, you were there
        at the passage
                when our ship arrived.
The sea, heavy as oil,
        heaved unbroken
                        on the reef,
the stars
        lay in clusters
                on the water,
and you wept
        when you laid
                the Southern Cross
upon our eyes.

VII   Brother Shark

The black mango
                is a priest
in his marae
                of blazing coral
where Ataranga's sunken house
        tilts
                towards Savaiki
and the setting sun.

VIII   Omoka

It will be like this one day

when I sail home to die—
the boat crunching up on to the sand,
then wading through warm water
                    to the beach,
the friendly voices
          round me in the darkness,
the sky dying out
          behind the trees of Omoka,
                    and reaching out of hands.

I   A Stranger from Rakahanga

A stranger has arrived from Rakahanga.
          Nobody knows how he came:
                    no strange canoe has been reported—
none could survive in such a sea.
          Our villages are awash, and our dead groan
                    as they sit up to the chin in water.
Such a stranger, you would think, would be
          so singular, so arresting,
                    once seen, nobody could forget him.
Nobody remembers a single thing—
          the look on his face (if he has a face),
                    his size, or if he is young or old.
He arrived, some say, a few hours ago,
          others claim it is more than a week,
                    since he was first seen at Omoka.
On one thing, though, all are agreed:
          he is a traveller from Rakahanga—
                    but why Rakahanga, they can't say.
They stand around in silent groups, expecting
          the worst—but not a thing happens.
                    No deaths or accidents are reported.
They will turn soon to urgent tasks, repair
          the storm damage, but strangely empty
                    as if nursing a disappointment.

Sina

You were a tender girl, Sina,
          fragrant as the *komuko*
                    of the young coconut tree.
Throughout our adolescence
          our entire universe
                    was the bottom of a canoe

where we lay together
        drifting among the *motu*.
                Every night I would pluck
for your breasts and hair
        the flowers of the sky.
                And then one night
we drifted far from shore
        through the scented darkness,
                oblivious of the reef
until too late—*aue!*
        Now you are a woman
                lovelier even than the girl
that loved me long ago,
        and another lover
                drinks from your calabash.
Ru the fisherman
        knows all the secret places
                in the ocean floor.
His spear is probing
        for an answer.
                I watch and wait.

Akaotu

Surging over the reef,
        surging over the reef,
                the sea has breached
the canoe of Akaotu
        and now she lies becalmed
                in the shallows of Sanganui.
Her splendid lovers have fled,
        leaving her to the mercy
                of her jealous consort,
red-haired Atea,
        Lord of Light, who grumbles
                in his sleep, causing
the sky to flicker.
        But the Lady Akaotu
                turns with the tide.
She smiles as she dreams
        of atolls in their green birth
                pricking the white horizon.

Mahuta

The gourd is overripe,
        but it is the yam you steal

from our ocean gardens,
Mahuta, lover of night,
            late of Rakahanga.
                    The beautiful young girl
sighs as she holds
            each heavy breast
                    within a heavy hand.
Stunned, stunned—
            the dragonfly bows its head
                    to the blows of the rain.
Lightning scribbles its name
            above Katea Village
                    where a young man lies
dying, who only yesterday
            was anointed ariki.
                    Mahuta, night-walker,
what are the fishermen saying
            as they wade hip-high in the sea?
                    It is easier to net the tide
than to trust in Mahuta,
            gatherer of souls.

W. H. OLIVER

In the Fields of My Father's Youth

1

In the fields of my father's youth, now bountiful and green,
I walked and stared, half-recollecting each
New but anticipated emblem of a past
once legendary, now more remote than legend,
remembering all he had told for the delight of children:
folk-habits, succession of seasons and lives,
the dim procession of my ancestors
walking through centuries this treadmill lane.

Its trench between stone bramble-plaited hedges
wound where the contour made a passage easy,
past fertile hills where he had worked all seasons,
last of the peasant line who broke this earth.
Mill and manor, farm house, cottages,
kept up an easy, sociable conversation:
a discourse of rank and degree, proud and humble
linked by its cautious line in a common life.

I celebrated every moderate hope
that lay embedded in the lane's hard clay
feeling myself made radical once more;
and celebrated, too, the manor house,
crown of the country, elegant, discreet
as well-worn riches, sweet as piety.

2

How many hopes were trenched in the secretive lane?
I populated every crossroad with
a host of suicides impaled on hate:
passionate, modest, impossible hopes, denied
in life and death the four unwinding roads
which lead, whichever way, to difference.
When it was moonlight, how many bones
jangled together at Black Cross and White Cross
as an army of lost liberators gaped for flesh?
How great a multitude of dreams? Not his,
at the end. They leapt across an era and a world and pitched
full-flighted, ready to flower, on an empty island,
travelled the dust and gravel of a new highroad
linking, not age to age, but moderate hope to hope.
Solitude, dream, their pinched and starving hopes,
his and my ancestors', he brought to breed
in the raw clay and timber of a settlement

new and elsewhere; not anywhere
the manor's grace could mock their stuntedness.

3

His dream is fulfilled in an acre of fertile ground;
took body in a house, a family;
in leisure, fruit and flowers, company;
work winning ease, children bringing home
children for grandparents, warmth for autumn.
The dream is fulfilled in an empty island town,
a street of stucco shops and iron verandas
perched on the site of a violated forest;
a temporary borough pitiable
beneath the winter snow range meditating
flood and disaster in the final spring—
not yet. Clay gapes in cuttings and the soil runs down
each winter river; land is dying; yet
there will be life in it enough for him,
enough for the dream to flourish and express
a permanent hope lodged in impermanence,
given, in one brief life, a chance to live
apart from that perpetual English rite:
one taken chance, then newness, all things strange.
Till that time fall from the mountain and the sky
I think the innumerable peasantry within
his hand and eye, the ground bass of that theme
particular skill and courage elaborate,
are strong and sappy in his acre garden
and, I expect, are happy as never on earth
moving in his disguises among strawberry frames,
directing the growth of flowers round a house.
They are prodigal there who died in paucity
and, having raised a county's fodder and crops,
delight themselves in more luxurious harvests.

And I think they talk through the words of poetry
he writes to me here in England, telling me
of the growth and profit and joy of his fruitful acre
as once in passion and in oratory
they stood on platform, soapbox, with the jobless,
full of the argument of state, rebelliously
talking down privilege, arguing equal rights.
That dream flower faded, cynically abused;
the song of equality became a bribe
offered abroad by immoral political apes,
while good men reeled in the wake of procureurs.

There is only the garden full of surprising fruit.

4

The lane led away to the by-pass, to the rail,
to the university town, this desk, these words.
Can I who live by his flight relinquish either
the peasant's dream or the eloquent manor house?
Both were his first and every birthday gift.
All those who sleep in tears within my seed
will reach, if I do not, the breaking point
where loyalties depart and go their ways
separate, hostile, taking up their arms
to meet in battle on the disputed field
of England's and our own heart's heritage.

That will be time for treasons and for faith.

Silent Revolution

Try it out with a bird or a fish. Though a woman would do.
They are well used to handling such weighty matters.
Like all the lesser creatures they have been
serious-minded since the first daub made them symbols.
Suppose, suppose, the bird took flight from the lectern
and swept through the nave wingtip to either wall,
or out of the font rose, huge, Leviathan
and it was all quite suddenly submarine?
Suppose, to bring it closer home, the mirror
you looked in every morning was removed
and there your image stood quite unsupported
by any frame, and subtly changed in ways
that changed the more you looked, would you
be able, even, to wonder who was there?

Counter-revolution

Did it go wrong just about a hundred
years ago? A ramshackle self-appointed
cast-off elite of first comers,
promoters, bent lawyers and sham doctors
set it up for themselves, a gentry of sorts,
saw it collapse and crept away with slim gains.
The cities grew, married men left home,
children were tall and wild, women restless.
Something had to be done. Seddon the burly
village policeman, a pattern for the future,
rose like a cork, admonishing finger aloft,
ponderously sly, licking his stub of a pencil,
selecting and rejecting, always with good humour,
not harsh in the least, but in the end obscene.

JAMES K. BAXTER

High Country Weather

Alone we are born
  And die alone;
Yet see the red-gold cirrus
  Over snow-mountain shine.

Upon the upland road
  Ride easy, stranger:
Surrender to the sky
  Your heart of anger.

The Bay

On the road to the bay was a lake of rushes
Where we bathed at times and changed in the bamboos.
Now it is rather to stand and say:
How many roads we take that lead to Nowhere,
The alley overgrown, no meaning now but loss:
Not that veritable garden where everything comes easy.

And by the bay itself were cliffs with carved names
And a hut on the shore beside the maori ovens.
We raced boats from the banks of the pumice creek
Or swam in those autumnal shallows
Growing cold in amber water, riding the logs
Upstream, and waiting for the taniwha.

So now I remember the bay, and the little spiders
On driftwood, so poisonous and quick.
The carved cliffs and the great out-crying surf
With currents round the rocks and the birds rising.

A thousand times an hour is torn across
And burned for the sake of going on living.
But I remember the bay that never was
And stand like stone, and cannot turn away.

Elegy for an Unknown Soldier

There was a time when I would magnify
His ending; scatter words as if I wept

Tears not my own but man's; there was a time.
But not now so. He died of a common sickness.

Nor did any new star shine
Upon the day when he came crying out
Of fleshy darkness to a world of pain,
And waxen eyelids let the daylight enter.

So felt and tasted, found earth good enough.
Later he played with stones and wondered
If there was land beyond the dark sea rim
And where the road led out of the farthest paddock.

Awkward at school, he could not master sums.
Could you expect him then to understand
The miracle and menace of his body
That grew as mushrooms grow from dusk to dawn?

He had the weight, though, for a football scrum,
And thought it fine to listen to the cheering
And drink beer with the boys, telling them tall
Stories of girls that he had never known.

So when the War came he was glad and sorry,
But soon enlisted. Then his mother cried
A little, and his father boasted how
He'd let him go, though needed for the farm.

Likely in Egypt he would find out something
About himself, if flies and drunkenness
And deadly heat could tell him much—until
In his first battle a shell splinter caught him.

So crown him with memorial bronze among
The older dead, child of a mountainous island.
Wings of a tarnished victory shadow him
Who born of silence has burned back to silence.

Wild Bees

Often in summer, on a tarred bridge plank standing,
Or downstream between willows, a safe Ophelia drifting
In a rented boat—I had seen them come and go,
Those wild bees swift as tigers, their gauze wings a-glitter
In passionless industry, clustering black at the crevice
Of a rotten cabbage tree, where their hive was hidden low.

But never strolled too near. Till one half-cloudy evening
Of ripe January, my friends and I
Came, gloved and masked to the eyes like plundering desperadoes,
To smoke them out. Quiet beside the stagnant river
We trod wet grasses down, hearing the crickets chitter
And waiting for light to drain from the wounded sky.

Before we reached the hive their sentries saw us
And sprang invisible through the darkening air,
Stabbed, and died in stinging. The hive woke. Poisonous fuming
Of sulphur filled the hollow trunk, and crawling
Blue flame sputtered—yet still their suicidal
Live raiders dived and clung to our hands and hair.

O it was Carthage under the Roman torches,
Or loud with flames and falling timber, Troy!
A job well botched. Half of the honey melted
And half the rest young grubs. Through earth-black smouldering
    ashes
And maimed bees groaning, we drew out our plunder.
Little enough their gold, and slight our joy.

Fallen then the city of instinctive wisdom.
Tragedy is written distinct and small:
A hive burned on a cool night in summer.
But loss is a precious stone to me, a nectar
Distilled in time, preaching the truth of winter
To the fallen heart that does not cease to fall.

The Morgue

Each morning when I lit the coke furnace
Unwillingly I passed the locked door,
The room where Death lived. Shadowless infection
Looked from the blind panes, and an open secret
Stained even the red flowers in the rock garden
Flesh-fingered under the sanatorium wall.

And each day the patients coming and going
From light jobs, joking below the sombre pines,
Would pass without looking, their faces leaner
As if the wintry neighbourhood of Death
Would strip the shuddering flesh from bone. They shouted,
Threw clods at one another, and passed on.

But when at length, with stiff broom and bucket,
I opened the door wide—well, there was nothing

To fear. Only the bare close concrete wall,
A slab of stone, and a wheeled canvas stretcher.
For Death had shifted house to his true home
And mansion, ruinous, of the human heart.

Poem in the Matukituki Valley

Some few yards from the hut the standing beeches
Let fall their dead limbs, overgrown
With feathered moss and filigree of bracken.
The rotted wood splits clean and hard
Close-grained to the driven axe, with sound of water
Sibilant falling and high-nested birds.

In winter blind with snow; but in full summer
The forest blanket sheds its cloudy pollen
And cloaks a range in undevouring fire.
Remote the land's heart: though the wild scrub cattle
Acclimatized, may learn
Shreds of her purpose, or the taloned kea.

For those who come as I do, half-aware,
Wading the swollen
Matukituki waist-high in snow water,
And stumbling where the mountains throw their dice
Of boulders huge as houses, or the smoking
Cataract flings its arrows on our path—

For us the land is matrix and destroyer
Resentful, darkly known
By sunset omens, low words heard in branches;
Or where the red deer lift their innocent heads
Snuffing the wind for danger,
And from our footfall's menace bound in terror.

Three emblems of the heart I carry folded
For charms against flood water, sliding shale:
Pale gentian, lily, and bush orchid.
The peaks too have names to suit their whiteness,
Stargazer and Moonraker,
A sailor's language and a mountaineer's.

And those who sleep in close bags fitfully
Besieged by wind in a snowline bivouac—
The carrion parrot with red underwing
Clangs on the roof by night, and daybreak brings

Raincloud on purple ranges, light reflected
Stainless from crumbling glacier, dazzling snow.

Do they not, clay in that unearthly furnace,
Endure the hermit's peace
And mindless ecstasy? Blue-lipped crevasse
And smooth rock chimney straddling—a communion
With what eludes our net—Leviathan
Stirring to ocean birth our inland waters?

Sky's purity, the altar cloth of snow
On deathly summits laid; or avalanche
That shakes the rough moraine with giant laughter;
Snowplume and whirlwind—what are these
But His flawed mirror who gave the mountain strength
And dwells in holy calm, undying freshness?

Therefore we turn, hiding our souls' dullness
From that too blinding glass: turn to the gentle
Dark of our human daydream, child and wife,
Patience of stone and soil, the lawful city
Where man may live and no wild trespass
Of what's eternal shake his grave of time.

The Homecoming

Odysseus has come home, to the gully farm
Where the macrocarpa windbreak shields a house
Heavy with time's reliques—the brown-filmed photographs
Of ghosts more real than he; the mankind-measuring arm
Of a pendulum clock; and true yet to her vows,
His mother, grief's Penelope. At the blind the sea wind laughs.

The siege more long and terrible than Troy's
Begins again. A Love demanding all,
Hypochondriacal, seadark and contentless:
This was the sour ground that nurtured a boy's
Dream of freedom; this, in Circe's hall
Drugged him; his homecoming finds this, more relentless.

She does not say, 'You have changed'; nor could she imagine any
Otherwise to the quiet maelstrom spinning
In the circle of their days. Still she would wish to carry
Him folded within her, shut from the wild and many
Voices of life's combat, in the cage of beginning;
She counts it natural that he should never marry.

She will cook his meals; complain of the south weather
That wrings her joints. And he—rebels; and yields
To the old covenant—calms the bleating
Ewe in birth travail. The smell of saddle leather
His sacrament; or the sale day drink; yet hears beyond sparse
    fields
On reef and cave the sea's hexameter beating.

Lament for Barney Flanagan

Licensee of the Hesperus Hotel

Flanagan got up on a Saturday morning,
Pulled on his pants while the coffee was warming;
He didn't remember the doctor's warning,
    'Your heart's too big, Mr. Flanagan.'

Barney Flanagan, sprung like a frog
From a wet root in an Irish bog—
May his soul escape from the tooth of the dog!
    God have mercy on Flanagan.

Barney Flanagan R.I.P.
Rode to his grave on Hennessey's
Like a bottle-cork boat in the Irish Sea.
    The bell-boy rings for Flanagan.

Barney Flanagan, ripe for a coffin,
Eighteen stone and brandy-rotten,
Patted the housemaid's velvet bottom—
    'Oh, is it you, Mr. Flanagan?'

The sky was bright as a new milk token.
Bill the Bookie and Shellshock Hogan
Waited outside for the pub to open—
    'Good day, Mr. Flanagan.'

At noon he was drinking in the lounge bar corner
With a sergeant of police and a racehorse owner
When the Angel of Death looked over his shoulder—
    'Could you spare a moment, Flanagan?'

Oh the deck was cut; the bets were laid;
But the very last card that Barney played
Was the Deadman's Trump, the bullet of Spades—
    'Would you like more air, Mr. Flanagan?'

The priest came running but the priest came late
For Barney was banging at the Pearly Gate.
St. Peter said, 'Quiet! You'll have to wait
    For a hundred masses, Flanagan.'

The regular boys and the loud accountants
Left their nips and their seven-ounces
As chickens fly when the buzzard pounces—
    'Have you heard about old Flanagan?'

Cold in the parlour Flanagan lay
Like a bride at the end of her marriage day.
The Waterside Workers' Band will play
    A brass good-bye to Flanagan.

While publicans drink their profits still,
While lawyers flock to be in at the kill,
While Aussie barmen milk the till
    We will remember Flanagan.

For Barney had a send-off and no mistake.
He died like a man for his country's sake;
And the Governor-General came to his wake.
    Drink again to Flanagan!

Despise not, O Lord, the work of Thine own hands
And let light perpetual shine upon him.

My Love Late Walking

My love late walking in the rain's white aisles
I break words for, though many tongues
Of night deride and the moon's boneyard smile

Cuts to the quick our newborn sprig of song.
See and believe, my love, the late yield
Of bright grain, the sparks of harvest wrung

From difficult joy. My heart is an open field.
There you may stray wide or stand at home
Nor dread the giant's bone and broken shield

Or any tendril locked on a thunder stone,
Nor fear, in the forked grain, my hawk who flies
Down to your feathered sleep alone

Striding blood coloured on a wind of sighs.
Let him at the heart of your true dream move,
My love, in the lairs of hope behind your eyes.

I sing, to the rain's harp, of light renewed,
The black tares broken, fresh the phoenix light
I lost among time's rags and burning tombs.

My love walks long in harvest aisles tonight.

Crossing Cook Strait

The night was clear, sea calm; I came on deck
To stretch my legs, find perhaps
Gossip, a girl in green slacks at the rail
Or just the logline feathering a dumb wake.

The ship swung in the elbow of the Strait.
'Dolphins!' I cried—'let the true sad Venus
Rise riding her shoals, teach me as once to wonder
And wander at ease, be glad and never regret.'

But night increased under the signal stars.
In the dark bows, facing the flat sea,
Stood one I had not expected, yet knew without surprise
As the Janus made formidable by loveless years.

His coat military; his gesture mild—
'Well met,' he said, 'on the terrestrial journey
From chaos into light—what light it is
Contains our peril and purpose, history has not revealed.'

'Sir—', I began. He spoke with words of steel—
'I am Seddon and Savage, the socialist father.
You have known me only in my mask of Dionysus
Amputated in bar rooms, dismembered among wheels.

'I woke in my civil tomb hearing a shout
For bread and justice. It was not here.
That sound came thinly over the waves from China;
Stones piled on my grave had all but shut it out.

'I walked forth gladly to find the angry poor
Who are my nation; discovered instead
The glutton seagulls squabbling over crusts
And policies made and broken behind locked doors.

'I have watched the poets also at their trade.
I have seen them burning with a wormwood brilliance.
Love was the one thing lacking on their page,
The crushed herb of grief at another's pain.

'Your civil calm breeds inward poverty
That chafes for change. The ghost of Adam
Gibbering demoniac in drawing-rooms
Will drink down hemlock with his sugared tea.

'You feed your paupers concrete. They work well,
Ask for no second meal, vote, pay tribute
Of silence on Anzac Day in the pub urinal;
Expose death only by a mushroom smell.

'My counsel was naïve. Anger is bread
To the poor, their guns more accurate than justice,
Because their love has not decayed to a wintry fungus
And hope to the wish for power among the dead.

'In Kaitangata the miner's falling sweat
Wakes in the coal seam fossil flowers.
The clerk puts down his pen and takes his coat;
He will not be back today or the next day either.'

With an ambiguous salute he left me.
The ship moved into a stronger sea
Bludgeoned alive by the rough mystery
Of love in the running straits of history.

Green Figs at Table

'To eat a green fig, my dear,
Torn from the belly of unreason,
Honey white or brown when you open it,
The female parts, a story, or a poem—'
　　'Perhaps.'

'The taste sticks in one's mouth. Even now
Barometer wounds begin to throb, simply
Because you are a woman, woman in her rubbed flesh
Dressed for carnage—' 'I thought there was
　　A better name for it.'

'Action. Society as undertaker
Measures us for coffins, plugs up the orifices
By which pleasure might enter or pity escape.
Mothers admire the handsome corpse
　　That cost so little

'To be tidied. They cover the rope mark on the throat.'
'You were talking of figs—' 'Yes, figs.
I would like to be, at length, Odysseus lounging
With loaf and wine-cup in the shade
    Of his daughter the bent olive,

'But I too roast in the brass bull
Of conscience, remembering at this autumn table
Women ganched in cupboards of the mind or
Geometrical on the black glaze of an urn—'
    'I burn in waiting

'For the sea to rise or the god to descend
And hear, in coffee shops, the mill of gossip turning.'
'Blood runs from my nail into the soya dish;
Oil boats rust, chained at darkened wharves.
    One movement could shake

'Us free, I think—' 'One should not say too much.
Enter, without knocking, the door of the fig.'

At Akitio

Consider this barbarian coast,
Traveller, you who have lost
Lover or friend. It has never made
Anything out of anything.
Drink at these bitter springs.

Fishing at river mouth, a woman
Uses the sea-drilled stone her mother used
For sinker, as big kahawai come,
As tides press upward to time's source.
This coast is shelter to the shearing gangs
Who burn dead matai in their kitchen.

Squirearch, straight-backed rider, built
An ethos of the leisured life,
Lawn, antlered hall and billiard room,
Glass candelabra brought from Paris,
The homestead foundered among fields.
Unhorsed they sleep.

A girl with a necklace of mako teeth
They dug from a sandcliff facing south,
Axe and broken needle.
Stay good under slab and cross

Thin bones of children burnt by cholera,
Made tidy by the last strict nurse.
As tributary of a greater stream
Your single grief enlarges now
The voice of night in kumara gardens,
Prayer of the bush pigeon.

One drowned at the cattle crossing,
One tossed and kicked by a bucking horse—
Who died without confession, wanting
No wafer in their teeth—
Does the toi-toi plume their altar?
Are they held safe in the sea's grail?

This gullied mounded earth, tonned
With silence, and the sun's gaze
On a choir of breakers, has outgrown
The pain of love. Drink,
Traveller, at these pure springs.

Remember, though, the early strength
Of bull-voiced water when the boom broke
And eels clung to the banks, logs
Plunged and pierced the river hymen.
Remember iron-coloured skulls
Of cattle thrown to the crab's crypt,
Driftwood piled by river flood
On the long beach, battered limb
And loin where the red-backed spider breeds,
By a halcyon sea the shapes of man,
Emblems of our short fever.

Pluck then from ledges of the sea
Crayfish for the sack. Not now but later
Think what you were born for. Drink,
Child, at the springs of sleep.

Perseus

Leaving them, children of the Sun, to their perpetual
Unwearying dance about the ancient Tree,
Perseus flew east, the bird-winged sandals beating
Smooth and monotonous; sauntered above
Fens peopled by the placid watersnake,
Flamingo, crocodile—

And those unfallen creatures, joyful in
Their maze of waters, watched; with reedy voices
Praised the oncoming hero; cried
And coupled in his path. But he felt only
Scorching his shoulders, the shield, Athene's love-
    gift—and the first
Wind of foreboding blow from Medusa's home.

So entered the stone kingdom where no life
Startled, but brackish water fell
Like tears from solitary beds
Of sphagnum moss, or spray from cataracts
Sprinkled the grey-belled orchid, feathered grass
And spider's coverlet.

Till by the final cleft precipitous
At a blind gorge's end he lighted, stood,
Unslung the heavy shield, drew breath, and waited
As the bright hornet waits and quivers
Hearing within her den the poisonous rustle
And mew, for battle angry, of tarantula.

Fair smote her face upon the burning shield,
Medusa, image of the soul's despair,
Snake-garlanded, child of derisive Chaos
And hateful Night, whom no man may
Look on and live. In horror, pity, loathing,
Perseus looked long, lifted his sword, and struck.

Then empty was the cave. A vulture's taloned body
Headless and huddled, a woman's marble face
With snakes for hair—and in the wide
Thoroughfares of the sky no hint of cloudy fury
Or clanging dread, as homeward he
Trod, the pouched Despair at his girdle hanging,

To earth, Andromeda, the palace garden
His parents bickered in, plainsong of harvest—
To the lawgiver's boredom, rendering
(The task accomplished) back to benignant Hermes
And holy Athene goods not his own, the borrowed
Sandals of courage and the shield of art.

Howrah Bridge

to my wife

Taller than the stair of Qtub Minar
These iron beams oppress the eagle's town.
Bare heels will dint them slowly.
And swollen Gunga's muscles move
Beneath, with freight of garbage,
Oar and sail, the loot of many lives.

In the unsleeping night my thoughts
Are millet falling from an iron pan,
While you, my dear, in Delhi lying down
Enter the same room by another door.
The rupee god has trampled here;
The poor implore a Marxist cage.
Dragon seed, the huddled bundles lying
In doorways have perhaps one chilli,
A handful of ground maize.
King Famine rules. Tout and owl-eyed whore
Whose talons pluck and stain the sleeve,
Angels of judgement, husk the soul
Till pity, pity only stays.

Out of my wounds they have made stars:
Each is an eye that looks on you.

On the Death of Her Body

It is a thought breaking the granite heart
Time has given me, that my one treasure,
Your limbs, those passion-vines, that bamboo body

Should age and slacken, rot
Some day in a ghastly clay-stopped hole.
They led me to the mountains beyond pleasure

Where each is not gross body or blank soul
But a strong harp the wind of genesis
Makes music in, such resonant music

That I was Adam, loosened by your kiss
From time's hard bond, and you,
My love, in the world's first summer stood

Plucking the flowers of the abyss.

Election 1960

Hot sun. Lizards frolic
Fly-catching on the black ash

That was green rubbish. Tiny dragons,
They dodge among the burnt broom stems

As if the earth belonged to them
Without condition. In the polling booths

A democratic people have elected
King Log, King Stork, King Log, King Stork again.

Because I like a wide and silent pond
I voted Log. That party was defeated.

Now frogs will dive and scuttle to avoid
That poking idiot bill, the iron gullet:

Delinquent frogs! Stork is an active King,
A bird of principle, benevolent,

And Log is Log, an old time-serving post
Hacked from a totara when the land was young.

Ballad of Calvary Street

On Calvary Street are trellises
Where bright as blood the roses bloom,
And gnomes like pagan fetishes
Hang their hats on an empty tomb
Where two old souls go slowly mad,
National Mum and Labour Dad.

Each Saturday when full of smiles
The children come to pay their due,
Mum takes down the family files
And cover to cover she thumbs them through,
Poor Len before he went away
And Mabel on her wedding day.

The meal-brown scones display her knack,
Her polished oven spits with rage,
While in Grunt Grotto at the back
Dad sits and reads the Sporting Page,
Then ambles out in boots of lead
To weed around the parsnip bed.

A giant parsnip sparks his eye,
Majestic as the Tree of Life:
He washes it and rubs it dry
And takes it in to his old wife—
'Look Laura, would that be a fit?
The bastard has a flange on it!'

When both were young she would have laughed,
A goddess in her tartan skirt,
But wisdom, age and mothercraft
Have rubbed it home that men like dirt:
Five children and a fallen womb,
A golden crown beyond the tomb.

Nearer the bone, sin is sin,
And women bear the cross of woe,
And that affair with Mrs. Flynn
(It happened thirty years ago)
Though never mentioned, means that he
Will get no sugar in his tea.

The afternoon goes by, goes by,
The angels harp above a cloud,
A son-in-law with spotted tie
And daughter Alice fat and loud
Discuss the virtues of insurance
And stuff their tripes with trained endurance.

Flood-waters hurl upon the dyke
And Dad himself can go to town,
For little Charlie on his trike
Has ploughed another iris down.
His parents rise to chain the beast,
Brush off the last crumbs of their lovefeast.

And so these two old fools are left,
A rosy pair in evening light,
To question Heaven's dubious gift,
To hag and grumble, growl and fight:
The love they kill won't let them rest,
Two birds that peck in one fouled nest.

Why hammer nails? Why give no change?
Habit, habit clogs them dumb.
The Sacred Heart above the range
Will bleed and burn till Kingdom Come,
But Yin and Yang won't ever meet
In Calvary Street, in Calvary Street.

from *Pig Island Letters*

2

From an old house shaded with macrocarpas
Rises my malady.
Love is not valued much in Pig Island
Though we admire its walking parody,

That brisk gaunt woman in the kitchen
Feeding the coal range, sullen
To all strangers, lest one should be
Her antique horn-red Satan.

Her man, much baffled, grousing in the pub,
Discusses sales
Of yearling lambs, the timber in a tree
Thrown down by autumn gales,

Her daughter, reading in her room
A catalogue of dresses,
Can drive a tractor, goes to Training College,
Will vote on the side of the Bosses,

Her son is moodier, has seen
An angel with a sword
Standing above the clump of old man manuka
Just waiting for the word

To overturn the cities and the rivers
And split the house like a rotten totara log.
Quite unconcerned he sets his traps for possums
And whistles to his dog.

The man who talks to the masters of Pig Island
About the love they dread
Plaits ropes of sand, yet I was born among them
And will lie some day with their dead.

The Beach House

The wind outside this beach house
Shaking the veranda rail
Has the weight of the sky behind its blows,
A violence stronger than the fable

Of life and art. Sitting alone
Late at the plywood table,

I have become a salt-scoured bone
Tumbling in the drifted rubble,

And you, my love, sleep under quilts within
The square bunk-room. When I was young
(Hot words and brandy on my tongue)
Only the grip of breast, mouth, loin,

Could ward off the incubus
Of night's rage. Now I let
The waters grind me, knowing well that the sweet
Daybreak behind your eyes

Will not be struck dead by any wind,
And we will walk on the shore
A day older, while the yoked waves thunder,
As if the storm were a dream. Sleep sound.

At Taieri Mouth

Flax-pods unload their pollen
Above the steel-bright cauldron

Of Taieri, the old water-dragon
Sliding out from a stone gullet

Below the Maori-ground. Scrub horses
Come down at night to smash the fences

Of the whaler's children. Trypots have rusted
Leaving the oil of anger in the blood

Of those who live in two-roomed houses
Mending nets or watching from a window

The great south sky fill up with curdled snow.
Their cows eat kelp along the beaches.

The purple sailor drowned in thighboots
Drifting where the currents go

Cannot see the flame some girl has lighted
In a glass chimney, but in five days' time

With bladder-weed around his throat
Will ride the drunken breakers in.

The Lion Skin

The old man with a yellow flower on his coat
Came to my office, climbing twenty-eight steps,
With a strong smell of death about his person
From the caves of the underworld.
The receptionist was troubled by his breath
Understandably.

               Not every morning tea break
Does Baron Saturday visit his parishioners
Walking stiffly, strutting almost,
With a cigar in his teeth—she might have remembered
Lying awake as if nailed by a spear
Two nights ago, with the void of her life
Glassed in a dark window—but suitably enough
She preferred to forget it.

               I welcomed him
And poured him a glass of cherry brandy,
Talked with him for half an hour or so,
Having need of his strength, the skin of a dead lion,
In the town whose ladders are made of coffin wood.

The flower on his coat blazed like a dark sun.

Summer 1967

Summer brings out the girls in their green dresses
Whom the foolish might compare to daffodils,
Not seeing how a dead grandmother in each one governs her
    limbs,
Darkening the bright corolla, using her lips to speak through,
Or that a silver torque was woven out of
The roots of wet speargrass.

               The young are mastered by the Dead,
Lacking cunning. But on the beaches, under the clean wind
That blows this way from the mountains of Peru,
Drunk with the wind and the silence, not moving an inch
As the surf-swimmers mount on yoked waves,
One can begin to shake with laughter,
Becoming oneself a metal Neptune.

               To want nothing is

The only possible freedom. But I prefer to think of
An afternoon spent drinking rum and cloves
In a little bar, just after the rain had started, in another time

Before we began to die—the taste of boredom on the tongue
Easily dissolving, and the lights coming on—
With what company? I forget.
                              Where can we find the right

Herbs, drinks, bandages to cover
These lifelong intolerable wounds?
Herbs of oblivion, they lost their power to help us
The day that Aphrodite touched her mouth to ours.

At the Fox Glacier Hotel

One kind of love, a Tourist Bureau print
Of the Alps reflected in Lake Matheson

(Turned upside down it would look the same)
Smiles in the dining room, a lovely mirror

For any middle-aged Narcissus to drown in—
I'm peculiar; I don't want to fall upwards

Into the sky! Now, as the red-eyed tough
West Coast beer-drinkers climb into their trucks

And roar off between colonnades
Of mossed rimu, I sit for a while in the lounge

In front of a fire of end planks
And wait for bedtime with my wife and son,

Thinking about the huge ice torrent moving
Over bluffs and bowls of rock (some other

Kind of love) at the top of the valley—
How it might crack our public looking-glass

If it came down to us, jumping
A century in twenty minutes,

So that we saw, out of the same window
Upstairs where my underpants are hanging to dry,

Suddenly—no, not ourselves
Reflected, or a yellow petrol hoarding,

But the other love, yearning over our roofs
Black pinnacles and fangs of toppling ice.

from *Jerusalem Sonnets*

Poem for Colin—1

The small grey cloudy louse that nests in my beard
Is not, as some have called it, 'a pearl of God'—

No, it is a fiery tormentor
Waking me at two a.m.

Or thereabouts, when the lights are still on
In the houses in the pa, to go across thick grass

Wet with rain, feet cold, to kneel
For an hour or two in front of the red flickering

Tabernacle light—what He sees inside
My meandering mind I can only guess—

A madman, a nobody, a raconteur
Whom He can joke with—'Lord', I ask Him,

'Do You or don't You expect me to put up with lice?'
His silent laugh still shakes the hills at dawn.

Poem for Colin—2

The bees that have been hiving above the church porch
Are some of them killed by the rain—

I see their dark bodies on the step
As I go in—but later on I hear

Plenty of them singing with what seems a virile joy
In the apple tree whose reddish blossoms fall

At the centre of the paddock—there's an old springcart,
Or at least two wheels and the shafts, upended

Below the tree—Elijah's chariot it could be, Colin,
Because my mind takes fire a little there

Thinking of the woman who is like a tree
Whom I need not name—clumsily gripping my beads,

While the bees drum overhead and the bouncing calves look at
A leather-jacketed madman set on fire by the wind.

Poem for Colin—18

Yesterday I planted garlic,
Today, sunflowers—'the non-essentials first'

Is a good motto—but these I planted in honour of
The Archangel Michael and my earthly friend,

Illingworth, Michael also, who gave me the seeds—
And they will turn their wild pure golden discs

Outside my bedroom, following Te Ra
Who carries fire for us in His terrible wings

(Heresy, man!)—and if He wanted only
For me to live and die in this old cottage,

It would be enough, for the angels who keep
The very stars in place resemble most

These green brides of the sun, hopelessly in love
With their Master and Maker, drunkards of the sky.

Poem for Colin—27

Three dark buds for the Trinity
On one twig I found in the lining of my coat

Forgotten since I broke them from the tree
That grows opposite the R.S.A. building

At the top of Vulcan Lane—there I would lay down my parka
On the grass and meditate, cross-legged; there was a girl

Who sat beside me there;
She would hold a blue flower at the centre of the bullring

While the twigs on the tree became black
And then slowly green again—she was young—if I had said,

'Have my coat; have my money'—
She would have gone away; but because I gave her nothing

She came again and again to share that nothing
Like a bird that nests in the open hand.

from *Autumn Testament*

7

To wake up with a back sore from the hard mattress
In a borrowed sleeping bag

Lent me by Anne—it was her way, I think,
Of giving at the same time a daughter's

And a mother's embrace—friend, daughter, mother—
These kids have heart enough to nourish the dead world

Like David in his bed—to wake up and see
The sun, if not the light from behind the sun,

Glittering on the leaves beside the graveyard
Where some of them cleared the bramble and placed on the
    bare slab

A jam jar full of flowers—to wake is to lift up
Again on one's shoulder this curious world

Whose secret cannot be known by any of us
Until we enter Te Whiro's kingdom.

18

Father Lenin, you understood the moment
When the soul is split clean, as a man with an axe

Will split four posts from one log of dry timber,
But then your muzhiks still had souls

That smelt the holy bread upon the altar
And knew their mother's name. The mask of money

Hides too well the wound we cannot touch,
And guns are no use to a boy with a needle

Whose world is a shrinking dome of glass
A drug from Hong Kong will splinter open

With a charging elephant on a yellow packet
For riding home to deep sleep. The dollar is the point of it,

Old Father Lenin, and your bones in the Red Square
Are clothed in roubles till the Resurrection.

22

To pray for an easy heart is no prayer at all
Because the heart itself is the creaking bridge

On which we cross these Himalayan gorges
From bluff to bluff. To sweat out the soul's blood

Midnight after midnight is the ministry of Jacob.
And Jacob will be healed. This body that shivers

In the foggy cold, tasting the sour fat,
Was made to hang like a sack on its thief's cross,

Counting it better than bread to say the words of Christ,
'Eli! Eli!' The Church will be shaken like a

Blanket in the wind, and we are the fleas that fall
To the ground for the dirt to cover. Brother thief,

You who are lodged in my ribcage, do not rail at
The only gate we have to paradise.

42

The rata blooms explode, the bow-legged tomcat
Follows me up the track, nipping at my ankle,

The clematis spreads her trumpet, the grassheads rattle
Ripely, drily, and all this

In fidelity to death. Today when Father Te Awhitu
Put on the black gown with the silver cross,

It was the same story. The hard rind of the ego
Won't ever crack except to the teeth of Te Whiro,

That thin man who'll eat the stars. I can't say
It pleases me. In the corner I can hear now

The high whining of a mason fly
Who carries the spiders home to his house

As refrigerated meat. 'You bugger off,' he tells me,
'Your Christianity won't put an end to death.'

48

The spider crouching on the ledge above the sink
Resembles the tantric goddess,

At least as the Stone Age people saw her
And carved her on their dolmens. Therefore I don't kill her,

Though indeed there is a simpler reason,
Because she is small. Kehua, vampire, eight-eyed watcher

At the gate of the dead, little Arachne, I love you,
Though you hang your cobwebs up like dirty silk in the hall

And scuttle under the mattress. Remember I spared your children
In their cage of white cloth you made as an aerial castle,

And you yourself, today, on the window ledge.
Fear is the only enemy. Therefore when I die,

And you wait for my soul, you hefty as a king crab
At the door of the underworld, let me pass in peace.

Shingle Beach Poem

There is (conveniently) a hollow space
Between the upper and the lower jaws

Of the world serpent. There, as if all days
Were one, the children whack

Their seaweed balls, brag, tussle, comb the shores
For little crabs. There's no road back

To the dream time, and I endure instead
This hunger to be nothing. I supplicate

Dark heaven for the peace of that woman they
Lifted out of the breakers yesterday,

With blue deaf ears, whom Poseidon banged on the
    kelp-beds
Though she was a good swimmer, her body oatmeal-white

Spotted with shingle. To and fro
She was rolled by the undertow.

This I understand. Sister, remember
Us who wrestle yet in the coil of life's hunger.

Winter in Jerusalem

The I Ching tells me T'ai, the sign of peace,
Is what I venture in. The pungas on the hill,
So lately loaded with snow, are green again
Though some branches were broken. Where many men gather
From need or friendship, truth begins to waken
As eels rise in the dark river.

If Heaven gives me this old house by a river,
It is not for myself, but for the purpose of peace,
As the thunder and rain of spring make green things waken,
A fence of poplar leaves between us and the hill
Who is our mother, or the chestnuts we gather
In autumn when the earth is warm again.

In our dreams it may happen the dead return again,
As if the earth spoke to us, because time is a river
On whose bank in ignorance the tribes gather
With emblems of battle, yet desiring peace.
The fathers instruct us from their holy hill
So that the warrior souls may waken.

In winter with a heavy mind I waken
And wait for the sun to lift the fogs again
That bind Jerusalem. Like a bridegroom above the hill
He touches with hands of fire the waves of the river
Like the body of a woman. Our words are words of peace
In this house where the wounded children gather.

We can go out with Maori kits to gather
Watercress, or some tough lads who waken
Early will break the veil of peace
With gunshots, combing the bush again
For young goats, or lift the eel-trap from the river
As fog shifts from the highest hill.

The times are like some rough and roadless hill
We have to climb. I do not hope to gather
Pears in winter, or halt the flow of the river
That buries in sludge the souls who begin to waken
And know themselves. Our peace can't patch again
The canoe that is broken, yet all men value peace.

Peace is the language of the pungas on the hill
Not growing for any gain. These images I gather
As eels waken in the darkness of the river.

The Dark Welcome

In the rains of winter the pa children
Go in gumboots on the wet grass. Two fantails clamber
On stems of bramble and flutter their wings
In front of me, indicating a visit
Or else a death. Below the wet marae
They wait in a transport shelter for the truck to come,

Bringing tobacco, pumpkins, salt. The kai will be welcome
To my hungry wandering children
Who drink at the springs of the marae
And find a Maori ladder to clamber
Up to the light. The cops rarely visit,
Only the fantails flutter their wings

Telling us about the dark angel's wings
Over a house to the north where a man has come
Back from Wellington, to make a quiet visit,
Brother to one of the local children,
Because the boss's scaffolding was too weak to clamber
Up and down, or else he dreamt of the marae

When the car was hitting a bend. Back to the marae
He comes, and the fantails flutter their wings,
And the children at the tangi will shout and clamber
Over trestles, with a noise of welcome,
And tears around the coffin for one of the grown-up children
Who comes to his mother's house on a visit,

Their town cousin, making a longer visit,
To join the old ones on the edge of the marae
Whose arms are bent to cradle their children
Even in death, as the pukeko's wings
Cover her young. The dark song of welcome
Will rise in the meeting house, like a tree where birds clamber,

Or the Jacob's-ladder where angels clamber
Up and down. Thus the dead can visit
The dreams and words of the living, and easily come
Back to shape the deeds of the marae,
Though rain falls to wet the fantails' wings
As if the earth were weeping for her children.

Into the same canoe my children clamber
From the wings of the iron hawk and the vice Squad's visit,
On the knees of the marae to wait for what may come.

PAT WILSON

The Anchorage

Fifteen or twenty feet below,
The little fish come creeping round the anchor chain.
I could not have it quieter now,
Not anywhere, nor could there be less movement
Anywhere at all than here.

The bay moves on into night.
The shadows come to watch and wait in every hollow
Till they have gathered-in all.
But moon comes over the rocks; she lights the little fall
And rise and fall at the beach.

Deep water, deep bay
So still and calm for one whole night in the south-east
That day has never come,
And I am still upon my knees out on the stern,
And you and I still watch
Down twenty, thirty feet below.

The Farewell

And so, one day when the tide was away out,
The gulls there dancing along the edge of the sea,
We walked across the sand, down to the boat
And began again—she to protest and appeal,
I to refuse, looking aside, and then turning
And smiling . . .
               for it was not as if I had
Whatever it was that she asked, but who could persuade
      her
Of that? nor was it true that I could pretend
For ever . . .
              and all the gulls there, crying and playing,
Hunting, and all the reds and browns and yellows
Of late afternoon, and the last tints of the blue
Going out with the tide, and the boat drawn up there fast
Becoming high and dry on the sand as we talked.

Cuvier Light

Perennial fluctuation,
Interior lift of the sea,
Mist or a light rain, and silence—

Suppose our breathing is this movement,
This mist, our wishes coming back to us,
The rain, some forgiveness of our rashness,
The night, all that is against us—

Land all along one side,
One lamp turned low in the cabin,
Two lights to sea and then great Cuvier,

Admirable light!
Swinging, like a discus
On the arm of its taut brilliant beam,
The whole massed weight of the night!

The Tree

The day the big tree went
There came two rather seedy-looking men
Full of mysteries of their craft.
They spoke loudly yet confidentially to each other,
Nodded to me and my brother,
Said good morning to my brother's wife,
Cleared away all the little children of the neighbourhood,
And addressed themselves
To their big, supple saw.

Two or three hours later under the tree
They were still only half-way through.
The cut had a tell-tale concave scoop
Where each had been pulling down at the end of his stroke.
There was much previous talk of wedges,
Much arranging of ropes,
Calculation of angles,
And my brother and I were taking turns at the saw.

And so we all got friendly there with each other,
Putting the mysteries away
Under the great macrocarpa tree.
And when it started to lift and heave
And when the earth shook and the great sigh went up
As it fell and settled,

Then all the birds came flying out in a cloud
And all the children flew in with shouts and cries
And started a battle with the cones
And made their huts and houses in the fir.

The Precious Pearl

The oyster shuts his gates to form the pearl.
He knows he has a saviour caught within him,
Poor fool, old oyster. And it works against him,
An irritant that's locked within his shell,
A single-mindedness that thins his heart,
Turns it to narrowheartedness. Yet he,
Poor fool, poor oyster, used to love the sea
In all its many forms, to every part
Open with tranquil, unassuming jaws.
Then that foul irritant was driven in,
And snap! the wounded tongue cherished its sin
Until at last by hard, immobile laws
     A shining, perfect pebble made from wrong—
     A perfect grievance—rolled from off the tongue.

ALISTAIR PATERSON
Birds Flying

What am I doing here—in this place where
there are spiders on the white-washed walls
and cryptograms outlined on the ceilings—
what am I doing here? Yes, you saw me
draw my pentagon, set up the phallic symbols
—you know all this—how Tom couldn't manage
it without my help, and how the children—
the children lit their candles every birthday.

FOR CHRIST'S SAKE STOP! It's getting dark
and I can feel the needles, the night-nurse
straightening sheets and smoothing blankets:
what's worse is he could never finish it and
I'd lie there sweating like a horse after the
Derby—PLEASE STOP! Why do the birds fly,
the cranes with their long necks delicately
scaled, and the lizard without ever moving?

And now we are forced to take sides for you
have become puffed up with pride, your hand
stirs the waters and your eyes watch each of
us indifferently: the trout moving by, how
birds build and their unlikely young lift
frailty and bone towards the impassive sky,
the trees choose their random wild canopies
of needle and leaf, bud, flower and berry.

But where were you on the eighth of December
when I turned and looked up from the rice
and the brown water, stared at the sky,
saw the clouds stretch arched and spreading
like small mushrooms after rain, saw how
the quick morning burgeoned into life while
the birds went on flying and the world kept
spinning, dragging after it all the turtles

and the water-buffalo, the fences and gardens,
the village and the road through the village,
the makers of fish-traps, stringers of kites,
all the huts, outhouses, fish, rice, fathers,
mothers and the world's youngest child? Where
were you when the earth flew up and the water
flared like a snake as it straightens and
strikes and there was no earth and no water?

I know it—that each and every last cell
must wither and die—but where were you
yesterday when I knew nothing and had neither
bone, sinew nor belly—when the womb cried
and somewhere in the red darkness the ovum
waited and the tired sperm shrivelled, flesh
had no substance and there was less than nothing
to measure you by—where were you?

They tell me the gardener grows grapes—the
sweet, green kind that are juicy, translucent—
and pomegranates, figs, peaches and apples,
but the grapes are my favourites. They are kind,
they are all kind and say I'll be cured
given time. But they've taken away all the clocks
and I cannot follow the slow flight of their hands
nor the little birds that sweep the hours away.

Overture for Bubble-Gum and Flute

When the bones are no longer curious
                        and the shells
                are no more than shells
the whale's way
the wine-dark waters
have been pricked out
                        for tourists
when the terrible children
                        Brunton
                Marx and
        the man who fixes television sets
have written all their books
finished their intricate fiddling
            ˙ have exhausted themselves
are
                no longer brilliant
                nor even very clever
Hephaestus
puts down his tools
                in bewilderment
                limps from his cellar
what will there be left to do
                on Lemnos?

A woman walks by the water
      talks to the wind and the sand
            she has combed back
the hair of her daughters
given her sons
                to the land:
on the rim of her horizon
rise
           office blocks and dormitories
the enclosures and the cages
            of the municipal zoo.
Her sister's in the nut-house
her brother died in gaol:
                though
      the sun still rises in the morning
the stars ascend at night
      the moon is what she married
      the moon provides her light.
What's to be done on Lemnos
when the merry-go
              won't
            go round?
At Chelsea
feeding
         the Sugar Company ducks
woman dwarf and child
         entice cajole and plead
play out their separate phantasies
         in secret
         as they must.
What the woman does
         you know
the child
attends mechanical toys
         in theatrical full-dress
the dwarf
      that's me
         of course
Narcissus-like examines
the woman in the child
and sees reflections of himself.
This hand holds out the bread-crumbs
         this eye
         concedes the womb
in a mirror wrought on Lemnos
a gargoyle-mask
        half-covers
      the waters of the moon.

Down on the lake
where algae
           leap blushing into bloom
the mayors of all the cities
       stir Lemnos with their spoons.
                  We wake
                     and
take the bus to Bristol
explore the public gardens
          examine Lenin's tomb
                admire
whatever's pretty
return to rented rooms:
        while Kitty gets the cholera
          Jack takes up the pill
we face with Agamemnon
the host of human ills
        the Great Pacific Ocean
          slides slowly
   down the eroded throats of shells.
What's to be done on Lemnos
when the merry-go
                won't
          go round?

C. K. STEAD

Carpe Diem

Since Juliet's on ice, and Joan
Staked her chips on a high throne—

Sing a waste of dreams that are
Caressing, moist, familiar:

A thousand maidens offering
Their heads to have a poet sing;

Hard-drinking beaches laced with sun,
The torn wave where torn ships run

To wine and whitewashed bungalows.
This summer sing what winter knows:

Love keeps a cuckoo in its clock,
And death's the hammer makes the stroke.

Pictures in a Gallery Undersea
I

Binnorie, O Binnorie

In Ladbroke Square the light on waxen branches—
The orange light through two veined leaves
Tenacious in frost.
                    Upstairs, she lit the gas,
And drew bright curtains on the whitened eaves,
And said (her hand above the slowly turning disc)
'I shall never go back'.
                    Mozart in the delicate air
Slid from her glass, beat vainly against the cushions,
Then took off gladly across the deserted Square.
'You too must stay' (loosening her sun-bleached hair)
'You more than I—you will defeat their fashions.'

Invisible fins guided her to my chair.

Pictures in a gallery undersea
Were turned facing the wall, and the corridors were endless;
But in the marine distance, floating always beyond me,
A girl played Mozart on her sun-bleached hair.

So that wherever I walked on that long haul, midnight to dawn,
Stones of a sunken city woke, and passed the word,
And slept behind me; but the notes were gone,
Vanished like bubbles up through the watery air
Of London, nor would again be heard.

II

Où tant de marbre est tremblant sur tant d'ombres

On steps of the British Museum the snow falls,
The snow falls on Bloomsbury, on Soho, on all
Cradled in the great cup of London.
On all the lions and literary men of London
Heaping in gutters, running away in drains
The falling snow, the city falling.

Snow behind iron railings, drifts, collects,
Collects like coins in the corners of Nelson's hat
(Newbolt from a window in the Admiralty shouting
'Umbrellas for Nelson' and waving a sheaf of odes)
And down the long avenue.
     There through her aquid glass
Circumambient Regina, turning slowly from the pane,
Is seen imperiously to mouth 'Albert, my dear,
How do we pronounce *Waitangi*?'
        And snow descends.

There I met my grandfather, young and bearded,
With thick Scandinavian accent, who asked me
Directions to the dock; and later departed,
Bearing me with him in his northern potency
South.
   South. Earth's nether side in night
Yet hardly dark, and I under this day
That's scarcely light.
      Flakes descending, dissolving
On the folds of a cape
       on a single blue ear-ring,
On a bowler beneath the great trees of Russell Square.

III

The prim lips, homing, round the wind,
Condensing news along the Strand.
Nerveless, the words assault, descend—
Stiff jaws convey them underground.

The verb that rackets through the mind
Transports the body far beyond

Expected stops.
            Swirled on the wind
The lost, chaotic flakes ascend.

IV

All evening the princess danced, but before dawn
Escaped from her ballroom's glass down the wide, white stairs
And walked among bare trees that spiked the lawn.

Far from her ears, airy and thin, the beat
Of goldsmiths' hammers rang in Devonshire Street,
And spent, above a quarrel of barrow wheels,
Songs on the night:

> *Flakes of the outer world*
> *Through London fly*
> *Together hurled*
> *Under the heavy sky . . .*

V

I dreamt tonight that I did feast with Caesar

Wilde had been lynched. His head, grown larger, grinned from
            the Tower of London,
Swung by its hair under the Marble Arch,
And looked out from the point of a spear down Constitution Hill.
South of the River they were roasting him slowly on a spit,
And in Knightsbridge several of the best families dined delicately
            on his battered parts.
He, in Reading, enjoyed the debauch by proxy,
Bored at last with the rented corpse of Art
Whose delicate lusts had never been near to his heart.

Snow fell—fell where Hueffer ascended
From Great Russell Street to meet the eyes of Garnett;
And heard the scholar's voice: 'Now it is all ended—
England shall breed no poet for fifty years.'

Yeats not a mile from where they stood

                    And Yeats
Drew down the dim blind of Olivia's hair
And dreamed of a great bird. Then woke
Calling 'Maud. Maud.' But the room was empty.
Across the narrow alley he drank coffee,
Bought his paper from me at the corner
(I only a few feet tall, in cloth cap and boots
Three sizes too large. He the toff of the buildings.)

And as he went a man approached me, shouting
'This paper you sold me—there's nothing in it'
(Waving the packed pages and snatching back his money).

And the toff, a hundred yards along the street,
And Ezra in billiard cloth trousers across the street
Wearing an ear-ring of aquamarine,
And old Possum hackneying past in a bowler to his funeral at
the bank,

Turned
    turned, and watching, faded from sight.

VI

Now it was time for the drawing of curtains.
The smoke climbed, hand over hand, its difficult way,
Rested, or sank back in the thick air.
The River swans nor sang for the dead day
Nor proudly departed; but each hooked
One leg across its back, displaying a dirty web,
And (strong beak poised on graceful neck) poked
The rubbish drifting at the water's edge.

VII

Chanterez-vous quand vous serez vaporeuse? . . .
And as the last orange of the sun was crushed
The River accepted its lights, from Kew to Battersea
On, winding, to the Tower.
                    It was winter, the year '58,
And many were dead. But into the same heart and out
Through channels of stone and light, the blood still pulsed—
Carried me with it down New Oxford Street
Through Soho to the whirling clock of the Circus,
Then down, on to the bridge. The snow was freezing.
A train stood middle-poised beside the footpath
Above the water. And in a corner, hunched,
An old man's unsheathed fingers struggled to revive
The dead years on a battered violin.

A Natural Grace

Under my eaves untiring all the spring day
Two sparrows have worked with stalks the mowers leave
While I have sat regretting your going away.
All day they've ferried straw and sticks to weave
A wall against the changing moods of air,
And may have worked into that old design

A thread of cloth you wore, a strand of hair,
Since all who make are passionate for line,
Proportion, strength, and take what's near, and serves.
All day I've sat remembering your face,
And watched the sallow stalks, woven in curves
By a blind process, achieve a natural grace.

from Quesada

"Je pense. . .

aux vaincus!"

I

All over the plain of the world lovers are being hurt.
The spring wind takes up their cries and scatters them to the
    clouds.
Juan Quesada hears them. By the world at large they go unheard.
Only those in pain can hear the chorus of pain.
High in the air over winds that shake the leaves
High over traffic, beyond bird call, out of the reach of silence
These lovers are crying out because the spring has hurt them.
No one dies of that pain, some swear by it, a few will live with
    it always,
No one mistakes it for the lamentations of hell
Because there is a kind of exaltation in it
More eloquent than the tongues of wind and water
More truthful than the sibylline language of the leaves
The cry of the injured whose wounds are dear to them
The howl of the vanquished who cherish their defeat.

2

Quesada on the dunes hurls himself at the elements
Howls at the sea, tries to shout down the surf
Pushes against the wind that fathers a mountain of sand
Catches at the sun with his glances
Throws his name away like a rose the surf casts back at
    him again and again.

The waves drive forward against an offshore wind
That turns their crests to banners.
They shake in the heat haze silver and white
Shaken against sunlight above the crack of broken rollers
Driving up the hill of sand again and again defeated.

3

Is there another poetry than the poetry of celebration?
When the defeated are silent there is only the song of the
    victorious.

Who plays on a broken pipe, who dances with a stone in his belly?
Sing holy wanderer, cry your anguish to wind and water.
Who but a Christian would celebrate the broken body of love?
Who but a lover would sigh to be a plaything of the gods?

4

Dulcinea walks
Through spears of grass
Her feet bare
Leaves embroidered about them
A girl in a dream
Quesada dreamed
How will she live
Outside his tortured sleep?
Hear the cicadas
Using their chain-saws
Listen to those birds
That seem to yap like dogs
Look at the vines
Binding her ankles
See where the spears point.
The spring is mindless
The sun is blind
She's a walking garden
Praise her.

7

He said God who gave the wound would give the cure.
He said there were many hours between one day and the next
And in one of them, even in a moment, the house falls.
He had seen rainshine, he had seen sunfall,
He had seen a man lie down at night who could not rise in
        the morning.
Whoever thought he could put a spoke in Fortune's wheel
Flattered himself. Whoever believed there was space for a pin
Between a woman's yes and no was deluded.
Then let Quesada wear his madness like a medal.
Copper would be gold, tears pearls, and westward, look—
Across the plain at nightfall a bonfire blazed for his coming.

10

Odysseus under wet snapping sheets
Quesada in the saddle—all men are travellers
Astride, under sheets, travellers and lovers, they go
To prize the world apart, to learn the spaces
In Circe's cave, on couches of blue satin
In brown grass under summer olives.
As long as seasons change don't look for stillness

Dulcinea, don't ask for kindness or rest—
Only the long reach of the mind always in love.

17

That the balls of the lover are not larger than the balls of the
     priest
That the heart of the miser is not smaller than the heart of
     Quesada
That the same sun warms the knight and the squire
That the long lance and the short sword open equally the
     passages to death
That the barber may wear a beard and the hangman have long
     life
These are the opaque equities of our world.

That the breast of Dulcinea is whiter than the driven snow
That the strength of her knight is as the strength of ten
     because his heart is pure
That the empire of true love is boundless and its battalions
     unconquerable
These are the translucent hyperboles of art.

Where was Quesada whose grapes fattened uneaten at his door
Whose fields were ripe, whose mill-wheels were always turning?
He was beyond the horizon, riding against the sunspears
Remembering the foot of his lady tentative as a white penant in
     the cold mountain stream.

Pictures in a gallery in his brain
Were turned facing the wall, his limbs jolted
Coming down into a valley, night coming down
Sun catching flax and pampas along a stream
A church white in the foot-hills, the dead on his mind
The empty world full of their singing ghosts.

Owls in the poplar candles, a pheasant dead on the road
Thunder over the treeless mountain burned brown by summer
Thunder over the flooded fields, thunder over the dunes
Thunder over the darkened ocean shafted with light
Thunder in the long line of the surf breaking against an
     offshore wind
Thunder in the long line
Exaltation in the defeated heart of Quesada.

Who but a Christian would sing the broken body of love?
Who but a lover would sigh to be a plaything of the gods?

from *The Yellow Sonnets*

6

(17th October 1974)

Spring is a recurring astonishment—like poetry.
So suddenly the oaks in Albert Park have assumed

Their bulk of green, so helplessly I find myself
With forty-two years notched up, my birthday presents

Hedge-clippers, screw-drivers, and *The Gulag Archipelago*—
And as I unwrap them a young man with a pack on his back

Knocks at our door wanting breakfast. His name is Blackburn,
Son of the 7th Fleet Admiral who rained down death

For years on North Vietnam—but the boy went to jail
Sooner than fight, and he's here to study mushrooms.

"He who forgets the past becomes blind." says Solzhenitsyn
In that bookful of Russian blood. "Cultivate your garden"

Say those Voltairean hedgeclippers. The quarrel of sparrows
Fills the silence of God that has lasted forty-two years.

From *Walking Westward*

Art has nothing to do with perfect circles
                    squares   parallelograms
they belong to the will
even the best of moons is hand-sketched
                    effulgence-blurred
but a rough triangle
                    that's different
the Nile Delta for example
or what Antony saw first and last in Cleopatra
a blunt arrow-head of crisp hair
                    pointing the way
down
        into another dimension
only perfect world
                    slippery sided
inward-enclosing
                    welcome
and welcome
                    and welcome
'die when thou hast lived'

and all the perfumes of Arabia couldn't rival what the lady made there
who called him infirm of purpose
talked of plucking a baby's toothless gums from her breast
and dashing its brains out
because he could not use a dagger
would not draw a circle about her brows.

Balmoral Intermediate
                    1945
learned to spell 'principal'
            (distinct from 'principle')
because it was on the headmaster's door
committed to memory that the chief was chiefly an adjective
(despite his great bulk)
                    not a noun
Pemberton
            who told me to ring the bell
because the War was over
            (50 million dead and half of Europe in ruins)
and ringing the bell I was worried
it had been War so long
            what would Peace be like?

This morning a quartz sky   an opal harbour
            late summer gardens in flower
            city of clean edges
and the little boys in black and the bigger boys and the big ones
gathering in tens in scores converging in hundreds
across the Domain   up from Newmarket   down from Mt Eden
staggering
            their bags full of what might be stones
but are free text books
to learn in English 'the 8 modes of language'

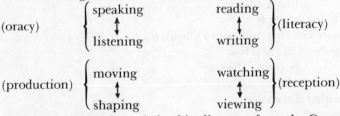

confusion of thought enshrined in diagrams from the Government
                                                    printer
tortured into text-books
small clear brows furrowed with incomprehension
            ' or ruffled in revolt
to be read as failure.

Peace was Korea
                    the Cold War
the CIA
          Vietnam
corruption of action because corruption of thought
corruption of thought because corruption of language

a white butterfly drifts across the tomatoes
a bell rings
              50 million.

October she phoned to say
for her at last it was   over
                          forgotten
                          irrelevant
3 nails meant for the heart

might have made use of the new maths
that has a cold beauty
like the beauty of a fiction

as for example that a survey of 19 love affairs showed
          17 were over
          7 were forgotten
          and 13 irrelevant
          but only 2 were all three
9 were over and irrelevant but not forgotten
5 were over and forgotten but not irrelevant

how many that were over were neither irrelevant nor forgotten?

to which a Venn diagram
viz:

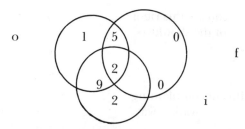

returns the answer 1
(rendered poetically: one only)
              irrefuteable
as to say in the language of another dimension
he had explored with her
the caves of generation and the terraces of the stars

From *The Clodian Songbook*

End of scene Catullus
                                            Cut!
Snap go the wooden boards on the brightest
days
                    when your wants matched
hers
flower-burst and leaf-
break
                                            twined vines
                    and a lurching tenderness shaking
                                            underfoot
your whole earth.

Phone   knock   urgent cable
nothing rouses her now unless it's to tell you
                            end of scene!
you're not wanted nor welcome.

Very well then
it's a hard school.

But you, girl
            have you thought of the long nights
the subtle notations of silence
those spaces between the stars
                    we used to populate
                    with songs and jokes?

            Who will ink poems on your pillow
pile your table with impromptu sculptures
phone you from the earth's end?

                    You see this rigor
                    of the shoulders?
It's what they call
the courage of a trooper.
More than a scene is ending.
                    Catullus uncomplaining
                    walks away.

        Air New Zealand
                    old friend of Catullus
        you offer a quick hike
                    to Disneyland
                    the South Pole

Hong Kong's hotspots
   to ease a jealous ache.

        Thanks brother
                but I'd rather
   you flew downcountry a message to Clodia.

Tell her she's known to her 300 loveless lovers
   as the scrum machine.
                Tell her
        Catullus loves her
   as the lone lawn daisy
                loves
                the Masport mower.

                15

Ianus I'm camped a hundred yards from your bones.
   The moths attack the lantern and die as surely
      as you did on that asphalt strip near home
      we used to burn up with our eager wheels.
   Defeated in love and in my dearest ambitions
   I've come to visit one who took the last blow first.
   The world's sweetest when it offers us nothing.
   Remember our eel-trap that summer polio closed
the schools and drove us north? These tears are happy.
      I wish you manuka on the eternal winds.
   'So long' we used to say, not knowing what it meant.

This May be Your Captain Speaking

Moon moon moon moon this
obsession darkness and clear
light over water the beach
Takapuna winds from all quarters

on vacation small waves
lifting with that breath-
catching moon-reflecting
pause its flash or shimmer

running down their raised
foil before falling the whole
Gulf across to Rangitoto
listening and over it a

huge havenless heaven alight
all the way out to the end
of the ever. But it's the sea's
particular talk these words

spaced out between wave-
break in every of its modes one
beach having one voice settlers
heard ancient Maoris came

upon a characterizing
untranslatable statement under
pohutukawas endlessly
varied endlessly the same.

GORDON CHALLIS

The Iceman

What happened to the iceman after all?
Amazing how we waited for his call
and ran across to pick up chips of light
as the iceman's hook would beak-like bite
deep into ice, which he shouldered on a sack
and carried to our veranda at the back,
invisible the winter halo round his head.

We have other means of freezing now instead
of ice; it only lasted half a day
unwinding summer's waterclock away,
filling the tank, falling on zinc
under the icebox.

      Nowadays I think
the nameless birds outside have hauled
some massive block of silence called
the morning to my door; with beaks well ground
have started chipping splinters made of sound,
have sung me almost unaware how sick
I felt one childhood day, the embryonic
pain of seeing yolk and shell all splashed
together yellow where a bird's egg smashed;
yet pain evolves, perception grows more keen
as fits the many-coloured bird that might have been.

What happened to the iceman after all?
Amazing, how we waited for his call.

The Man of Glass

Your least and lightest movement may be critical—
not only chip your limbs and leave bright shards
but bring bang down your dazzling tower too,
cascading like piano keys sprung loose,
peeled off their cobs of octaves scales or chords.

The brittle crystal structure of your silicon,
if shattered, lacks that green organic knack
of carbon which can give and grow again;
however deft your step a stone may slip;
in bracing for the fall a bone may crack.

There is no wool nor wave will cradle your fragility;
the kindest eyes, like flux of aluminium,
look safe yet have their flashpoint, oxidize
to ash with acrid taste of alkali.
There is no way of sealing all the million

crevices that daylight makes more evident.
By night you are both captain of your soul
and lighthouse-keeper too, at home with danger,
refracting feeling into pure hues of thought,
masking those million fissures still to seal.

Yet you allow no brother-keeper's company
for you admit no brother, who by dint
of thicker skin might ward off chance collisions
(though hedgehogs dead on distant roads at night
are never really killed by accident).

And so I do not fear for you, your clumsiness,
as much as that the heat of my hand may,
no matter how well-meaning on your shoulder,
disrupt the crystals, gripping tufts of splinters,
whilst making you, in my own image, clay.

The Shadowless Man

You have to be quick to stamp out your own shadow.

So first I got to know my shadow's ductile tricks
of transformation: jet-black dwarf, diluted giant
—sometimes both at once—rotated slowly
like clock-hands as I passed
beyond the last street-lamp toward the next one,
keeping double reckoning. Every time I pounced
my shadow dodged adroitly, ducked or swerved aside.
If only I could work one jump ahead, if only
I could beat his perfect sense of timing!

Then one day I used my lethal steel-stud boots
and caught him napping, flat-footed in full sunlight,
got him good and hard right in the guts. He disappeared,
went underground a goner and good riddance.

People said: 'See here this man without a shadow,
a man through whom light shines, lies all around him,
a man more pure than rain and more transparent.'

I, however, fear another explanation:
What if I have not fully stamped him out?
(Perhaps his absence is a mere delaying)
What if the lakes are low, the power failing,
and it is my own night that keeps him waiting?

Thin Partition

Someone next door is moving things about—
dusting the shelves which don't need dusting
making changes simply for the sake of change
or hoping that new order in the room will rout
those evil demons who resent what's new and strange.

Someone next door is singing as she moves—
maybe this tune will mark the turning,
work the trick for years-old resolutions
really to come true; but then she leaves
a word amiss and spoils the spell's relations.

Someone next door is thinking what to do—
wondering what meat to buy for Sunday
or shall she go back home and try again
to hide the fact that there she feels more lonely
and knows the reason yet cannot explain.

Someone is talking to us in her way—
her shadow gestures windlike through the scrim;
my wife and I are hurried, we are going out;
someone next door is asking us to stay,
someone next door is moving things about.

The Asbestos-suited Man in Hell

A homily for saints

I can indeed afford a pause of peace,
a brief abode in shade beneath my cloak
for those, inscription-blind or heedless,
who hope that love still functions, does not choke

like sulphur in the lungs. I cannot say:
'But blow you Jack,' knowing well how far
from fireproof I am. Even this five-ply
cone of woven wet asbestos cannot bar

out heat completely. Nor in this torment
can I claim: 'I know just how you feel'
unless I am to throw away my garment
which, once parted, would not even conceal

a single sufferer beyond the grasp
of flame's bright blind yet finding fingers.
Thus, one by one, my brothers come and clasp
my calves, like children. Each soul lingers

as long as possible but finds small aid
that I should come to hell—and suffer
at my leisure, seeing meantime others wade
in pain—simply to make myself tougher.

And it is easy for me to preach salvation:
'Bring all your burning world and let me hide
you for a little while.' This insulation
shields me from all mortal sins save only pride.

The Inflammable Man

Sequel to 'The Asbestos-suited Man in Hell'

If you should seek my footprints you would find
bright crocuses of flame which mark my way
but signify no birth and burningly deter
the touch of even creatures that are blind.
The scorchmarks of these flowers formed by day
are bleached away at night as if they were

reduced by moon's cool nickel. Inert night
should on the basis of statistics be
a safer time if danger might be met
externally—a spark from steel to light
high octane, camps abandoned carelessly,
the sun through glass, a half-stubbed cigarette.

Such be the hazards which I well might fear
if I could be ignited from outside.
The masks which I must chronically don
are not to shield me, though they may appear
the same as my asbestos friend's; he tried
to keep all evil out but I have long

forsaken such a view of hell and pain;
my masks are worn to stifle what's within—

the rabid flames whose fingers never tire,
which force apart the fissures till again
a new mask must be laid, where one burns thin,
to feed and hide the anarchy of fire.

The Postman

This cargo of confessions, messages,
demands to pay, seems none of my concern;
you could say I'm a sort of go-between
for abstract agents trusting wheels will turn,
for censored voices stilled in space and time.

Some people stop me for a special letter;
one or two will tell me, if it's fine, that I
have picked the right job for this kind of weather.
A boy who understands life somewhat better
asks where postmen live—if not our office, why?

The work is quite routine but kindnesses
and awkward problems crop up now and then:
one old lady sometimes startles passers-by
claiming she is blameless as she hisses
at people present in her reminiscent ken;

she startled me as well the other day,
gave me a glass of lemonade and slipped
me a letter to deliver—'Don't you say
a word to anyone, it's no concern
of theirs, or yours.' Nor no more it was, except

here was this letter plainly marked 'To God'
and therefore insufficiently addressed.
I cannot stamp it now 'Return to sender'
for addressee and sender may be One. The best
thing is burn it, to a black rose He'll remember.

The Thermostatic Man

The world could fall to pieces any moment now;
with luck it won't,
mainly because it hasn't yet. Though cracks appear,
I'll merely count
them leeway spaces left so masses may expand
to meet and don't.

But I, who used to walk bolt upright, this day bow
as meek as wheat:
how can I be sure I shall not always fear
to face fierce heat,
to face the sun, not watch my shadow lagging back behind,
and feel complete?

From strips of many metals am I made. I grow
beneath the sun
unevenly. I cannot cry lest the least tear
should cool down one
soft element and strain the others. I am bland,
bend to become

the thermostat which keeps my spirit burning low.
One day I shall
perhaps be tried by a more humble, human fire
which, blending all
my elements in one alloy, will let me stand
upright, ready to fall.

The Oracle

One-time liaison officer in Babel's tower,
I prophesy in any tongue; and in your voice
I hear both answers—one your question craves,
the other unacceptable. The prophets truer
to their trade would not shirk words that grieve,
nor care to be believed. However, their advice

is hard to come by and, when sought, neglected
like disused diamond mines where they retire.
They offer truth, more hard than any stone,
which trimmed to shape traps light within refracted
but when reduced to crystal thin-ness shows its own
extinction angle, just like any stone; its fire

is swampwards lost back in the lairs of time.
Meanwhile a lesser substance came from those swamp trees:
here I inhabit galleries where coal was mined
and, though the pit's redundant, people climb
down these shafts, like shifts of miners, bent to find
some little fuel for their dreams before they freeze.

Yet my advice is neither coloured black as coal
nor white as ash; the truth half-told suffices,
being the only kind that calls for full belief.
And if I say that you must seek your soul
where waves begin, beyond the hidden reef,
you still may choose to put away the crisis

of choosing till another day, the weather
being unpropitious and the route through pain.
Or, like most, you may interpret me to mean
'go such a way, seek this sign or that other,'
and then you'll thank me, ask what sacrifice has been
ordained. There was a sacrifice . . . You came.

KEVIN IRELAND

Parade: Liberation Day

Think of a tree-lined city street
on an early autumn day;
fashion placards and bunting;
imagine a display
of dripping clothes
drying among the flags and signs
hung from the balconies;
think flags on to washing-lines.

People this street;
create language and breed.
Then think of, say, twenty tanks,
cornering at a terrifying speed,
powdering the paving-bricks;
imagine parachutes, drifting like thistle seed
through the gusts of autumn leaves and sticks.

Now picture the infantry,
young, strong,
measuring with hobnails
their heroic song.
Yet make this song trail from the distance,
though the soldiers are near:
the rhythm is significant,
the words need not be clear.

Think of a happy street
on an early autumn night;
imagine tables and chairs beneath the trees,
and the gay light
of coloured globes,
swaying with flag and sign.

People this street;
create chatter and wine.
Then think of, say, a billion stars,
and a moon darting at a terrifying speed
from darkness, to darkness again.
Erase it all
with sudden drenching rain.

Now picture the infantry,
cold, damp,
measuring with hobnails
the way back to camp.
Yet make their tread trail from the distance,
though they are near:
gently imagine them,
their future is not clear.

Deposition

I cannot
give you words
which turned
as succulent as flesh
upon the nib:

thin men
write gaunt poems
and each word
sticks out
like a rib

Striking a Pose

we'll stock up books
and wine and pie
then stop the clocks
and never die

we'll nail the windows
brick up the door
and live on a mattress
on the floor

if death still comes
we'll strike a pose
and hold our breath
until he goes

A Hidden Message

her kiss on the mirror
was crushed and mute:
why couldn't she simply
leave a note?

I rubbed at her lipstick
and met my eye:
and got the message
hidden away

Educating the Body

when she asked
her sudden: why?
she tricked no answer
from my eye

when she tried
to make me slip
she forced no stammer
from my lip

she tried to joke
to sting to trip
her efforts could not
shake my grip

what should she do
with one so sly?
even my body
learns to lie

A Popular Romance

will you have me?
groaned the frog
my squashy love
is all agog

do you care?
complained the crab
a true heart serves
this horny scab

the prince exclaimed
if you agree
your love could change
the brute in me

they're all the same
the princess said
it's like a bestiary
in my bed

Caroline beside the Sundial

for a fraction
everything was stilled

camera-lens and water-lily

a droplet hanging from a leaf
undropped

the gnomon
idled in the sun

thistledown bristled

you said the dial
said one

for five-hundredths of a second
the shutter gaped

riplets pitched the lily-pond

droplets plopped
thistledown swarmed off

in that tripped moment
daylight blinked

time lay in a tray of fixative

Caroline and Eternity
are linked

A Guide to Perfection

you complain of your body
and make out a detailed list
of what you call your worst deformities

you start at your toes and proceed
to ankles knees bottom stomach
breast lungs jaw eyes hair skin

I reply that this is vanity:
you must have been inspecting yourself
too closely and with too much interest

low self-esteem is not aware
of how to turn this way and that
to show ill-favours quite so prettily

you won't agree: for far too long
you have denied your glamour: you won't
undress your eyes—and so I threaten

to hold you in the circus mirror of my mind
and by distortion warp you straight and show
how neatly blankly coldly perfect you could be

Auto-Da-Fe

yesterday you burnt your olden times:
proposals snapshots invitations declarations

your years of real and fake and flash affection
gusted into blushing flame

your lovers' hands across your shoulders
baked and blistered cracked then peeled away

your grinning moments at the horn-mad beach
fanned hot crackles then twisted into ash

yesterday you gave cruel riddance to the lot
and sent your past loves to the stake

but though I am impressed by ways or codes
so drawn to irreversible convictions

yet I am of that self-same faith which brought
these luckless men to their ordeal by fire

thus should I fear for our remembrance:
confess new fuel to a later blaze?

An Open Door

we forgot to close the kitchen door
a sycamore propels itself inside

spiders dangle from a shelf
a mould begins to mat across the floor

insects moths pour through a shaft
of glossy specks of dust and seed

tangled ferns and trees thrust up
the ceiling bursts the walls unseam and fall

our curtains deck out burrows nooks and nests
daddy-long-legs tinker with our radio

a minah-bird collects your lockets bangles
a weasel sticks its nose into my books

our Woolworth's clock that never used to go
beats like a gong beneath a mossy heap of bricks

From *Literary Cartoons*

15 A Literary Tag

those Romans tagged it right
he thought:
art is long
[and] life is short

but having neatly versed
the nouns
he turned their bearing
upside-down

and compared the brief
effects of art
to the endless torments
of his heart

18   The Literary Exile

he remembers more than twenty years ago
lying embedded to the thighs in sand
on a beach curved at the end like a hook

wishing to catch poems he could salt
and peg out on a line in the wind
to dry like Dally fish

but all he brought in that day was: Rangitoto
rises like an upper lip ... its teeth sink
into the sea's rim ... it gnashes the sun-scaled waves

images he keeps for good luck in his exile:
little nets of words to hold a moment and a view
as he grows older and closer to his past

21   A Serious Literary Slip

when the literary man
went soaring through the evening air
at a legal thirty miles an hour
(or very slightly more)

he had all the slow-motion time
in the world to formulate
a famous well-phrased
final thought

so imagine his embarrassed rage
not at the homicidal motorist
the broken motorbike torn shoulder
bruised wrist

but at the clown inside him
who suppressed his perfect set
of valedictory words and substituted
Jesus, this is it!

30   The Literary Man Observes a Window to the Sky

he remembered the street he walked along
but without being able to tell how or why
until he recognised the place where he had stayed:

first he noticed that the brickwork scored his absence:
cracked soot-dribbled grey: then—more disturbing—
saw how the windows seemed to contain no interiors:

they reflected the sky—as though they outlined gaps
in the walls which gazed at outer space: no longer
could he place himself inside—his talk his bed

his books: yet where had they all gone?
that part of memory which recollected his old rooms
had become a sky-blue window full of shapeless cloud

a two-dimensional illusion—like a film-set—
a false-front a prop an uninhabited sham:
it had become a frame for trick-effects and ghosts:

how could he foresee that it would come to this:
time would disembowel the structures of the town,
and his past become a window to the sky?

A Founder of the Nation

The round, plain, Limerick boldness in her glance
defies the eyeball of the lens:
'Try your worst. You shall see me as I judge.'

No lack of hostile courage in that look.
A childhood of famine, uprising, feud,
dispossession and her uncles hanged

and she had nerve to out-stare
the mechanical wink of the future.
Projecting herself in solemn, prosperous black,

she commands her descendants to respect the matriarch,
potent in piety, sovereign in success,
founder of nations. A fine performance

and a persuasive text: the advance party
of her kin had long struck it good on the Coast;
given their chance, position and substance

had come to them as naturally as their religion.
And why should they doubt it was sure to last forever,
their province astride the colony's pig's back?

When the girl had caught up with them it was to find
a Kumara which had everything: her townlanders,
her church, God's gift of gold, with more to come—

there were still the scatterings of the thousands
who had joined the first rush, ferried
by the skeleton ships whose sheets and chains

and shrouds had rattled the winds at Hokitika,
but whose doomed voyagings had already ended,
their remains sliding out of the old photographs

back into the white blizzards of the Tasman waves,
never to be seen again. Yet at the time it seemed
Providence had found the way to right their grievances,

advancing family prestige towards a destiny pregnant
with municipal buildings, dignified houses, avenues,
spires of stone, industry and boundless commerce.

So, we intrude upon the truth to resurrect
the stifled conspiracy of loyalty, luck, rich promises
and dreams which opened doors to a country girl

leading to a forbidden vacancy in a widowed bed.
Arrogance, cash and obstinate love
held the whole impossible affair together

until it became accepted then almost respectable.
And, since—because of her child—it would mean
the rest of her life should have to be spent

outwitting injustice, it no longer mattered
that the town became deserted, the money was blown
and the men drank themselves to death.

There is no smugness in the way she has gazed on us
for a hundred years, just a matter-of-fact,
slightly belligerent assertion of herself:

if she had fallen, then by Grace and Will
she had arisen, and opinion and institution
could shift over and make room. And, though

the Irish are a remembering tribe and skilled
at casting the first stone, who will now recollect
of that vast metropolis of gold-mad ghosts

the moonlight seduction of a teenage,
immigrant girl by a guardian old enough
to be her father? She was right,

there had been too much running away,
she had come far enough and now she would challenge
the times: 'See me as I judge.' The portrait

that remains testifies to trials and strengths.
It takes nerve deriving from her own to detect
in her glance the shadow of a voluptuous cunning.

PETER BLAND

Death of a Dog

Sally is dead, and the children stand around
Like small white lilies. Someone,
In a terrible hurry, has ground
Her red tongue into unaccustomed silence.
Now, all that was so much living
Lies like a mound of wet rags—freezing
Beneath my daughter's rough excited hands.

It is no risk for her, this going near
A silence she cannot understand.
Frank as forever she has wandered out
Beyond all thought of our complaining
And stands there pouting—puzzled to believe
That one who partners her adventures
Still lies at daybreak in a tangled sleep.

I tell her this is death, and leave
It at that. She does not weep
But runs repeating what she's learned
To all who'll listen. Women up the street
Spare kindness—grief quickens them
Like a cup of tea. Their men,
More urgently, cram early buses . . .

Life bursts into diesel oil and nicotine.
She feels her message meets with mild reproof
And so returns to that child-crowded scene
Where all was black and white, but finds
Someone's removed the death she runs to greet.
Tonight there'll be a burying, and tomorrow
A gap in the world to watch her cram with pleasure.

Mother

(*Died September 1950, Stone, Staffordshire*)

Last night came calling out of the dark
Your reborn image . . .
                    Mother, Mother,
Stretched between two wars and drained
By a crop of cancer . . . I thought I heard
Your brass voice laughing with my drowned
Sea brother. In my dream you nursed

His salt-lungs back to manhood; when
The guns exploded you blew back the waves
From his wrecked mouth. Again, I named
Your loud love to the factory hurt
And council-house heart of England—breathing
The warmth of your hennaed hair
Above the smell of earth. Beside your grave
I danced to your favourite tango and lowered
Your sky-blue pyjamas from the steeple,
While all about me sailors and factory girls
Coupled beneath the trees, and crocuses
Sprang from your buried death's black flower.

Past the Tin Butterflies and Plaster Gnomes

Past the tin butterflies and plaster gnomes,
The home-made garages, the weekend roasts,
The cats' paws delicate in new-laid concrete,
The cast-off sheaths and ice-cream cones
Outside the phone-box, and a mist of screams
Clouding the blue above the net-ball courts,
Past pastel avenues and rainbow houses,
Past father fuelling at the Bottle Store,
Past the Chemist Shop and the Corner Dairy
And the family photos on the kitchen walls,
Past clocks and mirrors and the coloured pictures
Of *Nature's Wonderland*—all sheep and snow,
And home in time to switch the radio over
From *This is New Zealand* to *My Orphaned Soul*.

Remembering England

Often the sudden smell of 'home'
sexed up in some angry northern novel
sours my blood. I remember most
wet council-house walls of pale distemper.
Was there anger there . . . in that fungus growth;
myself as a post-war adolescent?
I taste the damp, recurring thought
of being bred to expect so little.

No wonder, then, that our lives congeal
when we settle here like convalescents
to blink in this hard light and build
our hospital-homes of sun and butter.
What more *could* we want . . . the journey done

and hygiene triumphant over passion?
All that remains is to play the nurse
in this sanatorium for British anger.

Kumara God

Three days and still the slow fogged rain
Drifts inland—all along the valley
Light melts to clusters of steamed-up panes.
All's formlessness—a sharpened will
Won't chip us free of it. It is
A melting back, an elemental drift
Beyond time or season . . .

                            And so I bring
The little stone cramped kumara god
In from the garden . . . Take down the clock
And set him there, upon the mantelpiece,
To be my curled-in self, grown
Old in embryo, slightly sardonic . . .
Feeling around me this slow retreat
Of lives gone underground, of sleep turned solid.

So Many Cenotaphs

So many cenotaphs! As though a people
Had come here just to be remembered;
Finding no other future but to fall
Somewhere else and for some other quarrel
Than that which brought them. So,
To atone for leaving . . . to leave again;
And for that Fall . . . to Fall.

                            So much dead stone!
As though a people, turning back to wave,
Stepped out into their own memorials.

The Happy Army

The child has a vision of the happy army. He
has carefully sketched in my appointment book
the smiles, the fingers, the boots and guns
his happy army wave like rattles. No
one is dying, no one's bad or good
and even the one at the back has a medal

while the generals beam pure love. The sun
has rolled to the ground, has been caught up
in a growing air of excitement that runs
riot, filling the earth with faces, arms, legs
and bits of old tanks. It is natural
that everyone, everywhere, faces the front,
not out of discipline or to scare the enemy
but in frank expectancy of applause. And
of course this is why this particular army
is happy, why no one dies, why the sun
shares in the happy army's happiness
and rolls down to earth. It is why I run
towards the boots and guns, why I come
as far as I dare to the edge of the paper
to stare . . . to stare and to cheer them on.

FLEUR ADCOCK

Wife to Husband

From anger into the pit of sleep
You go with a sudden skid. On me
Stillness falls gradually, a soft
Snowfall, a light cover to keep
Numb for a time the twitching nerves.

Your head on the pillow is turned away;
My face is hidden. But under snow
Shoots uncurl, the green thread curves
Instinctively upwards. Do not doubt
That sense of purpose in mindless flesh:
Between our bodies a warmth grows;
Under the blankets hands move out,
Your back touches my breast, our thighs
Turn to find their accustomed place.

Your mouth is moving over my face:
Do we dare, now, to open our eyes?

For a Five-Year-Old

A snail is climbing up the window-sill
Into your room, after a night of rain.
You call me in to see, and I explain
That it would be unkind to leave it there:
It might crawl to the floor; we must take care
That no one squashes it. You understand,
And carry it outside, with careful hand,
To eat a daffodil.

I see, then, that a kind of faith prevails:
Your gentleness is moulded still by words
From me, who have trapped mice and shot wild birds,
From me, who drowned your kittens, who betrayed
Your closest relatives, and who purveyed
The harshest kind of truth to many another.
But that is how things are: I am your mother,
And we are kind to snails.

Note on Propertius I.5

Among the Roman love-poets, possession
Is a rare theme. The locked and flower-hung door,
The shivering lover, are allowed. To more
Buoyant moods, the canons of expression
Gave grudging sanction. Do we, then, assume,
Finding Propertius tear-sodden and jealous,
That Cynthia was inexorably callous?
Plenty of moonlight entered that high room
Whose doors had met his Alexandrine battles;
And she, so gay a lutanist, was known
To stitch and doze a night away, alone,
Until the poet tumbled in with apples
For penitence and for her head his wreath,
Brought from a party, of wine-scented roses—
(The garland's aptness lying, one supposes,
Less in the flowers than in the thorns beneath:
Her waking could, he knew, provide his verses
With less idyllic themes.) On to her bed
He rolled the round fruit, and adorned her head;
Then gently roused her sleeping mouth to curses.
Here the conventions reassert their power:
The apples fall and bruise, the roses wither,
Touched by a sallowed moon. But there were other
Luminous nights—(even the cactus flower
Glows briefly golden, fed by spiny flesh)—
And once, as he acknowledged, all was singing:
The moonlight musical, the darkness clinging,
And she compliant to his every wish.

from *Night-Piece*

2. Before Sleep

Lying close to your heart-beat, my lips
Touching the pulse in your neck, my head on your arm,
I listen to your hidden blood as it slips
With a small furry sound along the warm
Veins; and my slowly-flowering dream
Of Chinese landscapes, river-banks and flying
Splits into sudden shapes—children who scream
By a roadside, blinded men, a woman lying
In a bed filled with blood: the broken ones.
We are so vulnerable. I curl towards
That intricate machine of nerves and bones
With its built-in life: your body. And to your words
I whisper 'Yes' and 'Always', as I lie
Waiting for thunder from a stony sky.

Incident

When you were lying on the white sand,
A rock under your head, and smiling,
(Circled by dead shells), I came to you
And you said, reaching to take my hand,
'Lie down.' So for a time we lay
Warm on the sand, talking and smoking,
Easy; while the grovelling sea behind
Sucked at the rocks and measured the day.
Lightly I fell asleep then, and fell
Into a cavernous dream of falling.
It was all the cave-myths, it was all
The myths of tunnel or tower or well—
Alice's rabbit-hole into the ground,
Or the path of Orpheus: a spiral staircase
To hell, furnished with danger and doubt.
Stumbling, I suddenly woke; and found
Water about me. My hair was wet,
And you were sitting on the grey sand,
Waiting for the lapping tide to take me:
Watching, and lighting a cigarette.

Unexpected Visit

I have nothing to say about this garden.
I do not want to be here, I can't explain
What happened. I merely opened a usual door
And found this. The rain

Has just stopped, and the gravel paths are trickling
With water. Stone lions, on each side,
Gleam like wet seals, and the green birds
Are stiff with dripping pride.

Not my kind of country. The gracious vistas,
The rose-gardens and terraces, are all wrong—
As comfortless as the weather. But here I am.
I cannot tell how long

I have stood gazing at grass too wet to sit on,
Under a sky so dull I cannot read
The sundial, staring along the curving walks
And wondering where they lead;

Not really hoping, though, to be enlightened.
It must be morning, I think, but there is no

Horizon behind the trees, no sun as clock
Or compass. I shall go

And find, somewhere among the formal hedges
Or hidden behind a trellis, a toolshed. There
I can sit on a box and wait. Whatever happens
May happen anywhere,

And better, perhaps, among the rakes and flowerpots
And sacks of bulbs than under this pallid sky:
Having chosen nothing else, I can at least
Choose to be warm and dry.

For Andrew

'Will I die?' you ask. And so I enter on
The dutiful exposition of that which you
Would rather not know, and I rather not tell you.
To soften my 'Yes' I offer compensations—
Age and fulfilment ('It's so far away;
You will have children and grandchildren by then')
And indifference ('By then you will not care').
No need: you cannot believe me, convinced
That if you always eat plenty of vegetables,
And are careful crossing the street, you will live for ever.
And so we close the subject, with much unsaid—
This, for instance: Though you and I may die
Tomorrow or next year, and nothing remain
Of our stock, of the unique, preciously-hoarded
Inimitable genes we carry in us,
It is possible that for many generations
There will exist, sprung from whatever seeds,
Children straight-limbed, with clear inquiring voices,
Bright-eyed as you. Or so I like to think:
Sharing in this your childish optimism.

Composition for Words and Paint

This darkness has a quality
That poses us in shapes and textures,
One plane behind another,
Flatness in depth.

Your face; a fur of hair; a striped
Curtain behind, and to one side cushions;

Nothing recedes, all lies extended.
I sink upon your image.

I see a soft metallic glint,
A tinsel weave behind the canvas,
Aluminium and bronze beneath the ochre.
There is more in this than we know.

I can imagine drawn around you
A white line, in delicate brush-strokes:
Emphasis; but you do not need it.
You have completeness.

I am not measuring your gestures;
(I have seen you measure those of others,
Know a mind by a hand's trajectory,
The curve of a lip.)

But you move, and I move towards you,
Draw back your head, and I advance.
I am fixed to the focus of your eyes.
I share your orbit.

Now I discover things about you:
Your thin wrists, a tooth missing;
And how I melt and burn before you.
I have known you always.

The greyness from the long windows
Reduces visual depth; but tactile
Reality defines half-darkness.
My hands prove you solid.

You draw me down upon your body,
Hard arms behind my head.
Darkness and soft colours blur.
We have swallowed the light.

Now I dissolve you in my mouth,
Catch in the corners of my throat
The sly taste of your love, sliding
Into me, singing.

Just as the birds have started singing.
Let them come flying through the windows
With chains of opals around their necks.
We are expecting them.

The Water Below

This house is floored with water,
Wall to wall, a deep green pit,
Still and gleaming, edged with stone.
Over it are built stairways
And railed living-areas
In wrought iron. All rather
Impractical; it will be
Damp in winter, and we shall
Surely drop small objects—keys,
Teaspoons, or coins—through the chinks
In the ironwork, to splash
Lost into the glimmering
Depths (and do we know how deep?)
It will have to be rebuilt:
A solid floor of concrete
Over this dark well (perhaps
Already full of coins, like
The flooded crypt of that church
In Ravenna). You might say
It could be drained, made into
A useful cellar for coal.
But I am sure the water
Would return; would never go.
Under my grandmother's house
In Drury, when I was three,
I always believed there was
Water: lift up the floorboards
And you would see it—a lake,
A subterranean sea.
True, I played under the house
And saw only hard-packed earth,
Wooden piles, gardening tools,
A place to hunt for lizards.
That was different: below
I saw no water. Above,
I knew it must still be there,
Waiting. (For why did we say
'Forgive us our trespasses,
Deliver us from evil?')
Always beneath the safe house
Lies the pool, the hidden sea
Created before we were.
It is not easy to drain
The waters under the earth.

A Surprise in the Peninsula

When I came in that night I found
the skin of a dog stretched flat and
nailed upon my wall between the
two windows. It seemed freshly killed—
there was blood at the edges. Not
my dog: I have never owned one,
I rather dislike them. (Perhaps
whoever did it knew that.) It
was a light brown dog, with smooth hair;
no head, but the tail still remained.
On the flat surface of the pelt
was branded the outline of the
peninsula, singed in thick black
strokes into the fur: a coarse map.
The position of the town was
marked by a bullet-hole; it went
right through the wall. I placed my eye
to it, and could see the dark trees
outside the house, flecked with moonlight.
I locked the door then, and sat up
all night, drinking small cups of the
bitter local coffee. A dog
would have been useful, I thought, for
protection. But perhaps the one
I had been given performed that
function; for no one came that night,
nor for three more. On the fourth day
it was time to leave. The dog-skin
still hung on the wall, stiff and dry
by now, the flies and the smell gone.
Could it, I wondered, have been meant
not as a warning, but a gift?
And, scarcely shuddering, I drew
the nails out and took it with me.

Afterwards

We weave haunted circles about each other,
advance and retreat in turn, like witchdoctors
before a fetish. Yes, you are right to fear
me now, and I you. But love, this ritual
will exhaust us. Come closer. Listen. Be brave.
I am going to talk to you quietly
as sometimes, in the long past (you remember?),
we made love. Let us be intent, and still. Still.
There are ways of approaching it. This is one:

this gentle talk, with no pause for suspicion,
no hesitation, because you do not know
the thing is upon you, until it has come—
now, and you did not even hear it.
                                        Silence
is what I am trying to achieve for us.
A nothingness, a non-relatedness, this
unknowing into which we are sliding now
together: this will have to be our kingdom.

Rain is falling. Listen to the gentle rain.

Mornings After

The surface dreams are easily remembered:
I wake most often with a comforting sense
of having seen a pleasantly odd film—
nothing too outlandish or too intense;

of having, perhaps, befriended animals,
made love, swum the Channel, flown in the air
without wings, visited Tibet or Chile:
simple childish stuff. Or else the rare

recurrent horror makes its call upon me:
I dream one of my sons is lost or dead,
or that I am trapped in a tunnel underground;
but my scream is enough to recall me to my bed.

Sometimes, indeed, I congratulate myself
on the nice precision of my observation:
on having seen so vividly a certain
colour; having felt the sharp sensation

of cold water on my hands; the exact taste
of wine or peppermints. I take a pride
in finding all my senses operative
even in sleep. So, with nothing to hide,

I amble through my latest entertainment
again, in the bath or going to work,
idly amused at what the night has offered;
unless this is a day when a sick jerk

recalls to me a sudden different vision:
I see myself inspecting the vast slit
of a sagging whore; making love with a hunchbacked
hermaphrodite; eating worms or shit;

or rapt upon necrophily or incest.
And whatever loathsome images I see
are just as vivid as the pleasant others.
I flush and shudder: my God, was that me?

Did I invent so ludicrously revolting
a scene? And if so, how could I forget
until this instant? And why now remember?
Futhermore (and more disturbing yet)

are all my other forgotten dreams like these?
Do I, for hours of my innocent nights,
wallow content and charmed through verminous muck,
rollick in the embraces of such frights?

And are the comic or harmless fantasies
I wake with merely a deceiving guard,
as one might put a Hans Andersen cover
on a volume of the writings of De Sade?

Enough, enough. Bring back those easy pictures,
Tibet or antelopes, a seemly lover,
or even the black tunnel. For the rest,
I do not care to know. Replace the cover.

The Drought Breaks

That wet gravelly sound is rain.
Soil that was bumpy and crumbled
flattens under it, somewhere;
splatters into mud. Spiked grass
grows soft with it and bends like hair.
You lean over me, smiling at last.

December Morning

I raise the blind and sit by the window
dry-mouth, waiting for light.
One needs a modest goal,
something safely attainable.
An hour before sunrise
(due at seven fifty-three)
I go out into the cold new morning
for a proper view of that performance;
walk greedily towards the heath
gulping the blanched air

and come in good time to Kenwood.
They have just opened the gates.
There is a kind of world here, too:
on the grassy slopes above the lake
in the white early Sunday
I see with something like affection
people I do not know
walking their unlovable dogs.

The Net

She keeps the memory-game
as a charm against falling in love
and each night she climbs out of the same window
into the same garden with the arch for roses—
no roses, though; and the white snake dead too;
nothing but evergreen shrubs, and grass, and water,
and the wire trellis that will trap her in the end.

Against Coupling

I write in praise of the solitary act:
of not feeling a trespassing tongue
forced into one's mouth, one's breath
smothered, nipples crushed against the
ribcage, and that metallic tingling
in the chin set off by a certain odd nerve:

unpleasure. Just to avoid those eyes would help—
such eyes as a young girl draws life from,
listening to the vegetal
rustle within her, as his gaze
stirs polypal fronds in the obscure
sea-bed of her body, and her own eyes blur.

There is much to be said for abandoning
this no longer novel exercise—
for not 'participating in
a total experience'—when
one feels like the lady in Leeds who
had seen *The Sound of Music* eighty-six times;

or more, perhaps, like the school drama mistress
producing *A Midsummer Night's Dream*
for the seventh year running, with
yet another cast from 5B.

Pyramus and Thisbe are dead, but
the hole in the wall can still be troublesome.

I advise you, then, to embrace it without
encumbrance. No need to set the scene,
dress up (or undress), make speeches.
Five minutes of solitude are
enough—in the bath, or to fill
that gap between the Sunday papers and lunch.

Kilpeck

We are dried and brittle this morning,
fragile with continence, quiet.
You have brought me to see a church.
I stare at a Norman arch in red sandstone
carved like a Mayan temple-gate;
at serpents writhing up the doorposts
and squat saints with South-American features
who stare back over our heads
from a panel of beasts and fishes.
The gargoyles jutting from under the eaves
are the colour of newborn children.

Last night you asked me
if poetry was the most important thing.

We walk on around the building
craning our heads back to look up
at lions, griffins, fat-faced bears.
The Victorians broke some of these figures
as being too obscene for a church;
but they missed the Whore of Kilpeck.
She leans out under the roof
holding her pink stony cleft agape
with her ancient little hands.
There was always witchcraft here, you say.

The sheep-track up to the fragments
of castle-wall is fringed with bright bushes.
We clamber awkwardly, separate.
Hawthorn and dog-rose offer hips and haws,
orange and crimson capsules, pretending
harvest. I taste a blackberry.
The soil here is coloured like brick-dust,
like the warm sandstone. A fruitful county.
We regard it uneasily.

There is little left to say
after all the talk we had last night
instead of going to bed—
fearful for our originality,
avoiding the sweet obvious act
as if it were the only kind of indulgence.

Silly perhaps.
                    We have our reward.
We are languorous now, heavy
with whatever we were conserving,
carrying each a delicate burden
of choices made or about to be made.
Words whisper hopefully in our heads.

Slithering down the track we hold hands
to keep a necessary balance.
The gargoyles extend their feral faces,
rosy, less lined than ours.
We are wearing out our identities.

An Illustration to Dante

Here are Paolo and Francesca
whirled around in the circle of Hell
clipped serenely together
her dead face raised against his.
I can feel the pressure of his arms
like yours about me, locking.

They float in a sea of whitish blobs—
fire, is it? It could have been
hail, said Ruskin, but Rossetti
'didn't know how to do hail'.
Well, he could do tenderness.
My spine trickles with little white flames.

Crab

Late at night we wrench open a crab;
flesh bursts out of its cup

in pastel colours. The dark fronds attract me:
Poison, you say, Dead Men's Fingers—

don't put them in your mouth, stop!
They brush over my tongue, limp and mossy,

until you snatch them from me, as you snatch
yourself, gently, if I come too close.

Here are the permitted parts of the crab,
wholesome on their nests of lettuce

and we are safe again in words.
All day the kitchen will smell of sea.

Leaving the Tate

Coming out with your clutch of postcards
in a Tate Gallery bag and another clutch
of images packed into your head you pause
on the steps to look across the river

and there's a new one: light bright buildings,
a streak of brown water, and such a sky
you wonder who painted it—Constable? No:
too brilliant. Crome? No: too ecstatic—

a madly pure Pre-Raphaelite sky,
perhaps, sheer blue apart from the white plumes
rushing up it (today, that is,
April. Another day would be different

but it wouldn't matter. All skies work.)
Cut to the lower right for a detail:
seagulls pecking on mud, below
two office blocks and a Georgian terrace.

Now swing to the left, and take in plane-trees
bobbled with seeds, and that brick building,
and a red bus... Cut it off just there,
by the lamp-post. Leave the scaffolding in.

That's your next one. Curious how
these outdoor pictures didn't exist
before you'd looked at the indoor pictures,
the ones on the walls. But here they are now,

marching out of their panorama
and queuing up for the viewfinder
your eye's become. You can isolate them
by holding your optic muscles still.

You can zoom in on figure studies
(that boy with the rucksack), or still lives,
abstracts, townscapes. No one made them.
The light painted them. You're in charge

of the hanging committee. Put what space
you like around the ones you fix on,
and gloat. Art multiplies itself.
Art's whatever you choose to frame.

The Bedroom Window

A small dazzle of stained glass which
I did not choose but might have, hanging
in front of the branches of a pine tree
which I do not own but covet; beyond them
a view of crinkly hills which I do not
etc and did not etc but might have
in another life, or the same life earlier.

The cat is fed, the plants are watered,
the milkman will call; the pine tree smells like
childhood. I am pretending to live here.
Out beyond the coloured glass and
the window-glass and the gully tall with
pine trees I dive back to wherever
I got my appetite for hills from.

Icon

In the interests of economy
I am not going to tell you
what happened between the time
when they checked into the hotel

with its acres of tiled bathrooms
(but the bidet in theirs was cracked)
and the morning two days later
when he awoke to find her gone.

After he had read her note
and done the brief things he could do
he found himself crossing the square
to the Orthodox Cathedral.

The dark icon by the door
was patched with lumpy silver islands
nailed to the Virgin's robes; they looked
like flattened-out Monopoly tokens,

he thought: a boot, and something like
a heart, and a pair of wings, and something
oblong. They were hard to see
in the brown light, but he peered at them

for several minutes, leaning over
the scarved head of an old woman
on her knees there, blocking his view,
who prayed and prayed and wouldn't move.

Excavations

Here is a hole full of men shouting
'I don't love you. I loved you once
but I don't now. I went off you,
or I was frightened, or my wife was pregnant,
or I found I preferred men instead.'

What can I say to that kind of talk?
'Thank you for being honest, you
who were so shifty when it happened,
pretending you were suddenly busy
with your new job or your new conscience.'

I chuck them a shovelful of earth
to make them blink for a bit, to smirch
their green eyes and their long lashes
or their brown eyes... Pretty bastards:
the rain will wash their bawling faces

and I bear them little enough ill will.
Now on to the next hole,
covered and fairly well stamped down,
full of the men whom I stopped loving
and didn't always tell at the time—

being, I found, rather busy
with my new man or my new freedom.
These are quiet and unaccusing,
cuddled up with their subsequent ladies,
hardly unsettling the bumpy ground.

Double-take

You see your next-door neighbour from above,
from an upstairs window, and he reminds you
of your ex-lover, who is bald on top,
which you had forgotten. At ground level
there is no resemblance. Next time you chat
with your next-door neighbour, you are relieved
to find that you don't fancy him.

A week later you meet your ex-lover
at a party, after more than a year.
He reminds you (although only slightly)
of your next-door neighbour. He has a paunch
like your neighbour's before he went on that diet.
You remember how much you despise him.

He behaves as if he's pleased to see you.
When you leave (a little earlier
than you'd intended, to get away)
he gives you a kiss which is more than neighbourly
and says he'll ring you. He seems to mean it.
How odd! But you are quite relieved
to find that you don't fancy him.

Unless you do? Or why that sudden
something, once you get outside
in the air? Why are your legs prancing
so cheerfully along the pavement?
And what exactly have you just remembered?
You go home cursing chemistry.

VINCENT O'SULLIVAN

Elegy for a Schoolmate

On the other side of the world I heard
That she died in a Newton kitchen,
Her head in someone else's oven.

I'd never thumped her nor called her names
With the others, and so I had nothing
To sorrow or anger about.

                  Her big
Wet-nosed face just the same for me
As if she was sitting in the desk beside me.

Her clothes were always dirty
And she said stupid things.
The stupidest when she was trying hardest.

And I wish now that I'd thrown
A rock at her, had her caned for smoking . . .
Then I could feel pent-up for a day
            And forget her.

But she takes her place among immortal things.
With the potter's wheel at the bottom of a dry pit,
With the hands of Egyptian ladies held like thin,
    brown leaves,
Their collars of beaten gold, and a basalt dog.

Which Wing the Angel Chooses

Which wing the angel chooses
To flick us with, michaelean
Or post-satanic, is no casual quibble,
No field for aged divines to pasture on.
It is a thought our minds are hot with.

Provocation at the purest corners,
White vision in riot's crowded market,
You walk like the demon in medieval dream,
Saint to the eye, until night unbuttons
Your true intent.

Then oh your body burns like a candle flame,
Raises desire like an eager Lazarus,
While your crossings, all left-handed,
Your vestments black, draw blood
Like a thread of silk through coldest veins.

Conundrum, succubus, terror to small hours,
Daylight's appraisal places you again
In gothic niche, sets you on mind's reredos
Ready to summon prayer, promise
In your steady eye of gentler ways.

Like this, you could stand naked
In a crowd, and swing its lust to virtue,
Make temples of your either breast,
Incite to pilgrimage, entice response.
This terrifies as surely.

But to catch you in the quirky light,
One side turned rosy with demonic flares,
The other a jacket of civil graces,
Is our supplication; to find sanctuary
In your bosom, deceit in your joined hands.

Medusa

Sits at the window, waits the threatened steel
as any common housewife waits near dark
for groceries that should have come at four,
when it's too late to phone to hear they're certain,
to know the boy is pedalling up the hill
and not gone home. A boy who's late—
it could be simply that, so still her hands.

Two or three birds. Bare branches.
A thrush taps on the gravel, tilts its head.
Her eyes, she thinks, could hold it if she wanted,
could make it come up close, think this is home.
Sits there, her hands folded, her lips cold,
the expected blade already on her skin.

A piece of wind no bigger than a man
moves the dead leaves, bends the sopping grass.
A blind cord knocks the window like a drum.
'Perseus, stalwart, honest, comes his way,
his footstep nicks the corners of the day,
like something hard against a grey, chipped stone.'
The stone he says she makes with those grey eyes.
Jade in the dusk. Heavier than grey.

And when he comes, how talk moves like a mirror,
a polished shield, in shadows, then in light,
always his care to stay behind its hurt.
Talks of her greatest gift—to deck out men

in stone: stone heart, stone limbs, the lot.
Turns men to stone, turns them to herself.
'The only way to end, for both our good.'
And like a man who shows off coins or gems
he lets his words fall in the room by ones,
and twos, or if in piles, it's when
their rushing sounds and feels a streaming sword.
Edges in close with that, to do his work.
And all her strength, to keep her eyes from his.

Clown, and all the sea behind him

He's very odd, standing on yellow sand.
His grey and crimson, satin, three-inch diamonds

agitate the smallest children most.
The older ones keep saying it's plain silly,

but they know, these others, it's more elaborate madness.
It's planned before like the concrete tower's planned

to hide the sun in the mornings. See him turning now
like the steps that go round the tower and round the sky.

The diamonds over his heart are stained, like tea
that's spilt on a patchwork quilt, and made it run.

He shouldn't have ever come to the beach like that.
He's got sand as well in his pom-poms,

that ugly stain, and his hat's lost somewhere, surely.
Only spiky hair, a kind of dirty grass.

When you ask him to take a pigeon from under his arm
he lifts his arm and laughs when nothing happens.

'So, he's been drinking has he?' a father says.
The girls are called to come back and his coloured diamonds

go shiny click this way, dark, dark, that,
until he moves so quickly, going round,

he's winding the afternoon sun like a wire on him,
he's a reel with yards and yards of sunset to him.

His costume's gone to his mind. Leave him alone.
A clown, and all the sea behind him.

He's a bird turning his cage to another bird.

The Children

We are the children born
with tongues leafy as old lettuces.

Our green eyes are a fire
that had burned right down before we saw it,

our hands blue
like the Virgin's holy mantle

because we have held them up,
oh, ever so long,
against the sky.

Or brown, from pressing all night
against varnished doors.

When we walk along the road,
nothing ever happens.

The puddles stay as wet as ever,
dust falls from the pines onto our heads.
And the youngest of us say 'perfume, perfume!'
and will skip as the word pleases,
say '*bijoux*' and '*oiseaux*'
and in open daylight
jump at the sounds as though we were in a tunnel.

We are the children
who know the tricks of silence,
the cold minutes stacked to make an igloo.

Why do we think the sun
is a dirty coin?
why do we envy the yellow garters
on the skinny wasps?

Come inside, come inside,
it's late and we hadn't noticed.
Don't you know
the big white plates are watching for us?

I Have Taken a Thrush

I have taken a thrush from my cat,
I have left the cat un-natured

on the carpet, not comprehending,
and given the trees back to the mauled bird.
There is thin blood along my fingers,
the bird's wing is splintered.
Its eyes were bright then dull
while I handled it.
                              Full
with an act no animal ever ventured,
to square the unequal dangers
that rim cat, ring bird,
I have tried to strike *now* from blending
with everything more than now—featured
myself, as usual, PR-man for God.

For Where You Skill

The word I keep near me
like a rich disc of nephrite
I put down plainly for you.

It lies half-in half-out
of light, near your arm on the table
where you sew then shake

what you've sewn over your knees,
a sudden old lady
with your head tilted into shadow.

And then your head's raised,
the pins you hold in your mouth
a barricade of bayonets.

I say jade for my word, bayonet
for yours . . . my fancy envy
for where you skill: in cloth, in steel.

from *Butcher and Co*

Butcher in Sunlight

Butcher in sunlight picking at teeth with a combend
his eyelids half over his eyes
his left hand in his trouser pocket idling

gives late Friday a belch
from lung to lip *ah lovely*!
faces evening lean as a good carcase.

Oh Butcher how Friday latesun falls
touching the tip of your shoes with minute lighthouses
fetches bright stubble beneath your jawline.

For Sheila out the back still dredging beauty
from compact tube phial you're the very man
she could take you in slices like bacon

and no beg pardons. Butcher, her eyes grace you
gross there in sunlight. *You're miracle, man.*

Butcher Talks on Time

'Well' Butcher says 'they're all in for an end
the old stuff with its tall columns
the middle stuff with its pointy arches
the jumble of all the others
stations palaces airports racetracks.
That's the only vision *I* know.
Dust to dust.'
         His cleaver glints
up and down through the ribs. He breaks
the cage, there's nothing to fly out.
(A small blob of kidney in the sawdust
could though be canary's head, gone ruffly.)
Time's the sweat under his armpit
Sheila's quick grunt (lovely!)
it's the thin needle white as God
knocking the figures back
when your foot's right down.

'Well' says B. again 'we're all in for an end.'

Still Shines when You Think of It

Stood on the top of a spur once
the grunt before Sheila sharp beside him
a river shining like wire ten miles off
the sky clean as a dentist's mouth
jesus *Was* it lovely!
           and the hills folded and folded
again and the white sky in the west
still part of the earth
        there's not many days like that eh
when your own hand feels a kind of godsweat
fresh on things like they're just uncovered.

And not fifty feet from the spur
a hawk lifted
        and for two turns turned like one wing
was tacked to the air

and then she's away
beak a glint as she's turning
so the grunt sighs like in church
and even Butcher

                              yes Butcher too

thinks *hawkarc curries the eye all right*
gives your blood that push
while the mind corrupts as usual
with 'proportion' 'accuracy' etcetera
those stones we lift with our tongues trying to say
ah! feathered guts!
And she's closing sweet on something,
death, that perfect hinge.

It still shines when you think of it,

                              like that river.

Hold It

There's a high sweet figure
        inside every butcher

casually bent in his saddle
        lighting up against the wind

his hands cupping a match
        like a yellow stone.

He sits eyes grave as a camera
        his horse carved beneath him.

It's high up, he's sitting,
        the sky behind him, blazing.

Far off the river turns
        like a glass-backed lizard

the hills reach high in the blue
        where a few hawks stud it.

Butcher with luck will cross him
        say one dream in a dozen.

They gaze each other cool.
        Suck the same butt, sweetly.

Do You Ever Consider

In a former life Butcher may have been
so beautifully cut that Olympic athletes
hurried their clothes back on before they were seen
by *those* empyrean eyes,

in front of *those* limbs.
He may have been so priestly faced
a whore couldn't have seen him without shedding hymns.

And there's nothing a man on a dull winter morning
absently over the parsley he arranges neatly
can't have done in the line of brawling, of exotic spawning.

Where you see a striped apron there may hulk a hero
in two shoes the eleven feet of Capone and Spartacus, Don Juan
                    and Captain Ahab, M. J. Savage, Nero.
Between blade and block there may lie the head of Pharoah.

Here may be the horn
                    to outhorn Roncevalles
the boot to fill Eden Park
a heart so chocker with love for all things born
it shines self-contained as a host in a church's dark.
And his possible animal faces may fill the Ark.

        Lips of lords and ladies
        wait for the hands that sprinkle parsley.

Elegy

Today, because I am not dead,
I notice the red handbasin,
the green curtains,
the knot in the veins behind the leg
of the woman who pours our tea.
I see the world because my eyes are open, thus,
as nothing could stir me, being dead, thus.

Today, as you've guessed, a funeral.
The corpse was my first cousin.
I leaned forward in the cold, kissed my other cousins,
the corpse's daughters.
I said to one, who had lovers,
'There is no answer, no consolation.'
I said to the other, the virginal,
'Perhaps, somewhere, an answer.
We must let time drench us, its river.'

A day of a red bathroom,
of two women I have lied to,
of green curtains in the morning,
of bad weather, hills whose cows

mumble in a paddock next door
while the last prayer promises
the last dream:
the new, the eternal, the shining Jerusalem,
eternity brilliant as cow-spit
in the dripping wind.
The usual slipping of the coffin
into usual earth.

The angels whose wings are paper
we can see the earth through.

What Sheila Tells Him, Softly

Let me tell you my love the hardest things to learn:

the eye however it tries does not create the world;
'out there' for all our effort will elude us in the end.

Adolescence does not emerge as the fur on willows
it knocks the living shit from a child of 12.

The lungs choke themselves at the dance of loveliness.
A single petal on fresh earth puts paid to all talk.

(*Pasan los dias, pasan los dias*, know that foreign song?)

No one has ever heard the moon, not even the purest.
'Abundance' is a word makes sense only of food and money.

We've no choice at times but to leave it to flags, to gabble,
if the mouth of the wolf, say, is to shine blue.

My Butcher, you freckle with grief as a thrush's egg
yet for all that think of sky, of on and on . . . .

Let me tell you again. To expect prepares for nothing.

From *Brother Jonathan, Brother Kafka*

8

On the day my father died a flame-tree
with its stiff immaculate flares cupped over
the leafless branches outside the hospital window
said for us several things voice could not get round to,

yet not only and not foremost the riding of life
above the stark branches nor the perfect *Fin*
once the work is done, as though time's shining
is when the match is struck and is over, so.

It spoke, each opening red fist only feet from dying,
of small errors, of morning forgotten by afternoon,
of words taken or words put down lightly
as a glass, or laid like a single log on a fire,

or touched as the head of a child absently
while other words moved on; the looks,
brushings, immediate treasure, the cusps of morning
lifting as sky lightens the withholding tree.

13

To be in a place for spring and not have lived its winter
is to get things on the cheap—it is asking from sky
as much as taking from earth, what has not been earned,
it is food without its growing, pay without labour,

love and not its unpredictable effort
at kindness, tact—in fact, it is how we live.
I sit in a room where each day the heaters
burn for an hour less; I see trees

which I saw neither in leaf nor when their leaves
were called for, prepare for spring,
                  I am like a man
arriving too late for Friday's riddled flesh
or Saturday's dreadful inertia, and then on Sunday
     hearing

a corpse walks on the hillside, shining and placid,
asks 'What's so special?'
              A man in spring
without winter or the fear which is properly winter's
is Thomas's gullible brother,
                  so much sillier than doubt.

32

A young bee falls between my window
and the wire screen. It slips as it climbs at one,
is caught with legs and rough belly against the mesh
of the other. I raise the screen slightly and it shoots

across to sunlight, a small furred bullet.
So another, five years ago, I remember, catching
beneath an infant's singlet and stinging his chest.
The child clutched his breath, looked it seemed with
            appalling

wisdom at those who fussed about him, who
rubbed ointment on the red welt, carried
the bee to the porch in a scrap of paper
and stamped it on the boards.
                        The boy looked and moved

his head to take in the kitchen, the relations,
the afternoon of his first summer, the pain rising
on his body while he still forebore crying....
                    On, on through endless summers,
the look of the boy looking, the bee never crushed.

                        42

Life is a swollen magpie,
half-black, half-white
                    Ezra Pound

The magpie vicious or mute on his chosen tree
blocks day to parti-day, sits there speckling
night with stray pallors until light
again tilts dark streakings as fellow-feather;

he is canny magpie who offered a plate of bacon
prefers to rip deeply at the strings of the wrist;
the bird so feared by mothers who screech vivid
slanders on bright mornings, flap their sheets crudely

at his glassy beak slitting up sunlight.
In thinner light he has glided misread for dove
or for raven's sinister clatter in his frank
singing of guts warmed in the weather....

Yet on best days vision slings about like sun
round a filched bangle as magpie presumably dallies
a little with nifty beakwork on a high-up branch, there,
a circle dripping light as from gold, from offal.

                        43

There is a day when elaborate weathers ease down
to a harbour held so simply in the meeting of hills

as water cupped by the two hands of a child
who then stands, surprised that his hands hold it.

And so today: the air, the mild edging stumble
of sea beneath the highway, along the sand
which is unwalked on since the last tide smoothed it,
a few men leaning or sitting on the rail,

who spit across their shoulders or grab the bar
beneath them as gymnasts about to swing themselves
       outward.
A morning of intimations, on the point of mornings
when the backyard leaves may be suddenly yellow

and the cold grains of frost are on the steps like salt.
There is this delicate pause which is intricate, turning,
the day which is pivot to commissioned seasons.
I write it to let you know why I cup my hands.

From *The Pilate Tapes*
liberal

Consider this:
    A man who feels for the people.
    A friend to the ill-favoured.
    Never a word against the bar-
barians assuming Roman dress.

Reconcile this:
    A believer in man's potential.
    A voice raised against the games
    where human flesh is sport.
A man whose eyes fill at music.

You might at least concede:
    No man went hungry from my door.
    No woman was molested.
    No child was imposed on.
Humanitas inevitable as breath.

I who might have, have
    never raped, pillaged, extorted;
    abused office or position;
    concealed; interfered with art;
stood between any man and sunset.

And yet as you say,
    I have killed a god. I have made
    of impartiality, a farce.
    I have dabbled in chaos. I,
Pilate. Who vote as you do.

Sententiae

A place flickers. It always does.
There is anticipation. There is now.
There is lift off.
               Ergo, I proceed.
3 specks on a low hill
is a universe turning over.
              A girl with her goats
and then suddenly, *Ecce!*
The fat accountant dipped
as the other sheep, then half way
through supper strikes him
                    there's
lolly in this!
           The vanes have swung
completely. E-W/N-S.
Nuts flagellate in the desert
simply to change channels.
'Forsaken' he said on the cross
after all that palaver.
               Boundaries
haunt us Romans as we haunt
the rest. A foot steps
unbelieving—the temple's stuffed.
A woman embraces from habit—
infidelity's begun.
             A yawn
through a favourite poem means another poem.

It is all so small, once we've
left it.
       There is nothing,
no Troy with its splendid TV tatters,
no night's knocking the stars
for six,
        no god planting
himself before this Joker,
isn't a rolled map,
    a dated song,
        isn't raw statistic.

There is nothing we have ever seen
we are not leaving.

fault/line

Think   this. The first modern. The first striker of
        that   flaw across. Past chucked there like a meal we're
    sick of.   Future a hulk we whittle at we shape
        distort.   Your life is your own story—write out
that. The yarn   you spin as you say it, *novus,*
    neue, new.   Just make it. 'Each of you is the
cosmos. Each of   you is His just as much as I. We of the
    Father.& so on.   So on.' (Contract that. Son.)
His two paws stretch   ed. God's crab, noticed? The red
pincers embrace you.   He scuttles you, deftly. This is *grace* then
    making it new—that   fresh word for hunt. Thus the
    one man colosseum.   See how things pack up?
    First Catullus tossing   epic for a whore's canary,
        lyric's quick erection   the Muse's trendy stand-in.
    Now 'I' for 'I', not *Imper   ator.* Slaves high on eternity! *Cae-*
sar snapped like a biscuit   mere quotidian *nomen.*
        From a bored stinking   provincial evening, the torches
        bright clots in the table's   ewers, the bad-breathed
        rabbis, the accountant hoon   wanting his *Lord* strung up!
    How's that for impregnation-   history's guts swollen
with the new order. The borders   already destroyed. Rome
    dwindling to a postcard. Pilate   the slob figure in school
drawings of Easter! ('Raise Him Up'   the centurion ordered. Like
    the irony of that?) Longinus of the   Tenth Frotensis, the 'Old
        Dandies' in the service. He laughs   when I remind him. Says
    grinning, 'Just look what we started.   Unsprung the hinges. Mars,
        Venus, the *Pantheon*, little balls   of dung in ghetto corners! *Dei*
Romanorum. And you at the start, Sir. Un   decided. You, first
                among moderns.'

Rat at the Foot of the Cross

Rat says there is sugar or shit,
The wise suck the sweet.

Jix the great converter
thinks wine or water? So what?

Mr Pilate alone is troubled.
He likes words to stay put.

Yet Rat too gets toey
As the veil rends,

Mr P. edgy as a knife-drawer
When the sky burls up.

Jix is thinking the Company
May have called the deal off.

Consummatum est goes the call-sign.
Rat loves 3 o'clock.

TELEX FOR JIX RE SUNDAY

OPEN YR HANDS REPEAT OPEN
IGNORE TENDENCY TO STIFFNESS
REMEMBER INITIAL PROGRAM
THE ETERNAL FEEDBACK‖ MARKET
APPARENTLY ENDLESS‖ CONSUMERS
ANXIOUSLY WAITING FRIDAYS PRODUCT‖
PROGRESS SCHEDULED GEOMETRIC
ONCE FIRST STONE ROLLED
QUESTION OF TONGUES ENTIRELY
YR DISCRETION THOMAS NO
PROBLEM HANDLED CORRECTLY‖
PARALLEL LINES FINALLY CONVERGE
NEW/OLD MERGER FRESH DEAL
COMPLETELY‖ NO POSITION SO PRONE
RISE OUT OF THE QUESTION‖
SUNDAY REPEAT SUNDAY REPEAT
WELL DONE BELOVED‖ ∞

Them

Clarrie Smythe let's call him there was one of him
in Kotare Avenue I used to see him on my *Star-*
round sitting on a white veranda one hand slower than
the other, a daughter who called him 'Father' as though
old Clarrie gave a gippo's stuff for a bit of side; there was one
behind the shops he was Grace Wallace's grand-dad
that was enough for glory surely without the medals
he was supposed to have;
　　　　　　Arch Cook's uncle who sang on the trams
who took his teeth out so he could whistle a decent tune
was another of them;
　　　　　　there was one in Browning Street

down from the Weet-Bix factory he'd played in the Forces'
team after the Fighting; he liked more
than anything else to sit in the corner of a room
and hear someone do a turn on a tin-whistle or a mouth-
organ so long as the women bloody stayed in the kitchen
and no one asked him what he thought as he said
about bloody *anything*. Some good mates had died
for peace so let's have some shall we? (His fingers
mind you the ladies reckoned were ready
like a rake if you didn't watch where you sat.)

There were Clarrie Smythes but not many of them.
They were the old blokes who made sure the memorials
didn't hog the scene entirely. When they wore red poppies
they were letting on there's places bigger than Westmere,
places a danged-sight meaner.
        There's quiet streets though and white
verandas you think of when the poppies are budding in mid-
air and all you want is to get back there in one piece.
They let us in on that one too.
        If you watched them properly you knew
why they liked the reef's spread ink and the mangroves
changing colour a dozen times in a morning and to hold
a fish beating your hands down at Cox's Creek
was as good as an All Clear;
        Clarrie saying *By Christ boy*
it's a corker day knew what he was saying.

Meeting Up

When she walks through the door, at last,
it's as if the very clear line of memory
is suddenly rubbed: reality sets her
older, grosser, than you could have hoped.

You call her 'my dear', she answers you
'dear one'; after all the lies you've exchanged
the currency still floats. Was her hair
ever quite as bright as the script used to say?

That spread vein behind her knee, a kind of
carnation, shall we call it? Yet she's done
wonders since she's left you. Oh, lovers
who matter. Half a dozen new cities.

Another language she can read in.
She drops as you do facts carefully,
slowly, until the medicine glass is full.
You begin to enjoy it. She enjoys it.

You shove the little glass backwards
and forwards. Your lips shine with it.
You dip a finger in it. You write on the table.
Your hands actually brush across the words.

MICHAEL HARLOW

Paschal Transfiguration

Outside the café of mirrors
lambs turn, over a fine plume of ash

the light arranges tables and chairs

the priest sits under his bat black hat
he listens to the widow wake in her white room
he plays his beads
he waits

in the middle of the morning
he appears in the cool doorways of shops
he is a black flag waving from the balcony
he lands on the steps of the church

touched by an Easter fever
he makes a sign
he begins to multiply:

at midnight
a small mark under a swarm of candles;
blood-red anemones bloom in his arms

The Final Arrangement

The guards arrive in carts
drawn by blue horses

they climb down

they squat under the brushwork of trees
in the green weather of the Old City

they pry open the black boxes
they take out the prisoners
they take out needles, thread
they take out the wives and children
of the prisoners
they place them side by side

they prop them entirely in the sunlight
and one by one they stitch them together

Composition in Glass, for

the glass captain who has sailed away
the glass girl twitching in her sleep

this house, glass, wind whistling
in our pockets, tinkling the dark

the glass wish mutilated to pieces

on the wall saint malacoeur dances
behind the stub of a candle, one glassy

eye grinning, & the sea
at the window the sea licking
sleep from our eyes

at this table we are waiting, we wait
for the glass captain to return
for the glass girl to awaken...

The Witness Chair

Take a chair
drag it into the light
colour it
as ordinary, as blue as the sky
around it, draw
a square with shops, houses, a dog
curled inside an envelope
of shadow

Without losing count
one by one
let four men surround
that chair, watch
what they do

Watch, how they break
the legs of the chair, the arms
how they twist the spine-slats
out of its back
the head/rest cracked to bits
how they slip
one by one
into their pockets
a comb, a streetcar token, the stub
of a pencil, a gold ring

Now, tell
everyone in the city
to hide
in the corners of their rooms

K. O. ARVIDSON

The Tall Wind

He said to them, Look at this: you see
Where the tall wind leans against your window-pane?
And they said Yes; the cold has come again.
Which being true, he could not disagree.

Instead he said, If that wind once more blows
Like that, your house will fly away like straw;
But they, of course, had thought of that before.
And also, though he did not dare suppose

They might have done, they'd seen a dead man lain
For laundering on half a fallen tree.
He thought, How strangely that man looks like me;
And said aloud, With luck we'll miss the rain . . .

And just as he spoke it started in to pour.
One of them laughed, and one said, Thar she blows;
We'll find out now what this young charlie knows:
There's a tall wind out there, leaning on our door.

Fish and Chips on the Merry-Go-Round

In caves with a single purpose
Fish were drawn deliberately
From room to room.
Pallid Romans employed them
In a kind of masonry.
They even had their own day of the week.
Before that, though,
Presumably,
Before the nails from Calvary went back
Like bullets into the dove on Ararat,
There must have been a fish or two
Sharked many a household bare:
Great bloated sunfish, ogling octopi,
Between the bedstead and the hearth with relish
Tearing apart all shining arkless men,
Competing for the viscous eyeballs loose
Like opals on the suffocated floor.

A seasonable peripety assures
Contemporary hygiene,
Symbol and ancestor alike
Hosed out, or splintered off.

Little, or large as eels, fish
Fodder us; best of all
On the six days in between.
They build us up.

Still,
On a slow wheel, sharpening fins
Give glints.

from *The Flame Tree*

You might at one time, when you were young perhaps,
Have imagined that by holding out your hand
You could seize the moon.
Reconstructing the attempt, you might recall
How, silent at first, and single, the moon,
Avoiding your hand that moved like a cloud across it,
Prickled at length on the dryness of your eyes,
And split to a raffish galaxy, rapid and menacing,
Invading you at last through the holes of your head;
Acrid, intemperate brilliance
Racketing
With a scream of engines.
And in dense quiet then, the solitary moon
Watched
As the veins were flooded in your hand.

What gazing now can turn us into gods,
Lightning at our command?

The Four Last Songs of Richard Strauss at Takahe Creek above the Kaipara
1.   Frühling

(Hesse)

Waking's urgency, that sets
the day's track of desire, I deem
instinctive, right as the opening flower.
It surely leads me. Newer the sense of sky,
of skittering cloud, of new winds in the marram
murmuring. Gulls go blithely. And on the terrace,

north, and over the formal lawn,
the air itself sings freshly of my love,
its sweet betokenings, its fierce and morning
certainty.
                    In what sense is it I regret
the harbour's tranquility? Sun upon water,
and small lights murderously encroach
of elements at ease, in subtle harmony.
Eyes against eyes. And my eyes briefly wish
the whips of wind back, and the speed of rain,
the water's winter trepidation. Peace,
and the promise of this rising tide,
betray me; even in such a morning;
even in all this complement I find
to my conviction, fixity of dear pain,
anguish of the rose unfolding
in beauty once again.
                    But the time
does lead me; and I breathe
consuming fragrances.

2. September

(Hesse)

I am assembled here, at ease
in foreboding. I have measured the shadow
dying, and the brilliant wind
is alive with new things, lambs and petals and light,
asserting permanence. And yet,
this little thrush, that madly
flew through the scents of newness, now
grows cold within my hand. Strange noon,
to smite so casually, to freeze so small a thing
and drop it on warm grass!
I watched this little bird. It sped like a thistle
recklessly, bucketing on the air,
and very loud: implying, I think,
mortality, because I watched it all the way
from the long soft grass through that abandonment
to the tree so landmark-large, to the last and sudden
blindness, staggering ecstasy, light
singing
        death.
                    I am assembled here, at ease
in foreboding. And my desire?
My love should bury this with love.

My love would not. My love would
toss it in the air.

3. Im Abendrot

(von Eichendorff)

The far Brynderwyns heave across the harbour,
rising upon the second tide, mountains
in mangrove moving, weaving
the last complexities of the sun. These
are a tangle of reflections. Over them,
the next peninsula shines yellow,
pastoral century of slow change,
and the roofs of pioneers, like beacons, prophesy
the imminence of fishermen, their lights
alive and casting, quick
to be out before the strong tide sucks and runs.

> I sing of our long voyaging,
> and you who led me, at my side;
> I sing the saddest of all things;
> I sing the unaccomplished bride.

The hills will cease to float soon, and the mangroves
ripple themselves away.
The wandering flames of grass will calm, and the cattle
boom night's gullies up and down. My lights
will anchor a headland. Boats will take bearings,
seeking the channel; and then,
the Kaipara will move out.
A shag clap-claps in shallows.
I point the way to an open sea,
though all my doors are closed,
and I within.

> Go slowly, sun. A gentle death
> of day is in the birds that wheel
> in clouds to their accustomed rest,
> and in the racing of the keel
>
> before the racing of the tide,
> and in the crowding of dark trees.
> I sing the unaccomplished bride.
> I sing my death in all of these.

4. Beim Schlafengehen

(Hesse)

The fire of darkness, battle and desire,
the rising blood. Without, within,
sounds of continuance. The cattle do not sleep;

a lost bird quavers over the water, cautious,
ill at ease; the sheep in random companies huddle,
munching. Music overwhelms me, builds
and dissipates; my harbour, rising and falling,
song and ambience.
        Strange old man, man of my hemisphere,
spinning your daughters still, in such age,
deftly out of time and the lapse of time!
Tainted in wars, surviving; cause and cure;
your face unchanging—love alone, there? or music
richly ambiguous?—beauty with burden, beast
fulfilled and not fulfilled
in yearning. So am I.
        Northern, I think
you did not care for the dog-star greatly,
or else it rose in one eye, set in the other.
Here, still paradox, smiling and murdering,
restless lights locked in a softening cave
with sound that kills. Alarming spectre;
the sweetness of despair, the sandstone washed
and falling all aflame, its granite change,
and caught in fondling only, like a flower.

Of love elector and disposer,
of war creator and composer,
this music evades the season and month and hour.

RIEMKE ENSING

From *Topographies*

Already 5 drownings 32
rescues & various mishaps this season.

On the older map there are two houses.
Pine trees are also indicated.

Some things are constant
for a while.

Clouds scud past the moment-
ary sun. We are caught
up in the drift of things.

17 January 1982   This is the second Sunday after
Epiphany. You are locked in the sky,
on your journey east. I'm walking
west into the sun. The hills leave
awesome shapes against the red.

There is someone down there
weaving on the loom of the sea.
The currents shoot back and forth
the undertow shuttles in three
directions to pattern a fabric
of terror & joy.

What do you think of the weaving
I ask James. From where I stand
the foam & water crashes
an amazing spread of crochet.
I like his image. He tells me
use it.

You note the Greeks keep appearing oddly
congruous in this landscape.
Penelope & Orpheus. The memories
of Odysseus haunting rock
& shadows. Something old
here. Older.

As the poem has waited for the door
So the hills here also wait
and there is something ominous
in the way they bend their back.
The moment is there in the first curve
the rock follows, the bald blackness
cut by storm and scored to sharp-
edged presence.

You learn folk-lore here
and magic. Legends from the shapes
of stone. Where the stream takes a bend
you sense a message shifting
on the stretch of sand where the fires
burned and the wind whirls
in a column of glass. Yesterday
a house gutted. Today already
kikuyu through the ashes.

At night you notice how close the stars
are / and how they seem to breathe.

Northern Building Society Office Showing Police Headquarters, Auckland

If I told you corner of Grey
and Mayoral Drive just opposite
the Carpenters Arms and left
of Cook street where the markets are
you'd still have no idea
how this building shapes
itself squarely and not too tall
in the lee of the nineteenth century
tower telling you it's three o'clock
and the fountain tumbles over the green
copper slate brighter than summer
pollard showing off in the mirror
glass.
The only worry is the way
the sun reflects what you don't want
to see this blue day—
a concrete cloud.

MICHAEL JACKSON

Art Market: Leopoldville

Taking this painting at an appropriate distance
I see my critical eye was a loaded dice
in an empty cup looking for a winner
and his face comes back to me
the black fellow who spoke of poverty
and sat down as I sipped an iced martini
near the market, first day of the rains.

The four-month drought had broken
they said, as usual, according to a full moon
and when the downpour and the grey skies came
I knew the clouds in the blue one day before
must have inspired in me an old nostalgia
remembering closed windows, curtains drawn
in a warm room, and friends arriving to talk
and stay and hear Beethoven in the afternoon.

The painting is of a flood, a sunset
reminiscent of Turner, and some crudely delineated
fishing traps, giving on to a canoe
and its lonely occupant pushing an oar,
and it's a bad painting, lacks composition
and the colouring is poor,
water and sky contradicting, in fact
the whole thing the work of an amateur
and not worth nine hundred francs.

Yet that is what I gave and would have given
   more,
the first price named, broke as I was
when he bargained for bread,
and my head reeling with booze
told me against it as I said
I'll take it, you've a lot to learn
but you're young, hungry and untaught
and I've only money in Africa to burn.

Fille de Joie: Congo

Lips caked with lipstick
And the smell of booze

You dance with the man of ten thousand francs
Until the music moves him to
Take you to the room where the rite will be.

Preferring him not
To put out the light
You remove a bonnet of dead women's hair
Beneath which you jealously preserve
Stiff twirls of the African *coiffure*.

Down to your silken underthings
Breasts astir
And his own undoing scarcely seen
You are the cur under midnight heat
Of a mad dog doing it
For what in Europe would have been love.

Return from Luluabourg

My report is not of schools
we built out there, or market gardens
planted to help the poor
but of an evening after work
when through a ruined iron gate I saw
a garden overgrown with weeds
and entered it.

Before me rusted boats, swings
dislodged like giants on a dungeon rack,
seesaws split, unpainted, thrown aside,
a wall from which I could not turn my back,
my own hands tied.

That concrete prison drop was set
with broken glass along the top,
bottles once put to European lips
at evening on a *patio*.
I climbed a metal staircase,
looked across a land scarred red,
huts roofed with grass on which
bone-like manioc roots were dried
to rid them of their arsenic.

But poisons which had touched that place
still kept it out of bounds;
pleasures had gone; children's voices

were not heard
except beyond that wall, in villages
or in the dusk, the garden, one night bird.

Initiation at Firawa

It is better now that time
has re-entered this country, decked
in a mask, marked by the hurried syllables
of drumming;
the girls' plaits (secured by white shells
and beaded headbands) are
cultivated fields, their hands are wings,
their feet the impatient mimicry
of nightjars' courting.

The day drifts into the dark
and we are not ourselves;
in mask, dancing, drumming,
by identical fires parade
our ancestors in a shadow world.

Shape-Shifter

They said it was you
changed into a leopard, devoured
your neighbours' cattle,
and at this remove I think it likely;
you regarded even me
as part of your domain.

But I cannot prove a thing;
only that girl's death, not long before
I left, invites comparison.
I believe the boy
who glimpsed you in the bush,
half-man, half-animal,

In the dusk confirmed
something of your truth and ours;
and innocent like him
I ought to speak out now
and say I saw you too, dragging
her bloodied carcass through the trees.

A Marriage

In a room of black enamel, gold
filigree, two schemed to love;
often must they have been like us,
one stood at this window looking down
into a maze, the clouded waters of
the moat, the other recollected
something of that first far meeting,
a hunting party in the White Chateau
and the cold hills near Orleans.

Now it is all embellishment, grace
of swans, eglantine under snow
and barking hounds, is woven on
the legendary cloth that hangs
upon the spontaneity of dawn;
by a lucid river, how could our love
go on? I turn from revery
to welcome you, in whom the sound
of hunting in the forest ends
a pale fox dead on a green lawn.

River Man

Should have a name
months drowned
should be known by now
this pilfered remnant of a man
they pulled from the river

Should have a wife a girl a
mother who has listed him missing
this sack in its cold cabinet
they joke about it in the morgue,
that the eels enjoyed
that snags held up to ridicule
in the tow
that gravel by the bridge scoured
of fingerprint and finger,
whose mushroom skin
was the worms' home

Should have a name by now

But only this stretch of pebbled
water that yielded him,
all night and daylong

elbowing the shore
where tractors haul the eel traps out
in winter, and horses shy.

And his trade,
this lout of the weed and silt?
Scrubbing the stone
steps of the hill,
paving the sky
with the cement of his stare,
and with his pumice hands
rummaging through our lives
for a name.

The Moths

Our house had filled with moths,
a slow silting of lintel and architrave
a cupboard dust,
until I looked much closer
and found the wood-grain one,
the white quill paperbark, the blotched
shadow of a patch of bush,
an elbowing riverbank that had gone deep blue.

The soft perimeter of forests
had entered our house
fluttering around the moon.

Then for five days they drowned
in sinks and pools or seemed to wane
into sanded wood or ash on windowsills
until they became
what they were when I first noticed them;
fragments of a dull interior.

From *Fragments*

iii

Words like branches of a dead-
fall heaped with snow,
foot-prints detour. Birches lean
waiting for someone, some-
thing to fall through.
Then will I know? Hear
a voice out of icy silences,
words other than these
I try to use

as the rabbit tries the snow-
packed ground: love,
death, winter,
an empty hand...?
Nothing will do
but to go back and wait
for whatever is going to break through.

vii

Why I think of a cracked cup
I can't imagine
but the open-pored ceramic edge
where it got chipped
cuts into everything

So best accept it, take it up,
drink water tasting of
rust or tar

I crack
I cannot be drunk from
cannot hold water
convey this river to someone's lips

Dump me among sods
and coils of wire;
let me cut a child's foot
in the long grass.

ix

I think of you walking in the wind
I think of you as the wind

I stagger along a farm road
mud spattering my shoes, rain
beginning to unsling
itself over the gorge

Buffeted, I climb a gate
into a wilderness of green.

x

The wind has no source
no goal
neither is it in the trees it shakes
nor clouds it makes to move

I think of you
and through you to what you lived

Here at Makuri
using another language

And say *te hau*.

xi

The subject of poetry
is not itself
but leaving what we cannot live without

Then in a ploughed field
we see what we were looking for
and lost in looking

Nothing grows here
nothing can be said of these white stones
littering the ground

Memory will seize
on something like juniper, trying
to find its way back to words

I give up the past
and poetry,
walk on across this ploughed field.

Seven Mysteries

Now write down
the seven mysteries:
why you so young and beautiful should die;
why consciousness prevents
escape into the chestnut branches where
foliage goes soft
with God's vermilion;
why what is said is seldom what was meant;
why men and women work, come home,
cook meals, argue and renew
their vows of silence or revenge;
why we were different;
why there are seven of everything;
why I go on
broken-winded like that horse we saw
on the ridge above Waipatiki
by a bent tree
watching the waves roll in.

DAVID MITCHELL

windfall

th oranges in th bowl
really belong
to ward 7.

th nurse/however/has
brought them in here
'fr th children'

they don't amount to much
small, bruised fruit, still
there they are
        on th window sill. . .
familiar suns
against th willow pattern
dark blue & ice
& th 'sensuous rill' ah!
some kind of paradise.

th oranges in th bowl
are/undeniably/larger
than life
      to maureen fiona
             chantal. . .
yeah.
well, she's 4/nearly 5
still
glad to be alive/&

lucky.

     1 broken arm
     3 broken ribs
     fractured skull
     & massive shock. . . yeah. &

she
has lain there 2 weeks
beneath this world's crass clock
in th bruised pits of 'reality'
feeling/'a bit cold'
watching th dust motes dance
in th early sun (as of old)
& considering th gold cheeks

of th oranges . . .
she's lying there/alone/discreetly
watching th sun make time
with its own (as of old) & sweetly!
&
sweetly.

tomorrow th aliens come
th woman & th man
tomorrow is th birthday
(she's forgotten th other, darker anniversary)
tomorrow there will be gifts in th nursery
– – – according to th plan; yeah, looks
'of love'/& story books/with th pictures above
a doll
    an apple/maybe/& a ginger
    bread man. . . yeah. & voices; voices; voices
    from some star . . .
    (she's forgotten whose they are)

potato chips? licorice, darling?
    a
       mars
          bar?

ponsonby/remuera/my lai

th warrior's come home
there he goes!
right
    here
       & now

up queen street
in a gun carrier

palm to th clear brow
in th oldest, most obscene
salute
    & in th eyes
th mandrake root—

th blackened bone.

2 million years
have proved nothing

he did not already know
ah! there he goes!

th kiwi's come home.

he
sits in th barber's chair
'short back & sides'
& he
lingers in th chemist
buying coloured slides
& he
ponders on time/yeah. &
destiny; /
            also th fates . . .
& he
sits in th kitchen
playing poker with his mates
& he
contemplates his hand
& he
holds a king
            to each soft lip
in turn

& th others pass
(& he waits his turn)

& 30 seconds pass
& he
      plays his hand
&
      children burn.

RACHEL McALPINE

Zig-zag up a Thistle

i

A lot has changed here since the day
he left.
Fig trees have thrust up
their chubby fists,
tiny thumbs are dangling
from the sycamores,
cabbage tree rococo
in her blonde embroidered plaits,
fuchsia bleeding pointedly
from every joint.

Some things remain the same:
the cat is happy.

And my fridge is over-full
of half-forgotten love,
marbled with islands of mould.

ii

It's hard to fix your pronouns.
I was happy with 'me'.
Then we made an effort to be 'us'.
He retreated, I had to learn
'you' and 'him'.

I still say 'There are fig trees
in our street.'
I belong to many an us:
the family long and wide,
the human race.
Nobody lives alone.

Romans began their verbs incognito.
I (a part of us) got
two Christmas presents.
A Latin grammar once belonging
to my mother's grandmother.
A four leafed clover
which I keep between
'idem, alius, alter, ceteri'
and 'hic, iste, ille, is'.

I used to have a friend and people said
how strong she was. I sanded
the banisters yesterday.
If only she were here! Her eyes
are nimble and her fingers slick
with putty, brush, plaster.

Today you touched my breast and so
I must be near. Thank you, thank you.
If I could find my friend
I might supervise your loving.

A final decision every day.
I check the calendar:
so far, thirty-two—nil.
Poetry's algebra,
love is arithmetic.
Some people say we are living
lives with a shape.

iv

Sometimes you forget your lines
and have to act them out
again. This time,
should I flatter him, or cringe?

I have had such an urge to tidy up.
But I can work in a mess
and I usually do.

There is no
single perfect gesture,
and there is no amen.
The world will ad lib without end.

v

My children call me Mum.
I see the damn sun
jump off the hills
and fork the clouds again.
And Reagan's let me down:
where's his nerve?

I submit to the children
and the sun
and prod my black words
to grudging margins.

vi

Suddenly there are the words
I want to hear.
Sleep comes slopping,
belly's off the boil.
Please God let me think
like this tomorrow!

But others have also hosed me
with their insights:
Be firm. Be passive.
Be frank. Be quiet.
Be glad.
Each one dirties the one before.

The self-adjusting law of Lauris:
you may not have what you long for
till you cease to crave.

vii

On a dry hill I look
at small brave lives

A lark aspires to the orgasm
of a Pegasus. A ladybird
uses cocksfoot
for tightrope and trapeze.
Spiders zig-zag up a thistle.
Butterflies rely entirely
on their buoyant colours.

No one but the skylark travels
in a straight line.
The rest of us polka and pussyfoot.

viii

A dandelion opens twice,
first to a dominant gold.
Then discarding petals
it clamps up tight,
and leggy seeds develop
in its grip.
And later—froth.

Love must change or die.
The future needs no feeding,
no permission.

It is white.
It happens somewhere else.

Love, work, children.
Angels fly on
two wings.

                    ix

A good decision, that,
deciding to live, and properly.
Down on the beach it's hard to play
the tragedy queen for long.

Fathers watch their toddlers waddle,
lollipops laze in candy togs,
the sea explodes
with kids and yellow canoes.

You popping seed-pod of a world,
I love you, I love you,
let me come in!

Surprise surprise

I expected Sydney women
to be warm, lovely, sensible, lovely,
generous, lovely, and lovely,
lovely,
the way women are.

I expected the men
to have bristly necks
to leave me outside the pub
with the dogs
and to shout me an apron
for a real good time.

I was right about the women.
I was wrong about the men.

Now isn't that always the way?

ELIZABETH SMITHER

Man Watching his Wife in a Play

In the second scene she has to strip
To underthings. It shocks a bit:
The bedroom scene he ignores each day
Sending a ripple through the audience.
Those gestures that used to captivate
Captivate now a wider span
The indrawn breath sucks in his ear
He angrily searches out the sound
He's blasé by the curtain fall
Damn it all, he owns the lingerie!
No acting on the stage compares to his
As he meets her by the dressing room.

Temptations of St Antony by his Housekeeper

Once or twice he eyed me oddly. Once
He said Thank God you're a normal woman
As though he meant a wardrobe and went off
Humming to tell his beads. He keeps
A notebook, full of squiggles I thought, some
Symbolism for something, I think I've seen
It on lavatory walls, objects like chickens' necks
Wrung but not dead, the squawking
Still in the design, the murderer running.
He's harmless, God knows. I could tell him
If he asked, he terrifies himself.
I think it makes him pray better, or at least
He spends longer and longer on his knees.

Visiting Juliet Street

All the streets are named after Shakespeare.
Hamlet and Juliet are separated by an intersection
Down which floats Ophelia Street, very sleepy.
They are all such demanding people
Which lends the town an air of tragedy
As though Mercutio coming home after a party
Failed to dip his lights and ran over
Polonius Street right up onto the sidewalk.
Even Shakespeare thought it best to keep them separated.
At the end of long girlish Juliet Street

350   Elizabeth Smither

With limbs like Twiggy the air grows
Sleepier and sleepier as though
Juliet had anorexia nervosa and could hardly bear
A morsel of blossoms or any sap.

Fr Anselm Williams and Br Leander Neville
*Hanged by Lutheran Mercenaries in 1636 while out of their Monastery
on a Local Errand of Charity—from the Guidebook to Ampleforth
Abbey and College.*

'We'll see who can stick
Their tongue out first for God
Out of you two,' binding the hands
The flowers in the hedgerows starting
The sky turning over with a lurch
As when Brother Leander dropped the eggs.
They wouldn't be back to Compline
The hedgeroses looked askance now.
A swallow passed. Their hands touched
Just the fingertips like passing a note.
The tongues would come out later
Into an air gone blue, a world.

From Casanova's Ankle

Casanova's Ankle

Casanova was turned by an ankle
Over and over. His glance ascended
To towers of conquest, snares set
In the shade of trees. Too bad
He had to toil as well in the trap
To free the booty used
And stained by capture. Distasteful
Somehow what he possessed
When the time for possession came.
It was better in the stalking light
With the moon half-hid
Following the scented glove, the ankle.

Casanova the Technician

Call me in like a mechanic. I can fix
All malfunctions of the flesh
Who cares for love when I subdue
The will to an ache and a place?

Love is for time and I cannot spare
Longer than a ribbon or a song
But am I not more in tune
With the comings and goings of birds?

I was born a technician. Some might call in
A doctor, a quack or a surgeon
Only at love can they call me charlatan
My technique was perfection.

Casanova's Pied-à-terre

Time to take off the dust sheets and go through
The list of black addresses, code
The letters and file them, burn some
Wash the hands in ashes, hope the heart
Plucked from the fire will endure
In someone's pocket. Endure in a laboratory more like
Unless I sleep some nights single
On a camp bed, lamp lowered, diary gutted.

Casanova and the Shop Dummy

Yesterday I saw your torso
Carried by a clerk in a waistcoat
Levitating between alleys and dustbins.
I followed scenting a fish head.
Today behind a screen he dresses you
A tape over his shoulder divides the dandruff
His hands nervous and I observe
A pair of scuffed patent leather shoes.

Madam, I salute you.
So often was the process reversed
But this is proper, your deserts
Nakedness deserves covering in any case.

Casanova and the Residues of Indifference

At the amusement parlour
The fellatio clowns
Taking balls into their mouths
With the o of choirboys
Singing Palestrina

Remind me of calendars
Circles around and dropped clothes
Satin lamps, the latest books

And the night turned back
Like a quilt.

The Beak

He's a little man with a corporation who can say
Private parts as though it's butterfly cakes.
His mouth opens like a scissors and white air
Pours through smelling of ether. He's known for years
And years that words are the killer.
He chooses his carefully then betrays the jury
(Your accumulated experience) to decide.
Some days he calls the tea break early.
We rise to 'Stand for his Honour, the Queen's Judge'.
But he quickly asks us to sit, he dislikes
Honour and such words. Pressing his pale
Parchment fingertips together he says
You, the jury, will look for corroboration, believe no
    one.
At lunch under escort in a nearby restaurant
Where the police escorts amusingly eat through the
    menu
We see him pass in a black homburg, not eating
Himself, or speaking, just taking the air.

What the Dead Poets Know

All the dead poets know that
When you're buried you're in the dark
And they can all imagine for you
The stillness of a corpse under the park.
The sun comes up like a seeing-eye dog
All bounce and golden, faithful
On a leash like a planet, like God
But the poet playing possum has slipped the chain
And lies still, still under the leaves
Under the wood and the plaque and the rites
Frightened at opening his eyes like a child
Counting his fingers like commandments.

Finger to Finger

People comment on my cold fingers
But they are warm. They lay between
His that were white and translucent

In which the small injuries his fingers always had
Small bleedings, missing with nails, cuts
All his large economies, savings
My school shoes, ballet lessons, wasted music
Look up at me, like a leaf looks up at autumn.

Something has Swept over Him

Something has swept over him—not wind or wave
Though their sweeping may be parallel
A man on a beach, but that wave would run
Backwards and his hope would be at sea
To die ecstatically in water one must be at sea
And facing in the up sweep of a wave
To wear this look: likewise with wind
The look's directional: one would need to know
The exact wind path and lie there still.
More like a sculpture, where one plays
With fire of one's own fire that was in stone
And between the two the intent catches fire
Not that exactly but it closer comes:
He joined what he had in reserve to what came
Upon him, which was like the core, combusted and was gone.

Graves as Exercises

Back to each other, graves do not boast
To those in the know, what is written on
Dates and photos are the smallest view
Those that drive away may turn their heads
And see a class of exercises for the inspectorate
Of such pristine neatness—was nothing else taught
But how to rule and write and set things out
Where is the content, where the flight in that?
It is the immediate view the graves intend
Do not scratch your slate, spill ink, remove these blots
Upon these first impressions truth may come
Abacus sky, language grass, laureate sheep
Truth is easy when it is everywhere about.

PETER OLDS

My Mother Spinning

Sit too close
& the spinning bobbin cools you.
Leave the room
& the foot pedal beats
on a raw nerve.
Leave the house

& a thread of wool follows.

Thoughts of Jack Kerouac — & Other Things

I work nights at the University Bookshop:
Junior, Intermediate, Headman, Honorary Caretaker,
Master Cleaner. I work in every conceivable position
from toilets, Foreign Language to Herbal Cookery,

sometimes singing 'Oh What a Beautiful Evening' and
sometimes not. Mostly, I just race about like
Neal Cassady with an overstuffed vacuum
cleaner snarling on my tail, cornering fast on one

sneaker past SUPERWOMAN and gassing like a mad-
man up the BIOGRAPHY Oneway Section—chewing-gum,
cigarette-butts, paper-clips and brains dissolving before
my foaming fury.... Zap, out the back, empty a tin,

grab a bucket one mop one broom, flash back
past LAW, Modern PSYCHOLOGICAL Medicine, Heavy
Granite Colour-filled Graffito ART, Sex Cornered
PAMPHLETS, miles of wrapping paper and up the stairs

to the staff room for a coffee break at 8. Ten
minutes only. Into the toilets, scrub shine wipe
on hands and knees, sometimes thinking 'The Closest
I Come To God and Other Things' and sometimes not.

Mostly, I just thank the Lord for the Detention
Centre Experience many Rocky Youthful Years back
and get the hell out of there down the stairs (4 at
a time), jump over a hot PAN Paperback, switch off

the lights (5 second silence by the NZ POETRY
Section), scratch my backside, straighten the doormat,
lock up, slam the outside door tight, run to the pub
(9 PM), sweat, feel proud, get half drunk,

crawl home, sit down, try to write a love poem
to a girl who works in the Bookshop Office. . . .
Her typewriter and hairpin, her mystery yoghurt con-
tainers, her tiny footscuffed secrets and solitary chair.

E Flat

I've got this flat, see,
& it's got in it this piano
which I don't play,
but I've got a guitar—
you know, the lonely instrument—
& I use the piano's E Flat string
(which happens to be the only one that works)
to E Flat tune the guitar's 6th string.

Now, a guitar's got 6 strings
& a piano's got about one thousand & two,
while, on the other hand, this room
in this flat has no strings,
not even semi-attached.

I guess the E Flat string
must be the loneliest note I know. . . .
But I'm not silly, see—
when I play the guitar
I always pick the chord of D—

well, D Sharp, actually.

BRIAN TURNER

Late Winter Snow

The child has never been older
than in August
snow blanketing the countryside
and we never to be younger
greet the misty morning
sunlight spraying iridescent mountains
across the lake ...
               the birch trees sway
like frail dancers,
strings of light merge
and the violas of night put down their bows
as feet move in search of hands to clasp
and I say
       Lead me not into harsh ministrations
of cruellest spring
or the wells of inconsolable days
but down pathways leaf-lined to summer
in the absence of fog,
ladders of rain.

The Stopover

When the trout rise like compassion
it is worth watching

when the hinds come down
from the hills
with a new message

it will be as well to listen

The Initiation

Use a decent length of no. 8:

make sure you get it in deep, right
to the back of the burrow
if you have to.

Push and probe
until you feel the bastard
trying to squirm out of the way

then when you feel you've got it cornered
shove it in
and twist like hell
until you've got the bastard
really wound up
tight (it'll

squeal a bit) then
pull it out slowly
like you were pulling a lamb
from an old ewe's cunt,

then grab it
and break the bastard's neck,

the foreman said.

It wasn't *that* easy.

Trout

The river runs over
and under him slickly.
The bottom is green
and black and dull yellow.

You can hardly see him
for nature's camouflage; trout,
magnificent trout, darkly
speckled, toffee brown.

He lies and swings
with the current. He
pumps like a bellow, slowly.
The water swirls
and purrs over him.

He edges upstream
till his belly rubs gravel,
then he drifts back
and swings turning
downstream, returning
and sinking to nose
among mottle green and white
stones; then

he floats upward,
pouts, takes the fly
from the puckered surface.

Look out, trout.

A Drive on the Peninsula

Sunlight quivers on crater and cone
and shadows reach across the bays

where a sniping wind sweeps
over turbid water. The children

do not count species of birds
or notice sagging fences and derelict houses,

seem unmoved by what is past and passing
and the freedom of gulls

banking high in an empty sky.
The wind tinkers among flax

by the roadside; gravel squirts
from under the wheels; a kingfisher

flies ahead in spurts from wire to wire.
In the carpark at Allans Beach

I stand by the stile
cold as a nail in ice

forehead wrinkling in the shimmering air
while the sea booms beyond the dunes.

Tree-felling, Upper Junction Road

So rending
to come across a space
labelled death,

to see the
fallen trees,
trunks topped

and trimmed,
lying downhill,
no longer

standing
in the moonlight,
their branches

swaying, hosts
to armfulls
of crackling stars.

Country Hotel

One man with a frown ruining.
his once-young features, one woman
by his side and yet, one hopes,
by herself sometimes,
her body collapsing slowly, partly
because of the ravages of duty,
and partly through simple neglect,
her spirit not-quite-devastated
with weary camaraderie....
What use to ask or wonder
where have they been; what do,
and did, their lives mean
to each and one another.

Now that we should grow morose
and feel a swift *frisson*
at the sight of such ordinariness,
two people who happened to touch,
one day, for one moment
when something exciting broke
and left them reeling.

I can tell you this
because it happens to many of us,
because I know how random
whim and randomness are,
how opaque emotion conspires
to drive insight out the door.

Why, only the other day
I held two ducks who were
not quite ready to fly.
A friend had run them down

on the river bed, and rather
than killing and eating them,
decided on photographs instead.

I do not know, entirely,
what this tells of us, of ducks,
of what it *means*, but what I do know is,
that had it been the day before,
or the one after,
things might have been different.

Ashes

We had a view once.
We stood up for our rights
and we could see for miles
which isn't that far
but it's handy.
          It's a stranger world
now that we belong in the air
and nowhere else. Now we know
what real uncertainty is.
          We're no longer part
of a language of grunts, twitters, barks:
when a human speaks or a horse whinnies
we can't join in.
          The rain that streams
down skin and leaf rankles us, and when
we shine it's not with happiness.
          Now that we're independent
the wind whines and raps our knuckles.
Wind, rain, ice, snow, sun, earth, air,
what other words are there, that count,
except the ones we hate most of all, *at rest.*

Listening to the Mountain

The clouds lift off Flagstaff
relaxing in the sun
while the city gets on with dispensable business.

———

The cumulus jostle but not in earnest
and nor is the wind, teasing the sky's scalp
and ruffling the skin of the harbour.

———

Each day the sun's hauled further west
so there's no question
it's spring.

———

Late, the sun begins to shine
as cloud abdicates, and late
the spirit lifts, at last.

———

At a different magical time every day
the mountain comes into view
and frowns or shimmers.

The line of the ridge
dips then lifts and runs off
into the blue distance.

Sometimes I imagine the mountain
is sleeping in the sunshine,
sometimes I think I am dreaming

the mountain is dreaming
of places it will never get to see,
and sometimes I feel the mountain

knows what I am thinking
as it lies there smiling
and looking down on the city

and the thriving sea, and all
that I shall ever stand for
grows benignly like a mountain in me.

———

The blue burns and the mountains
turn blue and the streams
from the blue mountains flash wickedly.

———

Blue light clashes with white light
above where the rolling hills
are tanned and blistered beneath the sun.

———

A million tolerant stars or more
and one buxom full moon
look down upon the still dark waters of the pond.

————

Whatever I was thinking when the cirrus
touched the tops of the mountains
left me wondering where to go from there.

————

If we listen long enough
the mountain wind sifting through the tussock
will bring the music of water leaping from stone to stone.

————

The lark, so high it's but a speck
in the blue, sings a song to remember
when you feel despair.

————

Celmisia have no voice
except to sing of the flowers
that are not here.

————

The mountains know that many people
have lain among them and listened
to the yearnings that reverberate

from age to age, between the races
and shiver like fire and water, and shake
like stone among the creatures of the world.

————

The river issues from the mountain and gathers confidence.
It has the assurance of one who knows
that it will return to where it belongs.

————

The birds are so curious
they could be our friends.
Only the mountains know

where they have come from
and where they are going
and what will happen when we are gone.

A School Report

Working with these young kids in the pastel
clay frontier, we live near bulldozer blades.
The school I came to yesterday had loads
of children waiting: that was all.
The road up the valley still a shingle path.
The town planners never predicted such birth.

They write short poems, the kids. 'I wish I was rich I
wish I had gold wings I am made out of sky' . . . .
They paint houses pastel, and the houses
smudge. I told them this morning how wild horses
and moonshiners lived here once. Late on today
a group of them made a model city of clay.

A Valley Called Moonshine

The lights in the farmhouses
go out. The inlet is out.

An iron shack on the shoreline
floats its light on the water.

A grandfather up Moonshine
remembers the first daughter.

Dreams are easy. Wild horses.

My Father Scything

My father was sixty when I was born,
twice my mother's age. But he's never been
around very much, neither at the mast
round the world, nor when I wanted him most.
He was somewhere else, like in his upstairs
Dickens-like law office counting the stars;
or sometimes out with his scythe on Sunday
working the path through lupin towards the sea.

And the photograph album I bought myself
on leaving home, lies open on the shelf
at the only photograph I have of him,

my father scything. In the same album
beside him, one of my mother.
I stuck them there on the page together.

A White Gentian

Remember Ruapehu,
that mountain, six months ago?
You sat in an alpine hut
sketching scoria, red
rusted outcrops in the snow.

I climbed some southern peak
and made up the sort of song
men climbing mountains sing:
how, no longer your lover,
I knew it was over.

I thought I'd try out my song
when I returned that evening
as though there were nothing wrong.
Instead I brought a flower down
smelling of the mountain.

Just Like That

So close, the poisonous berries
so close! Lying where you are
right this minute here, so close
you could reach out and pick
a cluster of the orange-red berries;
pop them in like jaffas. You
could be a child again, eat
more than's good for you . . .
Here! like this . . . you could die
this minute here now where you lie.
One two three, that's it,
just like that!

School Policy on Stickmen

It's said that children should not use
stick figures when they draw!
And yet I've lain all night awake
looking at this drawing here

of orange men, stick figures every one of them,
walking up a crayon mountain hand in hand
walking up my wall.

They're edging up a ridge
their backs against the mountain
pinned against my wall.
And every one is smiling.
They know the way a mountain laughs,
especially crayon mountains made of brown.
They know they're not allowed,
these orange men.

Stabat Mater

My mother called my father 'Mr Hunt'
For the first few years of married life.
I learned this from a book she had inscribed:
'To dear Mr Hunt, from his loving wife.'

She was embarrassed when I asked her why
But later on explained how hard it had been
To call him any other name at first, when he—
Her father's elder—made her seem so small.

Now in a different way, still like a girl,
She calls my father every other sort of name;
And guiding him as he roams old age
Sometimes turns to me as if it were a game. . . .

That once I stand up straight, I too must learn
To walk away and know there's no return.

BILL MANHIRE

The Elaboration

there was a way out of here:
it went off in the night
licking its lips

the door flaps like a great wing:
I make fists at the air
and long to weaken

ah, to visit you
is the plain thing,
and I shall not come to it

A Death in the Family

His face is gone golden with the dusk
You would think he burned, he burned

We came without invitation
We did not follow the highways

Trees we went beneath, bending
Then climbed the stone walls

Golden, golden, and he has not spoken
We sent so many missives

Let us go brother, let us go sister
Open the gates, how can we remain?

He will not answer us
His eyes blaze out beyond us

His face is gone golden with the dusk
You would think he burned, he burned

The Old Man's Example

These drifting leaves, for instance
That tap my shoulder
Come along with us, they say
There are one or two questions
We should like to ask you

Pavilion

The house was in the mountains
Perched on the moon's wrist.
We sung, we sang.
I have forgot it.

All day you drew ladies dancing on clouds,
One falling into the open mouth of a book.
It was in the mountains
And I prayed for the swan.
I forget it.

The red pavilion, the red pavilion.
A tree climbed back in its leaves.
Love, good morning,
Your body was all freckles.

The Song

My body as an act of derision,
eating up the answers to life.
There is the bird-song, now,
elbowing through berries while
the hairs in my nose catch
at the little bits of existence.

And I know you go on living
because you need to be cared for.
I embrace you, I kiss you,
trusting in an ordered development,
watching the small explosion
under your wrists.

Oh we survive merely by good fortune,
by random appetite: going
outside to lie on our stomachs
as if we meant to swim in the earth,
floating near the dazed horizon,
giving this music into the light.

The Prayer

1

What do you take
away with you?

Here is the rain,
a second-hand miracle,
collapsing out of Heaven.

It is the language of
earth, lacking an audience,
but blessing the air.

What light it brings
with it, how far
it is.

I stayed a minute
& the garden
was full of voices.

2

I am tired again
while you are crossing

the river, on a bridge
six inches under water.

Small trees grow out of
the planks & shade the water.

Likewise, you are full of
good intentions
& shade the trees with your body.

3

Lord, Lord
in my favourite religion
You would have to be
a succession of dreams.

In each of them
I'd fall asleep,

scarred like a
rainbow, no doubt,
kissing the visible bone.

In the Tent, Elche

Since I need something else,
a machine with gold stars

in it, an ocean tossing with
fish, I hold you in my arms.

The rain was stopping just
as we began to talk about it.
How we complain to enter the earth,
like water falling from its cages.

Red Horse

The red crayon makes us
happiest, selected out with care
and making the outline of a horse
when once it's there complete
a rare delightful business;
then colouring the horse in
red as well, occasionally
going over the edge
but mostly filling up the space
without dismay or panic
and reaching in the box
eyes closed for something more or less
surprising for the sky and finding
deepest blue by accident.

Last Sonnet

There is this photograph of you dancing
Which keeps on arriving in the post.
Every morning I send out the dogs,
But they come back whimpering, broke
Boned: i.e.

The mails always get through.
Anne is laughing.
She turned into a tree.
Jane went to Europe,
A death to rocks and flowers.
Carol has had all her hair cut off.

What do you want, waving and
Waving, your hands flung
Right out of the picture?

It is Nearly Summer

A rubber duck is paddling up the sky.
The world is a constant amazement,
always on the move.
It is nearly summer. It is nearly autumn.

The Kiss

The damp sky is eating your hair.
The day drags its branches over.
There is no beautiful rest in which
you can do no wrong. Give me the teeth,
says the universe. You are neither here
nor there, but walking.

The direction you are taking
cries a low welcome
and darkness sinks its bone
in your shoulder. Under the stars
you are fed somewhat on stars.
Their popular wounds light your body.

A tale of grasslands under the sky.
A tale of hesitation.
The tale of a woman, pressing
her breasts against the window.
A tale of hesitation.
A tale of grasslands under the sky.

The Proposition

the week it
snowed, the day the
footpaths didn't matter,
I wanted to get

a number of things
straight, but didn't:
and the next day, when
people were out

again, driving, you said
let's take ourselves
off, into the country,
to a cave, or that

kind of expedition: I bent,
tentative, over the
table, and cracked my
knuckles: would you

care to be more
precise about whatever
it is you are
saying, I said

The Cinema

The Americans make many spectacular movies:
the surroundings of the town are beautiful,
the lake is enclosed by trees.

The other night we went
to a realistic, pitiless film. The spectators
cried, 'Encore!' Afterwards, we felt
we had risked everything.

Early in the morning, we weighed anchor.
We were on board a Russian steamer,
trying to find our sea-legs.

On shore there were many hardened criminals.
Many fields were under water,
many faces lit by summer lightning.

The Pickpocket

We get on well together.
We vie with each other in politeness,
promising no special treatment.
We contradict ourselves constantly.

Look at those people. She leads him
round by the nose, they are always bickering.
He is nurturing a viper in his bosom:
she must have applied for the post.

But, what a day! The favourite lost
by a neck. We lost everything but the clothes
we stood up in! I wish you
good fortune with all my heart.

A Song about the Moon

The moon lives by damaging the ocean
The moon lives in its nest of feathers
The moon lives in its nest of clamps
The moon lives by aching for marriage
The moon is dead, it has nothing to live for

The bodies are dangerous, you should not touch them
The bodies resemble our own, they belong together
The bodies are weapons, someone will die of them
The bodies will not lack for wings, someone will find them
The bodies are maimed but you will not remember

Do you still suffer terribly?
Do you always speak French?
Do you stare at the moon for you cannot forget it?
Do you long to be emptied of nothing but feathers?
Do you want to go on like this almost forever?

You must abandon everything after all
You must abandon nothing at least not yet
You must abandon hilarity
You must abandon your flags
You must abandon your pain, it is someone else's

You must abandon poetry for you cannot forget it
You must abandon poetry, it never existed
You must abandon poetry, it has always been fatal
It is like the moon, it is like your body
It is like the ocean, it is like your face

What It Means to be Naked

As you will know
the hands join hands to sing

and then you are naked.
Under the snow, the hands and chest

are draped, and with them the belly;
the thighs are pure bone

sunk without trace. Likewise
the eyes,

the mouth, the nose
sink in the face, while the teeth

are left surprised
by the pain which has vanished.

Also, as you will know,
the tongue leaves

its voice and taste to the snow
and the room at once

grows chilly. The hair,
of course, stays on the pillow.

Then the penis is removed
and shaved, as you will know,

and is buried subsequently
in snow: and this latter,

covering the earth is always,
as you will know,

and being no more
than the usual snow

under the snow
the snow will eat it.

Wingatui

Sit in the car with the headlights off.
Look out there now
where the yellow moon floats silks across the birdcage.
You might have touched that sky you lost.
You might have split that azure violin in two.

Children

The likelihood is
the children will die
without you to help them do it.
It will be spring,
the light on the water,
or not.

And though at present
they live together
they will not die together.
They will die one by one
and not think to call you:
they will be old

and you will be gone.
It will be spring,
or not. They may be crossing
the road,
not looking left,
not looking right,

or may simply be afloat at evening
like clouds unable
to make repairs. That
one talks too much, that one
hardly at all: and they both enjoy
the light on the water

much as we enjoy
the sense
of indefinite postponement. Yes
it's a tall story but don't you think
full of promise, and he's just a kid
but watch him grow.

A Scottish Bride

Long division and underprivilege,
sweets in a paper twist; or later,
hiking in the hills, days

like the fizz of flowers in a vase
she carried to a neighbour's house,
a war bride with a photograph of home,

and her own house on a single pulse
of stone, lapped by the tidal starlight.
Whose days were those?

A lit hearth, the flames trod water,
and on the dresser a wedding-cake
ascended like a genealogy towards

the two small figures on the top,
standing beside a silver flower
which gave them back a blurred reflection.

Were those the circumstances
which would have to change? A daughter
rehearsed expressions in the mirror,

choosing the face she might prefer to hold,
another touched the perforations
of a stamp, a profile she was saving.

*You cannot imagine, halfway
across the world,* her father wrote,
the sorrow of the undersigned. Was that her mother

then, who made those numbers on a slate?
Were those her children, almost finished eating,
blowing upon their faces in the spoons?

She Says

She lived there once where you were once,
in coastal light and gusts of stone.
Eventually, she says, you're left alone,
and the place is a gap in conversation.

She says you find things out in words:
the sadness of the emigrating master
is ornament-in-darkness, another sort

of language. The heart might be
a field or river stranded in the window,
someone carving a boat there. Beautiful

people, the landscapes of a friendly land.
The poor are as passionate as charity,
surviving in everything they spend.

The Distance Between Bodies

Sheets on the floor, a stick
of lipstick on the table,
bits of coastline almost visible at the window.

The distance between bodies
is like the distance between two photographs.
The star on the boy's chest.
The girl's head resting on the star.

Zoetropes

A starting. Words which begin
with Z alarm the heart:
the eye cuts down at once

then drifts across the page
to other disappointments.

*

Zenana: the women's apartments
in Indian or Persian houses.
Zero is nought, nothing,

nil — the quiet starting point
of any scale of measurement.

*

The land itself is only
smoke at anchor, drifting above
Antarctica's white flower,

tied by a thin red line
(5000 miles) to Valparaiso.

London 29.4.81

How to Take off Your Clothes at the Picnic

It is hardly sensuous, but having
Eaten all the cold meat and tomatoes
You forget to remove your trousers

And instead skip stones across the river
With some other man's wife
Until, finally, the movement

Of a small wind, no larger
Than the reach of a finger
& thumb, makes it

Impossible, carefully lifting off
Every item of clothing.
Then you may share an apple and watch

From your side of the river
Shoes & socks coming down
To rest on the other.

IAN WEDDE

King Solomon Vistas

1

Gazelle-girl/gazelle
your small breasts leap to your dancing
at the crest of the mountain.

Your feet play upon the brink
knocking the quartz pebbles together.

Your flank draws taut along lithe sinew.
Your narrow breasts leap to your dancing.

The rattle of pebbles down the mountainside,
ankle cymbals at the rim of space . . .

2

You are borne up
by the love of others.
You put words in their mouths.
You the king enter the bodies of women

& speak through them
in the flat
clonic syllables of trances.
Their dark eyes roll up.

They dance before you
groaning your impersonal strophes
clashing their ankle-cymbals.
Their fine joints turn back impossibly.

3

At the rim of space
                    mind's
archimedian point

on which it tosses
itself up & over
                    like the long
flung back hair of a dancer whose

spine cracks like a whip or
a quartz boulder striking half
way down the mountainside
& sailing outward.

from *Losing the Straight Way*

2

That Autumn day suddenly broken into
by pale sunlight   a hearse
glittered darkly across the intersection
between two buildings
which seemed to lean aside
as light drove between them.
& lately: atavistic dreams: flying/
water/swimming against the stream.
If I compound these images
I compound too much since
I know how we like to make dialogues thus
& thus, her voice floating
from her mouth, the bed full of
blood, the second heart silent,
the wave suspended, the
wave falling, the moment before
we cry out, our fires
licking into each other. I know
how we like to imagine this hiatus
endures like the process
it's only part of. Why
then does some vestigial part of me press &
press to believe
there's a price for everything.

3

I imagine the womb as a honeycomb

I imagine the womb as a kind of lung
& the child within breathed into
'part & not part'/stirring as if with
breath in the roseate glow of daylight
strained through blood

I imagine the womb as an early morning
in Autumn   filled
with the weary movements of trees

I imagine the womb as a city
where you might meet a friend or enemy
& be unable to embrace him or
make your peace with him because the crowds
moved on & moved on

I imagine the womb as a universe
& the child as an asteroid

travelling so swiftly it is motionless
across distances so vast it stops forever

I imagine the womb as a gourd
rattling against the house wall

I imagine the womb as a pod
which must rupture to ease the hungers of mankind

I imagine the womb as a kind of deep river pool
in which the river's currents become invisible
unless the eye can detect a dead gnat moving down the surface
unless the palate can taste the timeless alluvia
of what sustains us

I imagine the womb as the blank centre of a girl's eye
which the world
penetrates with its images

I imagine the womb as a honeycomb

as a lung

as an Autumn morning

as a moving city

as a universe

as a dry gourd

as a bursting pod

as a pool

as the pupil of an eye

from *Earthly: Sonnets for Carlos*

1 Madonna

The world stretches out
                        time yawns
                                    your head, lost
hours, on the pillow burns in its halo
of boredom. So what are we waiting for?
A birth, naturally.
                    O forgive me, this

is no light matter... you no she stretches
till your joints crack. You, I do not know you.
She watches little fists & knees in your
belly, I watch her watching your famous
blue tits. She yawns with your mouth,
                                    with your voice
she tells me 'it's not long now', her halo,
lost hours, burns east of me in bed, I think
this lovely strange madonna has no choice

I think that in the end she will whelp you,
biche, it will be so good to have you back.

2   It's Time

A beautiful evening, early summer.
I'm walking from the hospital. His head
was a bright nebula
                    a firmament
swimming in the vulva's lens... the *colour*
of stars/ 'Terraces the colour of stars....'

I gazed through my tears.
                    The gifts of the dead
crown the heads of the newborn   She said
'It's time' & now I have a son   time for

naming the given
                    the camellia
which is casting this hoar of petals (stars?)
on the grass... all winter the wind kept from
the south, driving eyes & heart to shelter.
Then came morning when she said. 'It's time, it's
time!'   time's
                    carelesss nebula of blossom/

3   paradiso terrestre

The room fills up with smoke. Their faces are
imprecise with the imprecision of
their perfect intentions, all that loving
menagerie which the old man's left for
good & which the newborn entered in a
rage & through which he now sleeps: a profound
indifference he will lose the knack of
in spite of love or because of it more
likely . . . oh, I'd be glad if he became
a carpenter & built a house for my
old age: a *paradiso*, well . . . but earth-
ly anyway, straight planks above a plain

or seacoast, the trees & mountains known, high
familiar stars still bright in heaven's hearth.

9

'If thy wife is small bend down to her &
whisper in her ear' (Talmud)

                              —what shall I
whisper?   that I dream it's no use any
more trying to hide my follies. If trees &

suchlike don't tell on me I understand
my son will & soon, too. His new blue eyes
see everything. Soon he'll learn to see
less. O the whole great foundation is sand.

But the drought has broken today, this rain!
pecks neat holes in the world's salty fabu-
lous diamond-backed carapace & doubt comes
out, a swampy stink of old terrapin.

What shall I say? 'I hid nothing from you,
but from myself. That I dream, little one,

10

by day & also by night & you are
always in the dream . . . . ' Oh you can get no
peace, will get none from me. The flower smells so
sweet who needs the beans? We should move house there
into the middle of the bean-patch: a
green & fragrant mansion, why not! Let's do
it all this summer & eat next year. O

let's tear off a piece. It's too hard & far
to any other dreamt-of paradise
& paradise is earthly anyway,
earthly & difficult & full of doubt.

I'm not good I'm not peaceful I'm not wise
but I love you. What more is there to say.
My fumbling voices clap their hands & shout.

17 For a Child who Turned Back

The world's full of the toys you will not
play with ever
                    the old dredge making slow
headway up-channel under its yellow
smokestack (rakish as the dainty rosebud

in an old man's lapel) for instance—should
I be reminded by such visions how
you turned back again with nothing to show
you'd been, no recognition & not

even the minimal gift of a name?
Or should I say I'll always love you
& grieve for you as we do for a friend
good enough to thank in time for the same
savage blow that sets the tilting heart true
again on its fulcrum, so that we send

18

in time a message back, like this, to say
'I love you. You are present, a known weight
upon the tender lever of the heart
to move the world or prise open a way
out of the dream-world. . . .'

The rain drifts
today

untidily on the old gay dredge that
would have been your plaything   & I regret
no single part of all this, but only

that you will not claim your live place with
us
among the unruly facts & fragments
which now crowd in daily through the space
you helped to clear, on your brother Carlos,
on all here who balance with such moments
thoughts of turning back, present embraces.

26   power transformer

Dozens of wrangling sparrows have built their
shitty serviceable nests high up Three
Mile Hill in a power transformer. I see
them every day unscorched & lusty where
they're getting on with it in that airy
crass penthouse with its fine view of the sea,
shouting & breeding among the deadly
grey buzzing conduits . . . oh you were born there
first of all little Carlos, in the mind,
& there you live now in faith & in hope
before a horizon that could skate right
up to you! (closer than *this*, than these lines,
& closer than the thought of love, the 'shape
of things to come')

— let them see/
who have sight.

Precocious spring how beautiful you are!

Let them see
            who can.
                              Barberry puts out
fiery buds early flowers prepare to shout
cold sere hills exhale the yellow colour
of births & marriages: spring, piss, sulphur!
Io Hymen! gorse, broom, lupin, ragwort:
the tough surviving 'noxious weeds' hang out
their crass banners all around the harbour
where this time last year seabirds crashed into
frozen slush

            when memory, a former
lover come to wish you well, left early
went home & wept alone . . . you never knew . . .
you forgot!
            O these battered weeds have flowers
as delicate
            & sweet
                  as any

      37   land-mine casualty Amman 1970

Because he was a man he retreated
instantly 'inside'/
                  His extremities
flipped off: feet genitals chin fingers nose.
Then he was sealed in what was left, a kind
of atavic stump. He had been erased
from the personal familiar surface
of his skin. I couldn't look him in the face.
When to greet him I took him by the hand
or what was left of it it was glossy

as though the gorgeous facets of minerals
were cicatrices.
            He'd become stone
warmed by the sun. It was the kite season.
Above scorching hillsides whose flint scars blazed
his childrens' weightless toys quivered & spun.

                  39

Right now the elm seeds whisper to the ground.
You can hear them. Oh there are other things
that strike first like the city's tawdry songs,

phlegmy hooters. The seeds fall to the sound
of their own whispers

                      whisper coming down
on to sooty grass, asphalt, among throngs
of people who don't hear them, these pale wings
of seed, gliders, thick on the earth, with round
scarlet detonators at their centres.
This sound people don't hear, is it voices,
or bodies touching, falling   or is it

like the forgotten subversive whisper
of blood slipping through the guarded spaces
of hearts set to a time to detonate?

Beautiful Poultry

Slipped it under a mothering
hen while she slept, thought
she might not turn it out
& next morning

her brood was larger by one
which one, 'my one', who knew:
survival's anonymous
& ungrateful & we need

more than that, we need
Beauty, Mandelstam's
'plain carpenter's fierce rule of eye',
intuitive alignments with the Infinite, oh

boy! we say, this egg's
so beautiful! & we gild it, it's
exquisite. It has
a dead chicken inside.

Dark Wood

1

The phrase goes on growing in my head
a tree fixing its roots in me:

            'in the middle of
            the journey of   *our* life'
            articulated

logging trucks hit low gear

down the main road.
                    masts of those hills
riding at anchor on their strata, compactions
                    of generations: the food
of the living

                         whose tissues I hear
tearing before the
bright saw.   the masthead
tipping, the earth-sea
shaking at the fall:

                    a swath
mown through the fleet: a thousand
of them skilfully
                    'taken out': a tithe

of what I think is beautiful
a commingling of elements
though another forest once grew there/

                    but *this* usurping
                    dark wood
where no birds live, where the foot-
fall's also silent in the
sour detritus, siftings
upon siftings
              & a sea smell, piercing,

cloacal.   where fungi
grow like rotten coral from the sea-bed/

                    but this
                    dark wood

's a seeming, a symbol, whose
mystery.
              whose mastery
I enter   whose masts   whose airy
corruptions I enter & am lost in

                    2
              : as a man might be lost
in that space where the battered hull's
held tenderly against the wharf-buffers
where the same deep redolence rises
              where the same light sifts

& the logs
swing over.   the iron tackle
clangs, the chains are loosed.
The logs drop to their allotted place.
They will cross the Ocean of
Conrad's dark heart.
They will be whittled into matchsticks

        & sent back.   little
masts.   mysteries. to light
        your fire.

3

If you know anything
you line the grain up & strike to the side.
I get short ends from the wharf
for winter. I saw them up.
Then I split them & stack them.
The bright blade
breaks the grain   the timber cracks   I
breathe its sea-gasp.
Stacked, a spring tide.   the dark shed
sails in a reek of pitch

        airy fragrance
of destruction.   the wood
burns bright & quick. the
        ash goes
back to earth   the gas
        to air.   A handful
a breath
of what the tree fed on.

4

        If you know
anything.   *in*
-spiration: whatever comes out at last
& must be purified

        again.   I split Language
        to make poems burn.   to have
        beauty usurp
        beauty.   comminglings of elements.
the broken ends of tithes of airy masts
split/lit by little mysteries.   a handful
a breath
        of what the dark
        wood took.

Driving into the Storm: The Art of Poetry

The music leads you out
        into a uniform evening landscape
    with a wide shining blue-
                grey body of water
                        dark smoky mountains
in the distance:
                a pale mantle, breath of its
thousands, reveals the city
                at the far side of the water:
        close up
the white cotton-head dry flowers
                of Old-Man's Beard clematis—
the music takes you out into
                all this—the music plays
    from some radio
                in some house
behind you up the hillside—
                some 'semi-classical'
trash. Next
        it's the
flatness of the landscape fools you, so that
when you first see the mountains
                they seem
        impossible obstacles, until you begin to ascend
when you realize they're lifting you up
into the rainy architecture of the storm.

                All language is a place, all
            landscapes
        mean something. In the back seat
one passenger is taping up his knuckles.
A less violent carload of travellers would be hard
        to find, but we too
                have places we arrive at
and sometimes we can't
drive through.
        We have to
    stop, we must let the hidden meanings
out. The confrontations that may hurt us
into original thought.

                If you've been everywhere
this was worth waiting for. If you've been nowhere, this
feels like everywhere, your free brochure
'How To Get Lost & Found In New Zealand'
            where you stop for lunch at a

'tavern' that plunks you into Europe
         till you get the bill. $8. *For two*! Where you
                  travel through farmland, 'cattle
     ranches' and
'meadows' full of sheep.
                  If you believe this
              you're really
nowhere, the language sees to that
whereas somewhere
                  you're still driving
into storms the mountains are about
to hurl down upon the nowhere brochure
imported trees and washbrick haciendas.
                     Places the earth's crust is so thin
you may even meet the natives
              and be unable to resist buying their wares.

                 The back-seat passengers are checking their
                        helmets and groin guards
and some kind of ignorant fear
         has begun to enter the trip
the way a conclusion can bleed back toward you
through a narrative.
                 The confrontations where
            you stop driving, you get out and stand
under hard rain and feel
storm waters burst through
                   the rotten barricades
of your heart. You're up there
                   you can see
where you come from.
               André Kostelanetz
playing footlight favourites
will not save you now
though not much art can manage such
              immaculate conjunctions, the uniform blue-
grey vista
            awaiting your recognition
     back then, that
trashy muzack

14/8/81

TONY BEYER

Cut Lilac

the dead smell the rain gives
to bunches of cut lilac
in bay windowed living rooms

is another version of the skull
your mouth feels when you kiss
a lover's or a child's clear forehead

but these are impetuous blue
upon the stems that throng
the vase's throat and splay from it

half captive or as free
as wands of light the recent sun
by peering wetly forth outside

has interspersed among them
divining paths like ours in time
that sprawl and gather haltingly

towards the next blind cervix
of the grave the best of us
will shoulder through with joy

Visiting

I hold the glass door wide
and watch my dad lurch crabwise
down the wheelchair ramp

on the flat path outside
between magnolias I am pleased
how well he walks again

he tells me the food is good
and points out which idle men in
wicker chairs are his new friends

who snores and who has
nightmares or the shakes they
all sweat through in here

his gestures are those of an
emperor in exile as he
shows me the ample grounds

where younger patients crowd
the smears of sunlight on the grass
like cultures in a petri dish

but no deeper talk than this
or sign that I am more
than some detached avenger

appointed by the family
to calculate the value
of his head before it rolls

so courtesies are performed
the sugary tea and malt biscuits
crueller than any quarrel

until his mercy or his boredom
prompts a game of pool in
the deserted recreation room

then his battle stance returns
and the eager eye he's tried
on me before and won with

and for an afternoon we stalk
the pockets bickering over fouls
and mock each other's flukes

sharing the frayed infinity
of the cloth between us
while we wonder

if we are saying goodbye

Rain Games

1

no need to look up
or put out a hand
when it starts

it just feels rainy

and puddles go *dip dip dip*

    2

    rain birds on the roof

    rain snakes on the window

    rain horses treading the path

    rain secrets and stealth

    rain accusing itself

    rain changing the subject

    rain the same

    loud rain silence

        3

        I like how the first
        few drops

        play dominoes

        with dry grey stones

From *Surviving the Journey*

3 Word of Snow

as if we swam in air
and breathed sea
this news of salt on the roads

the entire landscape blocked
like your children's noses

and my wife who was born
in your northern
hemisphere can't read

the book of wolves without trembling

VIVIENNE JOSEPH

Woman '77

today I wear my boots
take the whip from the wall
there'll be no more

          moonswinging
          wineslinging
I was once Hecate's cat
learned mythology's curses
from her lap
there'll be no more

          stroking
          hotpawing
and when the light turns on
I'll enter your window
drive you blind
          or mad
I've oil for the flesh
          or mind
but when the cock crows
the grey rat of dawn humps out
I'll go flying
          fur
          wet
          gleaming
deaf to your cries

A Desirable Property

When I open the door & let them in
          the real estate agent quotes:
'Handy to the shopping mall, adjacent to schools
          with a charming rural view.'
It appears that I must play the role
          of Devil's Advocate
I say: 'A woman lived here for years & years
          raising children in the shagpile
watching the hills move closer
          & pressing her dollars with an iron
to make them travel further.
      One day she fed her family daphne leaves & flowers
—a fragrant, though toxic brew—
          after which she cut her throat

the razor was blunt, the dying slow
        her neighbours went about their closeted affairs
and the grass continued to grow.'

'There's no mould on the ceiling,'
                        says the real estate man.

Sex Films

I go to school with my daughters, wearing a dress
                                        (not jeans please)
they giggle in the front row—I, with a sudden
                                preference for darkness
sit at the back, remember books my mother gave me
                                        to be read
then tossed up in the wardrobe with
                                        decapitated dolls
                                        stamp album
                        shoe-box nest of sparrows' eggs
we blew life out needle-holes
                        as bubbles through a pipe
the teacher puts the film on backwards
                                        everyone laughs
                                        the priest loudest
                                        (then he departs)
Later, their eyes night-huge
                                wasn't the girl pretty
                                didya see the flowers
                                & that cute baby
the outside air tastes good
                                as we walk I hold them close
Next day, under a hanging sky
                        we see a dog
running on leaden footpaths
                                his masculinity unsheathed
                                        screaming red
the background suburban grey
                        & not a flower in sight.

By Return Mail

Because there's a Monarch butterfly
                        on my foot
I can't move
                & have to sit as still as a stone

watching that open hinge
                  these freshly-painted wings
upon my skin
                —the advancing army of starlings
their beaks the stab of bayonets
                        here & here
& here a thrush, wild-eyed
                skewers a worm, seems to say:
                    We have our orders....
Your letter is written in another country
    you write (in a house with many empty rooms)
             of how I should leave my children
& join you there.
             My reply must be tactfully-phrased
I will try to tell you about butterflies
             how they feel against the skin—
                of their heaviness....

JAN KEMP

Poem

A puriri moth's wing
lies light in my hand—

my breath can lift it

light as this torn wing
we lie on love's breath.

In Golden Smock, Walking

Is this her in golden smock, walking?
She's no hostage, and he, then so pale and thin,
now smiles so, his brilliance startles—

Her green veil falls and waves
over dust brown and stark
skeletons of trees—

A quiet white world vanishes
under her feet, as she, bending
scatters light from sheaves of her arms—

Out she steps, brightly,
into the unbroken blue
from the cracked shell of her sleeping,

Where he'd lain with her winter-long
and breathed on her
her saffron season.

Cinderella

She lives in ming-blue daymares
And dresses in crackled wax,
She dreams of mermaids, flaxen-haired,
White horses at their backs.

One day she drove a Bambina
Down a narrow cul-de-sac,
A giant grey stallion straddled the road,
The Bambina would not drive back.

She fainted there on the macadam
And revived on a harnessed trapeze,
Flying to and fro over a cobbler's bench,
When the cobbler began to wheeze.

Then, as though through a rocketing slipstream,
She slid into a lady's closet,
Where sloe-eyed cherubs cavorted in silks,
And Freud left five dollars deposit.

O give her robes and plume her hair,
Allow her to go to the ball,
For inside her pocket's a slipper,
And outside's a castle wall.

Atalanta

He keeps tossing her
those golden apples
just as she draws level
with his elbow—

indifferently
she lets them fall.

She wants to range with him
a huntress
and let fly her brilliant arrows—

but she's enchanted
by the slow arc
of his arm
and his enticing smile.

If You're My Friend for Life

If you're my friend for life
don't arrange to meet me as if your wife's
back's a wall
and the field we'll sit in is small
and golden and strewn with straw don't tempt
me with kindnesses your understanding and far sight don't
let me let you take me into the light
on the other side and leave behind earthly anxiety don't

kiss me as if I give you another horizon.
I can't fit you in on a Wednesday between the train timetable
your wife's burgeoning interest in computers
and my contemplation of hedges.
Your propositions make me feel grubby round the edges.
Go back and tell your wife you love her and life and
rearrange your pattern to include champagne breakfasts
and the moon on Sunday mornings.
Go off now and contemplate new dawnings.
Leave me to play the sibyl.

My Return to Czechoslovakia

1

This is my return to Czechoslovakia.
Twice in my life I have felt utterly
foreign, staying in a place.
The first was in Prague.
I felt the need to leave behind me
a book I had written myself
—a present for the people I stayed with.
It was as though time stopped
and I needed to rest, and in their house
I rested. At night I rested
and listened to the one cold water tap
running all night in Prague,
running on and on like silence.
By day they took me by the hand
and showed me the churches, the palace,
the cathedral with the tiny window
up high where Kafka wrote and looked down
and saw the drama of K. and the priest.
They took me in hand and led me
down that long side street by the Vlatva
to a place where on a brick
at the corner of a building
at the height of my eye
someone had scratched the name Dubček.
Because nothing seemed to correspond
I needed to leave something complete
that would stay there,
that would live its own life there.
This is my return to Czechoslovakia.

2

The second place I left a book behind me
was Christchurch, night of a lunar eclipse,
and I sat alone in the middle of a garden
perched on a chair, a singular point
in the whole of the Canterbury Plains.
I watched the moon disappear
and thought of myself as the sum
of all the people who went into my making
—my father's stoop, my mother's hands,
grandmother's hips, my Scottish soul,
doctor, preacher, grocer, weaver,
silent, dead, mad and drowned,

and not one present beside me
to watch the moon turn black.
The tide of everything being born and dying
stopped for a time in the eclipse
and I looked right through the window of the moon
—right through into Czechoslovakia.

From *Poems of the End Wall*

House

Last night as I lay beside you all the desire had gone out of me
and I was cast up like a heap of sand, porous, shapeless, shifting,
a thing of shape, an entity, only by virtue of its million parts.

Here I live on a cliff in a tiny house at the end of the island
and in the face of the wind from the north and the wind from the
      south
I surround myself with this thin wall of wood, this shape in space
and you are there asleep in the bed, curled to the end wall of the
      house,
your breathing blowing shapes in the cold air, your dreams dreaming,
your dreaming holding up the whole fabric of paint and wood and
      tin.

If you stop wanting to dream it will collapse. Your desire to dream
      holds it up,
all the bare longing of the imagination holds it up, the desire of the
      nail
to enter the wood, the desire of the wood to embrace the nail,

the desire of the paint to hide the wood and reflect the light,
the desire of the roof to contain a secret shape of darkness,
the desire of the glass to shine like the sun in the face of the sun.

And the earth desires to lie asleep under the house and dream,
it dreams the very shape of the house as though it was something
      organic,
whole as a body, breathing and seeing and standing cold in the wind.

The house is the container and you are the thing contained.
Its membrane protects you and your life gives it energy
and stops the walls from collapse. And the moment of seeing this

and the moment of saying this are two separate moments:
the first, the moment of seeing is a moment without desire,
at night, by the bed watching you sleep, alone, still, chill,

but not cold, watching, as the silence of space watches the grinding
     earth,
when all the desire has gone out of me and I get up,
get up out of the bed, go out the door, out through the end wall,

and grasp hold of the string on the balloon and rise slowly, steadily,
shimmering like a giant eye over the house, the whole town, the
          capital city,
rising over the island and the ocean, the earth opening like a flower.

But the second, the moment of saying, involves me in the grammar of
     desire.
I have to touch you with my speech to be heard.
And grammar itself is a thing of desire, announcing its capacity

to evolve infinitely more complex systems out of bits of nothing,
to put together the grains of sand to make rock and the rock to build
a cliff and the cliff to hold a house, many houses, a city

to stand at the end wall of the island, the end wall of the land
turned like smooth wood in the yielding shape of the bay
to embrace the random desiring waves of the sea.

Somewhere a child is sacrificed and buried at the foot of the posthole
which comes to hold up the whole house. Building walls for the
          compost heap
I smash a post in half and in its rotted core a weta lies, soft and sleepy,

hiding until its new exoskeleton hardens enough to let it safely live,
to let it grow vulnerable, as earth to light, as sand to sea.
Tonight I embrace you and trust the roof will hold up till morning.

Shack

I read the word shack.
I like it.
It is a good solid small word.
It would be good to live in a shack.
In inflationary times a shack
would be a good place to live.
Welcome to the shack.
It hardly exists.
You are out the exit
before you are in the entrance.
Turn it sideways—
               it disappears.
Just a few upright bones hung with flesh.

The beating brain like a soft bunch
of kapok tossed on a derelict floor.
Love this shack, take it to your breast,
wrap your legs around it, it is the best you'll get
this year, next year, never.
Come, let us put ourselves out on the hillside,
let sunbeat drain and dry us,
windbeat drive out the loving heat,
there's more we can make
when we light up the fierce furnaces
of this rusty shack.
Let us be done with concrete and steel,
plastic and formica and all the festoonings
of luxury and comfort, all the false triptrap
gadgetry of glamour.
We can boil potatoes in the middle of the floor.
We can stoke the fire.
We can shack it.
This glorious tiny unstable living heap
which hugs the hillside.
In a week of looking for the cheapest
chintziest, ritziest, ripoff place to live in town
I got sick in the mind, sick at the heart
like Lord Randall returning to his mother
from all the agencies who own the land,
I was sick in the balls
from the way this city was dressed up,
a series of Christmas treats under the richman's
tree I wasn't allowed to unwrap.
Until I found this word shack.
I took a good bath in the word,
washed myself clean with it,
let its pure language force pour down over me
and give me back the smell
of salt and earth and iron
and the sweet wood smell burned grey by the sun.

CILLA McQUEEN

Matinal

Alice on the croquet lawn
is nibbling   at the morning
high   as a tree   she is
appropriately placed for
contemplation.
                    In the garden
held down by webs
                              anchored on
leaves,
              quiet as trickling
the wind unknots its branches.
Alice goes in   to the garden
leaf by   leaf:
                        such small things
as transparency in the sun's light
move her.
                    The blackbird directs an eye
at veins   under the
skin: she watches a moment, and
laughs her
                    disappearing laugh, unpicking
nets of shadows.
                        Alice's balance
is delicate;
              yet see
the quiet spider journeying
from point to point,
repairing her small wounds.

Living Here

Well you have to remember this place
is just one big city with 3 million people with
a little flock of sheep each so we're all sort of
shepherds
                    little human centres each within an outer
circle of sheep around us like a ring of
covered wagons   we all know we'll probably
be safe when the Indians finally come
down from the hills   (comfortable to live
in the Safest Place in the World)
                                        sheep being

very thick & made of wool & leather
being a very effective shield as ancient
soldiers would agree.
                        And you can also
sit on them of course & eat them
so after all we are lucky to have these
sheep in abundance   they might
have been hedgehogs—Then we'd all be
used to hedgehogs & clothed in prickles
rather than fluff
                        & the little sheep would
come out sometimes at night under the moon
& we'd leave them saucers of milk
                                        & feel sad
seeing them squashed on the road
Well anyway here we are with all this
cushioning in the biggest city in the world
its suburbs strung out in a long line
& the civic centre at the bottom of
Cook Strait   some of them Hill Suburbs
& some Flat Suburbs & some more prosperous
than others
                        some with a climate that embarrasses
them & a tendency to grow strange small fruit
some temperate & leafy   whose hot streets lull

So here we are again in the biggest
safest city in the world   all strung out
ovesr 1500 miles one way   & a little bit
the other
                        each in his woolly protection
so sometimes it's difficult to see out
the eyes   let alone call to each other
which is the reason for the loneliness some
        of us feel
                        and for our particular relations
with the landscape   that we trample
or stroke with our toes or eat or lick
tenderly or pull apart
                                and love   like an
old familiar lover who fits us
curve to curve   and hate because it
knows us & knows our weakness
We're calling fiercely to each other
through the muffled spaces   grateful for
any wrist-brush
                        cut of mind or touch of music,
lightning in the intimate weather of the soul.

To Ben, at the Lake

See, Ben, the water
has a strong soft skin,
and all the insects dance
and jump about on it—
for them it's safe as
springy turf. You see,
it is a matter of ensuring
that you are lighter
than the medium you
walk on: in other words,
first check your meniscus.
And also, to hell with the
trout—you can't afford
to look down, anyway.
You and I have lots of
golden sticky clay on our
gumboots—the world
is holding us up
very well, today.

ANNE FRENCH

Simultaneous Equations

All day I try out simple sums
such as *in 1967* a year I can almost
remember as a shareholder with voting
rights *you were only four years older*
than I now am

or complicated ones, a kind of higher
mathematics of the heart *since you can offer*
her a house with an extra room and a Dishmaster
will she fulfil her half
of the bargain?

But my new differential calculus
cannot solve pairs of simultaneous

$$x = \begin{cases} \underline{\text{she will come}} \\ \text{if she came you would want her} \end{cases}$$

equations

$$y = \begin{cases} \underline{\text{my love can make no claims}} \\ \text{she will reclaim you} \end{cases}$$

which it renders as $\quad x + y = \begin{cases} \underline{\text{I love you}} \\ \text{she is your wife} \end{cases}$

It is midnight, the storm that blustered all day
has blown itself into stillness, the fire has died
to embers, and I am no closer to the answers
than when I began *when did I begin to love you?*
and *is it too late now to pull out?*

A Summer Storm

Last winter I tore up poems full of animals—
possums, eyes glazed, blood congealed on claws,
dead faces grinning, entrails spread for yards.
Today in Cornwall Park it was business as usual—
nature doing everything it does
without fuss. Only a deep litter of leaves,
drifts of pine-needles, a few branches down,
to show for Saturday's storm. In the garden
yesterday we collected fallen wood
from the jacaranda. 'This will make good kindling,'
I tell my son, 'when autumn comes.' 'Autumn,'
he repeats, not knowing what I mean, the seasons

of his two years' confused by travel. Today
there are no furry bodies thrown clear into
the gutter. Just the pale khaki shape
of a hedgehog, flattened out, dessicated, brittle,
lifting and curling like a sheet of paper.

Writing

I could have written, 'I left
you standing in the street;
it was dawn; the northwest arch
promised wind off the mountains'

—but this is hindsight. Or I
could describe it, how the light
fell on the land, and the land lay
under it, beautiful and meaningless.

But in fact I stared
out of the window most of the time
and tried to write. Five hundred
and ten miles an hour is a good

clean quick way to exit in anyone's
language. The writing on the wing
said REVERSE THRUST LEVER but I can't
see anyone getting out there at that speed.

An Evening in November

Eight hundred of them, and this as ordinary
as any. A sea breeze worries at the windows,
sunlight illuminates Rangitoto's flanks,
and in the next room, unimaginably, my son
sleeps in a basket. Seven days ago
he was still tucked inside; we were
bean and bean-pod, egg and egg-shell
a bellyful of rare fruit. Then
my son who was once an axolotl
once a little fish leapt
into his own life. His lungs
ballooned, his heart closed up,
his clear eyes fixed mine, his fist
grasped my finger. As if it were
an ordinary day the sun rose.

ELIZABETH NANNESTAD

My Mother's Mother, Dearly Beloved

My mother's mother, dearly beloved
heap of downwards sliding parts
though not mean of mind or mouth
ties six knots in a rubber band
six times broken.
Oddly female
scrapbag on her arthritic throne,
she rewrites her life daily
so that her memories rise
around her, like smoke-rings.
In her home she is indispensable
to generations of jampots, and the
fly swat on the twenty year nail.

Portrait of a Lady

Some people are incurably gentle.
I am thinking of one. She
is thin as a bird
as if she might
be taken up by the wrists and ankles
and stolen, so light.
She is the lady of the house
though her face moves
like the face of a thief
at the window of her house.
She is laying the table,
making a bed,
it all turns
to ash.

Imagine her

by a wall, in a church where
the roof is bombed out and
the choir missing. Why wait?
Already you could say, turning away, Yes.
It was a growth, internally.

Here the boat set me down, and I wait. The oarsman swung on the pole
and we came to the bank, lifted my belongings, and I got out.
Four days and five nights, the canoe does not return.
I waited at the river bank. Oh, the river. How I wept, and now how dry I am.

        This is only a tributary, and a thousand miles to the sea,
a lifetime to the other side. The river bends, or is it that my eye
bends what I see with distance and time.

                The military walk in the town.
The old giantess behind her stand in the market refuses to bargain
selling fallen fruit smelling of diarrhoea, golden and black.
She looks down. The tiny captured monkeys
tethered to her, they also look down.

In the evening I walk to the river, at the end of town
and I watch the sun set in equatorial calm.
I see the circles on the slow-swift stream
and I hear the monkeys scream. It is all one.
I walk back to my hammock and lie down.

Opposite in the street is the tailor's shop, a carbox with an open side
where the tailor works through the night. In the evening
his family comes and sits with him, a laugh breaks, and one sings out.

Outside my room the night has turned to flowers. The tailor's daughter
lines up her back with the side of the shop, looks down the street.
The military drift, looking in at bars.

               I am the queen of the River
and I go as I please. The river is as wide as this arm of mine,
I reach out and measure the river with my arm and touch on the far side.
I will leave now. Why should I not go down?
A mosquito steps on my arm and clings.
My arms are bitten by the dark bougainvillea
and ignored by the spines.
               I am the Queen of the River,
and I know by now the one song they play, over and again,
down in my throat I know them, all the songs to this hour in time
and I will drive the oarsman mad.

The tailor's little daughter kicks a foot at midnight.
It is cool now, and I who have flown in my dreams and died
stop sweating, pull the sheet up onto a shoulder, and sleep.

Portrait Across a Room

When I see you moving in a room with other people
your lips outlined
shining and going from one to another

I think the first of your line was a marketeer
and poor, who fought in crowds
for part of a carcass
and won the tail, or the eyes.

GREGORY O'BRIEN

Riverbend for Damien

(Trappist Monastery, Kopua)

It is enough that you visit the earth
and bless it, bones warming in the sun
the river coiling around itself and up

against the monks' diving-board where the
wide-awake contemplate murky depths and Christ
is an armless swimmer in the ocean above the sky.

All in its ordinary time, the tracks of sandals
are absorbed by the moist ground you will
one day disappear beneath (but not yet).

You might ask why the willows weep
but it is not for themselves, or why the glass-
eyed eel will never ask how tall an aeroplane is.

It is enough that you visit the earth
and in the unaccustomed storm that is silence
you can hear the sound of another voice

in the river, very deep and very wide awake
and you can make out the chugging of a motor
propelling us on to no-one knows where.

Her Voice is the Tidying of a House

A woman is kneeling in a stream—
        the mist is a sponge drawing the town
up into itself. Dogs lie around the park
like battered violins
        their music scattered
among the long grass. Trees grow straight

only the leaves curl like dollar notes
on the arms of a skeleton. A man is standing
        beside the stream
cold as charity, beautifully shaven
a dove is whispering into his ear
        a drizzle of light descending . . . .

Now it is night, the woman is climbing out
of a car. The string of pearls around her neck
        breaks and the man crawls down the road
trying to scoop the beads up
out of the darkness. Later, on a couch
the woman realizes he has handed
        her a palmful of tiny wet stones

by now the pearls have rolled
miles away
        into the hands of a child
on the pavement who is waiting for her mother
(she will recognize a woman with nail polish
        on only one finger)—her voice
is the tidying of a house, her handclaps like rain
the patter of her feet like the first
                fall of snow as she recovers
pearls from the streets of the moon—
and two shadows move
        further up the road
leaving the child who wishes
        their hands held more
                than hands could ever hold.

The Uses of Clouds

Clouds from Matiatia Bay
to Motutapu Island, a red

dinghy tied to the branches
of a tree—someone talking

the split tongues of magpies.
Mention me to the used-car lots

the death columns of newspapers.
I'll be inventing airships and

arguing over guests at Ostend
hands wrapped inside a cardigan

considering the plight of small boats
the still floating wharves, a girl

aged four walking past in yellow boots
bus-ticket stuck to her forehead.

From *Bride of the Disappearing Man*

9 The Fable

The fox is out of breath
the long tooth of the sky
    has punctured his back
hounds are looming—
the sound of a trumpet.

There is a vase in the woods—
the fox slips through
    its clay mouth—
the dogs bark
the huntsman takes the vase home.
He cannot understand why
the hounds make such a fuss
      over a beautiful vase.

At midnight the fox
leaves his hiding place
    on the mantelpiece.

Next morning the blankets
have disappeared from all the beds
the huntsman's dogs
    have had their throats cut
his daughters are dancing
trance-like in a circle
    on the crown of a distant hill.

10 The Light

It was the light that first caught his eye
    an intense burning somewhere
over his left shoulder
at first he thought of oil
    in the kitchen
but it was more than that.

Walking towards the flame
he imagined one thing:
    a figure on the horizon
with two flags
spelling out something
    in semaphore

but he could not read semaphore

as he walked up to the flame—
    and it could have been
the burning of a forest
or perhaps only
    the flashlight of a child

as he walked on into it.

A Visiting Card

How lightly we
carry ourselves

that stirring in
the long grass yes

five minutes ago
that was us.

A Painting Entitled Love and the Pilgrim

Tate Gallery, London

The woman has wings all the pilgrim
has is a moustache and feet full of
thorns. A butterfly alights
            on her countenance
the wine trembles in its moonlit
glass. His feet are bound
to the earth
            she drifts solemnly over
and there is love enough to
evaporate a cathedral. He cannot
believe where the time has gone.
The pilgrim is crawling with bugs
moths fly through his clothes
and hair. Her face is a
            sculpture being made
in the studio of an almond.

Comfort for the Sick Child

If there was a sequel to the life
you are living as, say, the island
    becomes a fist releasing birds

which fly through the broad grin
of the harbour bridge, cars like
        teeth travelling north, summer

would be a bicycle with two wheels
and nothing between and that's about
        where you happened along

I wanted to name you Little Hat or
Speckled Red but, by way of Bo Weavil
        and Sleepy John, we arrived

at Jack then drank your health
another feather plucked from the
        Great Bird. The whole time

you never lost your step, feet never
touched the ground. Now you are realising
        the movement of a tiny fish through

the many fissures of a rock, narrow
body tucked inside a towel. We understand
        each other. It takes time.

In general, place names and proper names have not been included.

Aoteaa roimata o Ranginapa here are the tears of Ranginapa

Akuroa Earth Mother in Tongarewan mythology

ariki high chief

Aorangi tohunga (priest) ancestor of the main Tongarewan line

Ara Sky Father in Tongarewan mythology

aue alas

E moe, e whaea wahine tangimarie sleep, mother, woman of peace

te hau the wind

Io supreme god in Maori pantheon

kahawai, a fish, *Arripis trutta*

kai food; a meal

karaka broad-leafed tree, up to 10 metres high, found in coastal forest. Its distinctive for its orange berries

kauri a massive coniferous forest tree, prized for its timber. Sites of ancient kauri forests have been extensively worked for deposits of kauri gum

kea a species of native parrot, found mainly in mountainous regions of the South Island

kehua ghost

komako growing tip of young coconut tree

kotiro girl

kowhai small tree, with golden blossom in spring

kumara sweet potato

mahuta death

mako, mango shark

maoa mulberry poultice

manuka shrub or small tree; its aromatic leaves were used by early settlers for manuka tea, and it is also known as tea-tree

Maoritanga Maori traditions and culture

marae surround of a Maori meeting-house, forum; a common area/ life of Maori

matai species of forest tree; black pine

Maui mythological Maori hero, one of whose exploits was to try to kill the Death Goddess by entering her body, and was killed in the attempt

mere club, used in hand-to-hand combat

Moriori name of Polynesians thought to have inhabited New Zealand and Chatham Islands before the Maori

motu island

t'moko a rima tribe of Tongarewa

pa fortified Maori village, by extension, Maori settlement

Pakeha New Zealander of European descent

piupiu Maori skirt of grass or flax

pohutukawa evergreen coastal tree, with bright crimson blossom in summer

pukeko swamphen, *Porphyrio melanotus*

punga tree fern

puriri tree, yielding hard, durable timber

GLOSSARY OF MAORI AND POLYNESIAN WORDS AND PHRASES

In general, place names and proper names have not been included.

Aanei nga roimata o Rangipapa here are the tears of Rangipapa
Akaotu Earth Mother in Tongarevan mythology
ariki high chief
Ataranga tohunga (poet); ancestor of the main Tongarevan line
Atea Sky Father in Tongarevan mythology
aue alas

E moe, e te whaea: wahine rangimarie sleep, mother: woman of peace

te hau the wind

Io supreme god in Maori pantheon

kahawai a fish, *Arripis trutta*
kai food, a meal
karaka broad-leafed tree, up to 10 metres high, found in coastal forest. It is distinctive for its orange berries.
kauri a massive coniferous forest tree, prized for its timber; sites of ancient kauri forests have been extensively worked for deposits of kauri gum
kea a species of native parrot, found mainly in mountainous regions of the South Island
kehua ghost
komuko growing tip of young coconut tree
kotiro girl
kowhai small tree, with golden blossom in spring
kumara sweet potato

mahuta death
mako, mango shark
mana authority, prestige
manuka shrub or small tree; its aromatic leaves were used by early settlers to make tea, and it is also known as 'tea-tree'
Maoritanga Maori traditions and culture
marae courtyard of Maori meeting-house, forum or centre of social life of Maoris
matai species of forest tree, black pine
Maui mythological Maori hero, one of whose exploits was to try to kill the Death Goddess by entering her body, and was killed in the attempt
mere club, used in hand-to-hand combat
Moriori name of Polynesians thought to have inhabited New Zealand and Chatham Islands before the Maori
motu island

Omoka main village of Tongareva

pa fortified Maori village, by extension, Maori settlement
Pakeha New Zealander of European descent
piupiu Maori skirt of grass or flax
pohutukawa evergreen coastal tree, with bright crimson blossom in summer
pukeko swamp-hen, *Porphyrio melanotus*
punga tree-fern
puriri tree, yielding hard, durable timber

te ra the sun
Rakahanga atoll in the northern Cook Islands, west of Tongareva
raupo bulrush
Ru Tongarevan earthquake god, disrupter of the natural order

Savaiki the Cook Islands name for Hawaiki, the legendary homeland of the
    Polynesian people; also the world of the dead
Sina daughter of Rongo, the god of agriculture

taiaha long wooden club, used now for ceremonial purposes
tangi funeral (n); to cry (v)
taniwha mythical beast inhabiting waterways and lakes
tapu (under) religious restriction, sacred
tauhinu a scented shrub, often infesting poor soil
tohunga Maori or Polynesian priest or expert in ritual, art and lore
toi-toi tall tussocky grass with whitish-yellow plumes
Tongareva an island in the northern Cook Islands, also known as Penrhyn
    Island
totara large coniferous forest tree, prized for its timber
tui largest of honeyeaters native to New Zealand, rather larger than a
    blackbird, with distinctive and beautiful song
Turua an overlord of Tongareva

waiata song (n); to sing (v)
weta large wingless long-horned grasshopper, of alarming appearance
whanau family, extended family
Te Whiro personified form of evil, darkness, death

ACKNOWLEDGEMENTS

For permission to reproduce copyright passages grateful acknowledgement is made to the publishers and copyright holders of the following:

Arthur Adams, *Maoriland: and other Verses* (The Bulletin Newspaper Co., Sydney, 1899). Fleur Adcock, *The Eye of the Hurricane* (A.H. & A.W. Reed, 1964). *Selected Poems* (Oxford University Press, Oxford 1984); *The Incident Book* (Oxford University Press, Oxford 1986). B. E. Baughan, *Reuben and Other Poems* (Constable, 1903); *Shingle-short and Other Verses* (Whitcombe & Tombs, 1908). James K. Baxter, *The Lion Skin* (University of Otago, 1967); *Jerusalem Sonnets* (The Bibliography Room, University of Otago, 1970); *Autumn Testament* (Price Milburn, 1973). Mary Ursula Bethell, *Collected Poems* (Caxton Press, 1950). Tony Beyer, *Dancing Bear* (Melaleuca Press, 1981). Peter Bland, *My Side of the Story, Poems 1960-64* (Mate Books, 1964); *London Magazine* (vol. 6, February 1967) and the Author. Charles Brasch, *Disputed Ground, Poems 1939-45* (Caxton Press, 1948); *The Estate and Other Poems* (Caxton Press, 1957); *Ambulando* (Caxton Press, 1964); *Not Far Off* (Caxton Press, 1969); *Home Ground* (Caxton Press, 1974). Alistair Campbell, *Blue Rain* (Wai-te-ata Press, 1967); *The New Zealand Listener* (vol. 61, 1969, and the Author); *New Zealand Poetry 1974* (Pegasus Press, 1974) *Dreams, Yellow Lions* (Alister Taylor, 1975); *Collected Poems* (Alister Taylor, 1982); *Soul Traps* (Te Kotare Press, 1985). Gordon Challis, *Building* (Caxton Press, 1963). Allen Curnow, *Island and Time* (Caxton Press, 1941); *Collected Poems* (A.H. & A.W. Reed, 1974); *An Incorrigible Music* (Auckland University Press, 1979); *You Will Know When You Get There* (Auckland University Press, 1982). Ruth Dallas, *Country Road and Other Poems, 1947-52* (Caxton Press, 1953); *The Turning Wheel* (Caxton Press, 1961); *Day Book* (Caxton Press, 1966); *Shadow Show* (Caxton Press, 1968). Basil Dowling, *Signs and Wonders* (Caxton Press, 1944); *Canterbury and Other Poems* (Caxton Press, 1949); *Landfall* (vol. 30, 1954). Eileen Duggan, *Poems* (Allen & Unwin, 1937); *More Poems* (Allen & Unwin, 1951, and the Author). Lauris Edmond, *Selected Poems* (Oxford University Press, 1984); *Seasons and Creatures* (Oxford University Press, 1986). Murray Edmond, *End Wall* (Oxford University Press, 1981). Riemke Ensing, *Topographies* (Prometheus Press, 1984); *Ariel* (vol. 16 no. 4, October 1985) and the Author. A. R. D. Fairburn, *Collected Poems* (Pegasus Press, 1966). Janet Frame, *The Pocket Mirror* (Pegasus Press, 1967). Anne French, *All Cretans are Liars* (Auckland University Press, 1987). Denis Glover, *The Wind and the Sand* (Caxton Press, 1945); *Sings Harry and Other Poems* (Caxton Press, 1951); *Arawata Bill: A Sequence of Poems* (Pegasus Press, 1953). Michael Harlow, *Today is the Piano's Birthday* (Auckland University Press, 1981). Paul Henderson, *Unwilling Pilgrim* (Caxton Press, 1955); *The Halting Place* (Caxton Press, 1961). J. R. Hervey, *New Poems* (Caxton Press, 1940); *Man on a Raft, More Poems* (Caxton Press, 1949); *Landfall* (vol. 35, 1955). Sam Hunt, *Collected Poems* (Penguin, 1980). Robin Hyde, *Houses by the Sea and the Later Poems of Robin Hyde* (Caxton Press, 1952). Kevin Ireland, *Face to Face* (Pegasus Press, 1963); *Educating the Body* (Caxton Press, 1967) *A Grammar of Dreams* (Wai-te-ata Press, 1975); *Orchids, Hummingbirds, and other poems* (Auckland University Press, 1974); *Literary Cartoons* (Islands/Hurricane, 1977); *Landfall* (September 1986) and the Author. Michael Jackson, *Latitudes of Exile* (John McIndoe, 1975); *Wall* (John McIndoe, 1980); *Going On* (John McIndoe, 1985). Louis Johnson, *Poems Unpleasant* (with others, Pegasus Press, 1952); *New Worlds for Old* (Capricorn Press, 1957); *Bread and a Pension* (Pegasus Press, 1964); *New Zealand Poetry 1974* (Pegasus Press, 1974); *Land Like a Lizard* (Jacaranda Press, Brisbane, 1970); *Poetry New Zealand* (Caxton Press, 1974); *Poetry Australia* (No. 54, February 1975); *Fires and Patterns* Jacaranda Press, Brisbane, 1975); *Coming and Going* (Mallinson Rendel, 1982); *Winter Apples* (Mallinson Rendel, 1984); *Confessions of the Last Cannibal* (Antipodes Press, 1986). M.K. Joseph, *New Zealand Poetry Year Book* (Pegasus Press, 1954); *The Living Countries* (Paul's Book Arcade, 1959); *Imaginary Islands* (1950, by permission of the Author); *Inscription on a Paper Dart* (Auckland University Press, 1974). Vivienne Joseph, *A Desirable Property* (John McIndoe, 1984). Jan Kemp, *Against the Softness of Woman* (Caveman Press, 1976); *Diamonds and Gravel* (Hampson Hunt, 1979); and the Author. Rachel McAlpine, *Recording Angel* (Mallinson Rendel, 1983). Cilla McQueen, *Homing In* (John McIndoe, 1982). Bill Manhire, *The Elaboration* (Square and Circle, 1972); *The Young New Zealand Poets* (Heinemann, 1973); *Good Looks* (Auckland University Press, 1983); *Zoetropes* (Allen and Unwin/Port Nicholson Press, 1984). Katherine Mansfield, *Poems* (Constable, 1923). To Stanislaw Wyspianski (Bodley Head, 1938, the Society of Authors, and Alfred A. Knopf Inc.). R. A. K. Mason, *Collected Poems* (Pegasus Press, 1962). David Mitchell, *Pipe Dreams in Ponsonby* (Stephen Chan, 1971). Elizabeth Nannestad, *Jump* (Auckland University Press, 1986). Gregory O'Brien, *In Search of the Least Person* (Auckland University Press, 1987). Peter Olds, *Doctor's Rock* (Caveman Press, 1976); *Beethoven's Guitar* (Caveman Press, 1980). W. H. Oliver, *Fire Without Phoenix, Poems 1946-54* (Caxton Press, 1957); *Out of Season* (Oxford University Press, 1980). Vincent O'Sullivan, *Our Burning Time* (Prometheus Books, 1965); *Revenants* (Prometheus Books, 1969); *Butcher & Co.* (Oxford University Press, 1977); *Brother Jonathan Brohier Kafka* (Oxford University Press, 1980); *The Rose Ballroom* (John McIndoe, 1982); *The Butcher Papers* (Oxford University Press, 1982); *The Pilate Tapes* (Oxford University Press, 1986). Alistair Paterson, *Birds Flying* (Pegasus Press, 1973). Gloria Rawlinson, *The Islands Where I was Born* (Handcraft Press, 1955); *Of Clouds and Pebbles* (Paul's Book Arcade, 1963). Keith Sinclair, *Songs for a Summer* (Pegasus Press, 1952); *A Time to Embrace* (Paul's Book Arcade, 1963). Elizabeth Smither, *Legend of Marcello Mastroiani's Wife* (Auckland University Press, 1981); *Casanova's Ankle* (Oxford University Press, 1981); *Professor Musgrove's Canary* (Auckland University Press, 1985). Kendrick Smithyman, *The Blind Mountain* (Caxton Press, 1950); *The Penguin Book of New Zealand Verse* (Penguin, 1960, and Longman Paul, 1967); *Inheritance* (Paul's Book Arcade, 1962); *The New*

Zealand Listener (vol. 59, 1968, and the Author); *Earthquake Weather* (Auckland University Press, 1972); *The Seal in the Dolphin Pool* (Auckland University Press, 1974); *Stories About Wooden Keyboards* (Auckland University Press, 1985). Charles Spear, *Twopence Coloured* (Caxton Press, 1951). C. K. Stead, *Whether the Will is Free* (Paul's Book Arcade, 1964); *Quesada* (The Shed, 1975). *Walking Westward* (The Shed, 1979); *Geographies* (Auckland University Press, 1982). Edward Tregear, *Shadows and Other Verses* (Whitcombe & Tombs, 1919). Brian Turner, *Ladders of Rain* (John McIndoe, 1978); *Ancestors* (John McIndoe, 1981); *Listening to the River* (John McIndoe, 1983). Hone Tuwhare, *No Ordinary Sun* (Blackwood & Janet Paul, 1965); *Review '69* (Otago University Students' Association); *Selected Poems* (John McIndoe, 1980). Ian Wedde, *Made Over* (Stephen Chan, 1974); *New Zealand Poetry 1974* (Pegasus 1974); *Earthly: Sonnets for Carlos* (Amphedesma Press, 1975, and the Author); *Castaly* (Auckland University Press, 1980); *Tales of Gotham City* (Auckland University Press, 1984). Pat Wilson, *The Bright Sea* (Pegasus Press, 1951). Hubert Witheford, *Shadow of the Flame, Poems 1942-7* (Pelorus Press, 1950); *The Lightning Makes a Difference* (Brookside Press, 1962, and the Author); *A Native, Perhaps Beautiful* (Caxton Press, 1967).

We are grateful to Mac Jackson for his reading of the second edition for corrections; any errors that remain, however, are ours.

INDEX OF TITLES AND FIRST LINES

Titles are in *italics*; first lines in roman.